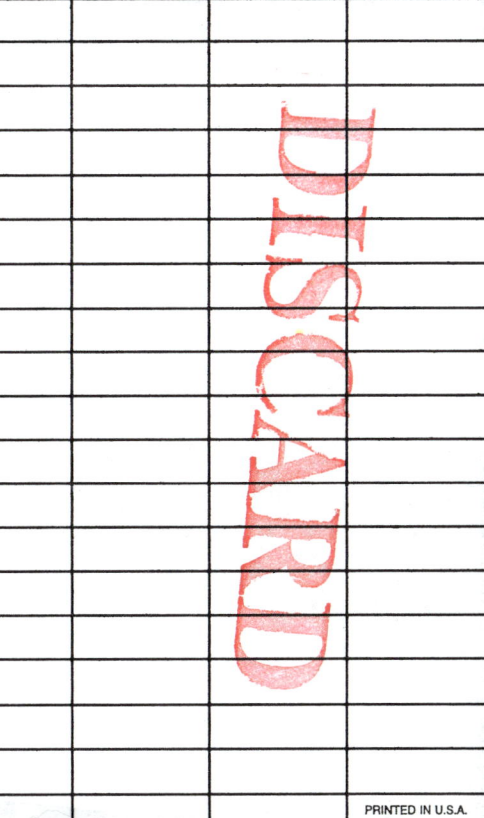

Che Guevara Icon, Myth, and Message

Che Guevara

Icon, Myth, and Message

David Kunzle

UCLA Fowler Museum Of Cultural History
in collaboration with the
Center for the Study of Political Graphics

Published in conjunction with an exhibition of the same name at the UCLA Fowler Museum of Cultural History, 5 October 1997 to 1 February 1998.

All posters unless otherwise indicated are lent by the Center for the Study of Political Graphics, 8124 West Third Street - suite 211, Los Angeles, California, USA 90048-4309.

Portions of the Introduction previously appeared in "Uses of the Portrait: The Che Poster" in *Art in America* 63:66-73, September 1975. Reproduced with permission.

©1997 Regents of the University Of California

UCLA Fowler Museum of Cultural History
Box 951549
Los Angeles, California, USA 90095-1549

Patrick Fitzgerald, *Design*
Corinne Lightweaver, *Editing*
Don Cole, *Photography*
Daniel R. Brauer, *Production Coordination*

Printed and bound in Hong Kong by
South Sea International Press, Ltd.

Library of Congress Cataloging-in-Publications Data

Kunzle, David.
   Che Guevara : icon, myth, and message / David Kunzle.
     p.   cm.
   "Published in conjunction with an exhibition of the same name at the UCLA Fowler Museum of Cultural History, 5 October 1997 to 24 January 1998"—CIP preliminaries.
   Includes bibliographical references.
   ISBN 0-930741-58-7 (hard). — ISBN 0-930741-59-5 (soft)
   1. Guevara, Ernesto, 1928-1967—Exhibitions. 2. Cuba—History—Revolution, 1959—Exhibitions. 3. Political posters—Exhibitions. 4. Guerrillas—Latin America— Exhibitions. I. University of California, Los Angeles. Fowler Museum of Cultural History. II. Title.
   F2849.22.G85K85 1997
   972.9106'4'092—dc21
                                                                          97-33307
                                                                                 CIP

Cover photograph. A twelve-year-old resident of La Higuera, the hamlet where Che was killed, poses for the camera outside his house in December 1996 with drawings he has made of Che Guevara, done in homage to the man who has inspired him in his life and in his studies. (He is not selling the drawings.)

Frontispiece. Roman Cieslewicz, *"CHE SI,"* magazine cover and poster, 81 x 55 cm. The importance of the design, apart from its simple clarity, lies in its being the only major portrait of Che outside Cuba (after the *Time* cover in 1960) known to me to be published before his death. Cieslewicz's design first appeared on the cover of *Opus International* 3 (October 1967), a French cultural quarterly of which the artist was artistic director. (The poster presumably came later.) The two lead articles of this issue are "La Havana: Peinture et Revolution" and "Che Si," both evidently based on an encounter of Cuban revolutionaries and European intellectuals held in Havana that summer. Che Guevara and Fidel Castro are credited with "reinventing the revolution," under the aegis of the slogan "Che Si."

    It is at this moment, when Che was known to be "somewhere in Bolivia taking incalculable risks," that he was, as far as I can tell, first apotheosized in art; the Casa de las Américas exhibited a large mural on which more than ninety artists collaborated in the form of a huge spiral, compartmentalized like a board game (reproduced in *Opus*, p. 17), including several images of Che by Raúl Martínez. The "Che Si" article by Alain Jouffroy was accompanied by an image of Fidel speaking before a huge photograph of Che at a conference for Latin American Solidarity (OLAS).

Lenders to the Exhibition

Freddy Alborta

Center for the Study of Political Graphics

Center for Cuban Studies Art Space

Alexis Esquivel

Fine Arts Museums of San Francisco

Stephanie Hagen

International Institute of Social History, Amsterdam

Monique Knowlton Gallery, New York

Michael Rossmann / The AOUON Archive

Jack Rutberg Fine Arts

Fabian Wagmister

One Anonymous Lender

Table of Contents

Director's Acknowledgment 8

Curator's Acknowledgment 9

Ernesto Che Guevara: A Legacy 10

Preface 11

Che and Me *Maurice Zeitlin* 12

    Che and Latin America 16

Ernesto Che Guevara: A Brief Chronology 17

    Che and Cuba 18

Impressions 19

Introduction 20

    The Volatile Face: Two, Three, Many Ches 26

Chapter 1: Che's Ideals in the Cuban Poster: OSPAAAL, Frémez, ICAIC 28

Chapter 2: Che as Landscape 38

Chapter 3: Che-Man ↔ Che-Project: A Collective Poetic Articulation *Fabian Wagmister* 42

Chapter 4: Symbols: Hair and Beard, Cigar, Uniform, Beret, Star, the Name 48

    Felix Beltrán, 4 Ches 55

Chapter 5: The Korda Matrix 56

    Che Multiplied 61

Chapter 6: Mederos's Life of Che 62

    The Mederos Paintings 66

    Cuban Murals 70

    Latin American Murals 72

Chapter 7: Che, Chicanos, and Cubans: The Struggle Over a Symbol *Shifra M. Goldman* 74

    US Murals 76

Chapter 8: Chesucristo: The Christification of Che 78

Chapter 9: Che Dead, Che Vive: The Alborta Photographs and the Belkin Variations 88

    The Dead Che in Art 91

    Weisberg's Deposition 91

    The Alborta Photograph in Film 92

    Christ-Che in Three Contemporary Works of Art *Christophe Blaser* 92

    Alternative Views 94

Chapter 10: Demythification: The Twentieth Century Fox *Che!* *Christine Petra Sellin* 98

    *Mis*Chellanea 104

Chapter 11: The Passion Of Che: Capture, Death, and Dissapearance 108

Gallery 112

Notes 118

References 122

Detail from a mural in Palacio de los Pioneros, near Havana (see fig. H.6, p. 71).

Director's Acknowledgment

I first encountered David Kunzle's commitment to politically motivated art when I was a graduate student in a twentieth-century Mexican art history course he taught at in 1972 the University of California, Santa Barbara. His tenacious enthusiasm for the subject matter made for a particularly compelling class, which has stayed with me longer than most of my educational experiences.

The socially concerned art of the Mexican muralists made a lasting impression and was the inspiration for an ambitious class assignment. In addition to lectures and readings, students were involved in a large mural project in the university's student union. David clearly wanted members of the class to be more than observers of art history, he wanted us to be active participants in its processes. I want to thank David for the education and for his extraordinary efforts on this publication and exhibition. His ideas and dedication are truly remarkable.

I would also like to thank the other contributors to this volume: Christophe Blaser, Shifra M. Goldman, Christine Petra Sellin, Fabian Wagmister, and Maurice Zeitlin. Each has provided a unique and thoughtful perspective that has enhanced our understanding of Che and his image.

This project would not have been possible without the collaboration of the Center for the Study of Political Graphics. This publication is just a small measure of their accomplishments over the past ten years. The leadership and energy of Carol Wells, executive director of the Center, are greatly appreciated. We are also grateful for the support of the Center's staff: Lisa Nunez-Hancock, research assistant; Liz Fischbach, assistant to the director; Hae Jin Lee, 1997 Getty intern; and Bony Toruno; and to Board Members Garland Kirkpatrick, Susan Martin, and Lori Zimmerman.

Our gratitude also extends to other lenders to the exhibition listed separately on page 6.

Within the University I would like to thank Larry L. Loeher and the Chancellor's Committee on Instructional Improvement Programs, and Carlos Albert Torres, director of the UCLA Latin American Center, for their support. Fabian Wagmister of the UCLA Film and Television Department developed the 4,000-image CD ROM on Che that was featured in the exhibition, a compelling addition to the project.

This is the third volume that Patrick Fitzgerald has designed for the Fowler Museum, and I continue to be impressed by his abilities. Likewise, Corinne Lightweaver has edited the text with her characteristic patience, finesse, and intelligence.

The staff of the Museum (listed on p. 23) has, as always, performed as consummate professionals. I would like to single out the work of Christine Sellin, director of Public Relations, who also served as a contributor to the publication. She wore both hats with style. Photographer Don Cole, who recently joined the Museum, turned around a large body of work in a very short time and his extra efforts are highly valued. Registrar Sarah Kennington and her assistant Farida Sunada also rose to the occasion to meet the unusual demands of this project. The irrepressible energy of Clarissa Coyoca, assistant director of the Museum, David Mayo, director of Exhibitions, and Betsy Quick, director of Education, sustained the staffwide collaboration that ensured whatever success the Museum has achieved.

Doran H. Ross, *Director*
UCLA Fowler Museum of Cultural History

Curator's Acknowledgment

My thanks go first of all to Doran Ross, director of the Fowler Museum, for agreeing to fulfill a dream of decades and to publish such a copiously illustrated catalog. I acknowledge also the staff of the Fowler Museum who helped in so many ways, especially David Mayo for an imaginative exhibition design. Patrick Fitzgerald, designer of this book, rose to the challenge and produced it most handsomely.

My thanks go also to the Center for the Study of Political Graphics, directed by Carol Wells, for lending the bulk of the material for the book and exhibition, and for assisting in so many ways to bring both projects to fruition. I owe much to Carol, a friend for two decades, for her collaboration and encouragement in the collecting of posters and her single-handed creation in 1988 of the CSPG, making it possible for me to donate my own collection in the secure trust that she would preserve and mobilize it much better than I could.

My UCLA colleague Fabian Wagmister has been a constant, active, and creative collaborator on many aspects of the projects, which overlap so happily with his own project: a CD ROM on Che. On trips we shared to Cuba and Bolivia, he made contacts, arranged and conducted interviews, and ran diplomatic errands and courier services. His friendship, inspiration, and energy have been very precious.

I received significant assistance on the OSPAAAL posters from Lincoln Cushing, who with Dan Walsh directs the Cuba Poster Project, and with Michael Rossmann has compiled the OSPAAAL posters catalogue. (Inquiries regarding reproduction of OSPAAAL imagery to Lincoln Cushing, 510-845-7111, lcushing@ipg.apc.org, and www.zpub.com/cpp.) Michael allowed me free access to his own fine collection of posters, and lent several for the exhibition.

Shifra Goldman was indefatigable in finding me sources and references, and answering questions; Jim Prigoff culled Che images from his own vast collection of slides of murals; six of his photographs are reproduced here and gratefully acknowledged.

In 1995–1997, I held several seminars at UCLA on Ernesto Guevara which helped to maintain the momentum. Among the many participants, undergraduate and graduate, whose research and thinking contributed to this project, I would single out (omitting names credited in the text): Sylvia Chivaratanond; Alestra Flores; Karen Frid, who also ran errands and found Che memorabilia; Natalya Golubchik; Varand Gourjian; Lisa Hancock-Nuñez, who also helped with the inventory; Lisa Hernandez; Deborah Himy, who also found the Haitian Che (fig. M.43); Salomon Huerta; Diane Lucero; Anita Morris; Sarah Nilsen of the University of Southern California, who compiled extracts from US films using the Che image and found videos of Cuban films on Che; Dara Rosenzweig; Donna Simchovitz; Jennifer Wirsching; and Mary Wolfgram.

Debts of various kinds are also owed to the following: Jacqueline Adams; Rune Andersson, who searched Scandinavia for Che; Patricia Belkin; Jon Lee Anderson and Grove Press for sending me advance copies of his magisterial biography; Cindy Bendat; Al Boime; Christophe Blaser; Dermot Begley, who gave practical help on my visit to Cuba of September 1996; Félix Beltrán, for sending magnificent Mexican posters; Beverly and John Berger; Luc Chessex; Steef Davidson; Tomas Essón; Antonio Frasconi, for lending a print; Rupert Garcia; Paolo Gasparini; Verenice Guaysamín; Marien van der Heiden; George and Valerie Kunzle, who kept me posted on Che in the British press; Sergio Michilini; Aurore Lombardo, for searching and sending French materials; Bruno Margadant; Susan Martin; Nina Moss, who helped with the translation; Liliana Porter; George Andrew Roth; Jack Rutberg; Ralph Schoenman (he and Roth spoke most movingly to my seminar); Christine Sellin; Stephanie Wood; Barbara Zeitler; and Maurice and Marilyn Zeitlin; a special thanks to Maurice for reading a typescript and correcting some errors.

In Cuba, a great debt accumulated, as usual, with José Fresquet (Frémez) and Alfredo Rostgaard, who since I first met them in 1973 were always so generous with gifts of posters and friendship. A special mention goes to Gerardo Mosquera and Erena Hernández, always so attentive to me and unstinting in their time, advice, and the run of their library. The spirit of my dear friend René Mederos who died in September 1996 informs this whole project. He was to have painted a mural for the exhibition. The book and exhibition stand as a memorial to him; in many ways he came as close to embodying the spirit of Che as any Cuban I have known. I owe much to his widow Elda and the attempts she has made, still ongoing, to recover his paintings of the life of Che.

The bibliographers of Cuban art José Veigas and Christina Vives gave me free access to their archive. Lesbia Vent Dumois, curator of the Casa de las Américas art collections, generously allowed me to photograph Che posters. I owe much to María del Carmen Ariet of the Che Guevara Foundation whose guidance in Bolivia was invaluable. Gladys Acosta of OSPAAAL, assisted by Patrick Hernández, showed me the latest OSPAAAL posters and gave me several.

The photographers Raúl Corrales, Alberto Korda, Liborio Noval, and Roberto Salas were generous with time and information. Thanks are also due to Che biographers Adys Cupull and Froilán González; Alexis Esquivel; Ismael Gómez and Estornino, for access to the work of Raúl Martínez; Gina López F., of the Historical Museums; Manuel, Waldo, and Sara Hernández of Matanzas; Aldo Soler and Isabel; and Erquidio Rodríguez Ortiz of ICAP, who gave us so many posters.

In Bolivia, my thanks go to Freddy Alborta; Carlos Gerardo Carrasco in Vallegrande, who opened up his archive of newspaper clippings; Loyola Guzmán; Anastasio Khoman; Walter Solón Romero; Carlos Soria Galvarro; Maggie Talavera; Juan Ignacio del Valle; Umberto Vázquez; and Dr. Buddy Lazo de la Vega.

All translations and site photographs, except where otherwise credited, are my own. All works reproduced are of Cuban origin unless otherwise identified. Photographs of posters are by Don Cole of the Fowler Museum or from the Visual Resource Museum Collection of the Art History Department, UCLA. Measurements are given to the nearest half centimeter.

This text was efficiently and speedily copyedited by Corinne Lightweaver. In April, at the moment when the manuscript should have been ready to go to press, I was suddenly struck down by a dangerous illness, which prevented me from making a scheduled trip to Cuba that would have allowed me to do some fine tuning of information. I was nursed through by my wife Marjoyrie who embodies to the full what may be regarded as Che's salient characteristic: selflessness.

David Kunzle
UCLA Department of Art History

Ernesto Che Guevara: A Legacy

Ernesto Che Guevara epitomized Latin America, and elsewhere the agonistic and emblematic figure of peace and war or, better yet, of peace through war. Che Guevara was known for becoming enraged when faced with what he considered an injustice. His definition of a revolutionary—someone who will rebel and fight against injustice wherever he or she finds it—became a moral foundation of revolutionary activism. But there was another Guevara—the man who could, in the midst of the hardships of the revolutionary war in the rugged Sierra Maestra, open a book of poetry, *El Siervo* by Spanish Republican poet León Felipe, a book that he carried always in his backpack and which he read aloud to his mostly illiterate campesino compañeros.

Guevara was known as an extremely ethical man who was ready to die and to kill for what he believed to be a just cause. His revolutionary commitment took him to Cuba, a country with a history that could not be more removed from his own political experience, to join the Granma expedition with Fidel Castro against Cuban dictator Fulgencio Batista. From the moment he set foot on a Cuban beach, the Guevara legend was born. When he was killed in Bolivia on 9 October 1967, his bearded face and beret were already a symbol of social struggles in Latin America. To be ready to die for what one believes seizes the high moral ground and creates the conditions for unselfish, generous social activism. It was not by chance that Guevara and his image became cultural icons of the Left and progressive movements. As such, Guevara has much to offer to art, literature, and music. His passion for change and his commitment to the cause exploded in Latin America at a time when social transformation was pursued with energy and optimism.

Che's passion in the pursuit of ethical change remains a central contribution to cultural history, a message that has already outlived his individual commitment to a particular political strategy or system. Ernesto Che Guevara's message still resonates, challenging us to believe that it is impossible to achieve lasting peace without justice, and that it is impossible to build a just and caring society without the construction of robust, ethical "new" men and women. This is Guevara's lasting cultural and moral legacy to us and future generations.

Carlos Alberto Torres, *Director*
UCLA Latin American Center

Preface

Che Guevara: Icon, Myth, and Message highlights two legacies of the Cuban Revolution, legacies which transcend its physical borders and which are undiminished, perhaps even rendered stronger by the continuing US embargo against Cuba: the omnipresent image of Che Guevara as a heroic figure, and the vitality of the protest poster as a weapon against injustice.

The charismatic visage of Che Guevara has become a political archetype—gracing posters, murals, T-shirts, banners, and album covers. Inspirational or irreverent, Christlike or sexy, realistic or abstract, his bearded face and starred beret constitute internationally recognized icons disseminated primarily by the political poster. For thirty years, protest posters have transmitted and promoted Che's ideals, hopes, and dreams and those of millions of others who dare to challenge the status quo.

Posters are one of the most democratic art forms and it is not surprising that they have been produced in every imaginable medium and visual language. Hastily slapped on walls "guerrilla-style" or carefully fashioned by recognized artists in well equipped studios, they communicate instantly and directly to both literate and nonliterate audiences. Graphic invention is the hallmark of the political poster, as this exhibition amply demonstrates in Pop- and Op Art-influenced posters from the 1960s, realistic portraits reproduced from photographs and paintings, and a variety of styles ranging from the professional to the amateur.

The 1960s launched a veritable tidal wave of poster making. Inspired by the Cuban Revolution and fueled by opposition to the Viet Nam war and other movements for social justice, posters became emblematic of both widespread discontent and new found—and hard won—freedoms. Leaders in the fight for self-determination and justice like Che, Ho Chi Minh, and Angela Davis commanded space on college dormitory walls alongside posters of the Beatles, Bob Dylan, and the Rolling Stones.

And nowhere in the world did posters flourish more spectacularly during the 1960s and 1970s than in Cuba. Sanctioned and subsidized by the new government, posters were used to educate and inspire the Cuban people to support the revolution within its borders and to promote liberation movements internationally. Folded into magazines or rolled into tubes, the Cuban poster quickly spread throughout the world. Expressing solidarity with revolutionary struggles in Africa, Asia, and Latin America, Cuban posters were mirrors held up to the foreign policy of the United States—transforming the international perception of the US from a democratic standard bearer to an oppressor supporting dictatorships throughout the world. An energetic graphic exchange ensued between Cuba and the US. The protest movements within the US inspired Cuban poster makers to produce stunning images demanding freedom for Angela Davis and condemning the murder of George Jackson. These posters could be found on the walls of Black Panther Party and anti-war activists from New York to California.

The posters in this exhibition are a small selection of the countless renditions of Che that were produced in Cuba and around the world after his death, and continue to be produced. Yet the context of a Che image produced in Cuba in 1967 is very different from that of a Che poster produced in the United States today. The visage of the hero who helped transform history has to a degree become a commercial logo in recent years. In the 1960s and 1970s, Che was a hero of Leftist and student movements throughout the world. His death was mourned and his life celebrated as Che became a larger-than-life, mythic personality who embodied their ideals and dreams.

But for today's youth who sport the rock group "Rage Against the Machine" T-shirts emblazoned with Che's face, he is not a contemporary. The struggles in which he fought are not hot topics...if they are known at all. And Che's history is certainly not made clearer in cinematic fantasies such as the "Everyman" Che haunting the film *Evita*. By showing the variety and continuity in the use of Che's image, this exhibition raises important questions about Che's enduring popularity. What is behind this fascination with Che? Why does he continue to appeal to generations who were not even born when he died? What is his particular attraction for US audiences?

Perhaps these questions cannot be answered, or may be answered only with other questions. The 1960s and 1970s had many cultural/political/revolutionary heroes and no lack of martyrs who were commemorated with posters. While few of these figures are recognizable today to those less than thirty years old, they have been replaced by new heroes and martyrs—such as Rigoberto Menchú, Subcomandante Marcos, Ken Saro Wiwa, and Mumia Abu-Jamal—whose faces and causes now appear internationally on posters. Yet Che continues to loom large. Why? Perhaps because he is a hero in a time when optimism is a rare gift, and pessimism and apathy paralyze too many. When "voting for the lesser of two evils" becomes a mainstream attitude, when communities link the CIA to the sale of drugs in their neighborhoods, when popes, presidents, and rock stars are equally vulnerable to assassination attempts, it is not surprising that cynicism too frequently outweighs optimism. But the heroicized Che is a reminder of high ideals and self-sacrifice, and the posters provide a link: a memory of a life lived large.

Political posters are social and artistic documents that bring together history, philosophy, and aesthetics into a coherent whole. They speak to us across time of the ideals and aspirations of the many groups and individuals who produced them. In the case of Che, while the context may change, the message remains clear: this one man—through his life and actions—has been transformed from a mere mortal to a transcendent symbol of liberation. At a time when ethnically defined nationalism is reemerging domestically and internationally —often with savage results—Che represents the ultimate internationalist, recognizing neither limitations of border nor of self.

Carol A. Wells, *Executive Director*
Center for the Study of Political Graphics

The Center for the Study of Political Graphics (CSPG) is a nonprofit, tax-exempt educational archive that collects, preserves, documents, and exhibits domestic and international posters relating to historical and contemporary movements for peace and social justice. The majority of graphics in this book and exhibition come from CSPG's growing collection, which currently contains over thirty thousand posters. Donations of posters to this archive are welcome.

Che and Me   *Maurice Zeitlin*

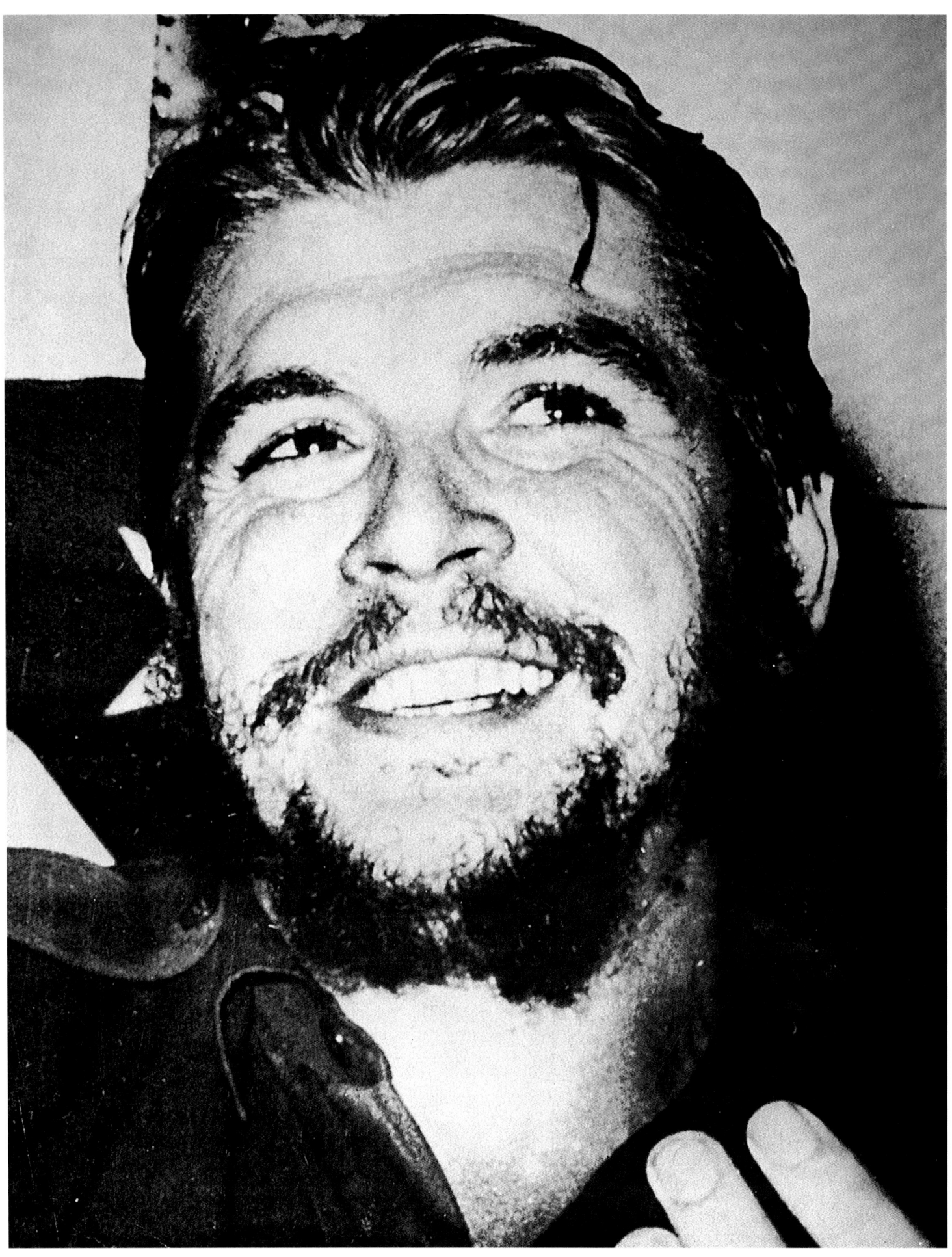

How did I meet Che? By the time I got to Cuba in the summer of 1961, I was already known as a critic of US policy toward the Revolutionary Government of Cuba. In late 1960, I was a grad student at the University of California, Berkeley, about to get started on my dissertation. My friend Robert Scheer had visited Cuba that summer. He came back incensed at the misinformation the American public was getting about the revolution and convinced me that we had to "do something." We were already deeply involved with the new student movement then emerging in Berkeley around the civil liberties protests against the House Un-American Activities Committee (HUAC) hearings in San Francisco and the boycott of Woolworth's in solidarity with the struggle for civil rights in the South. So it came naturally that we would organize and speak at protest rallies against US policy on Cuba. We wrote, mimeographed, and distributed thousands of leaflets around campus, and—spurred by an invitation from Beat poet and City Lights Books publisher Lawrence Ferlinghetti—we had begun to write a book about US-Cuba relations. I also decided to write my dissertation on the working class and the revolution in Cuba.

But getting to Cuba wasn't easy. It's hard now to recall the fear and hysteria in our country at the time. Our government had forbidden American citizens from traveling to Cuba. Only "bona fide" reporters could get passports valid for travel in Cuba. I went to Cuba as a reporter, in 1961 for the Pacifica Foundation's radio station KPFA in Berkeley and in 1962 for *The Nation*.

By the time I arrived there, given all the reading and research I'd been doing, I was something of an expert on Cuba. I spent every day all day talking to people—in the streets, in parks, in public squares, knocking on doors at random—about the revolution. I traveled all around the island without any restrictions. The revolution was so young. I was there at a moment of popular euphoria; it was only a few months earlier, in April, that the US-organized, -trained, and -equipped invasion force had been defeated at the Bay of Pigs.

By chance, when I came back to Havana from Cuba's interior, shortly before I was to return to the States, I met a young Chilean economist named Carlos Romeo. After three hours sipping strong Cuba Libres and debating the nature of the revolution, Carlos said.

"I think you should meet Che. Do you want to?"

"Sure," I said.
"Wait in your hotel room tonight."
"Right."

As it turned out, Carlos wasn't drunk. What he hadn't told me was that he was working as an assistant to Che. So, sure enough, at about 3 AM, a car came to my hotel to pick me up and take me to meet Che. This was standard practice for Che. He met reporters, diplomats, delegations, etc., only after working sixteen hours or more a day in his post as Minister of Industries.

When I arrived at his office, I discovered another link in the chain of coincidences that got me to Che. J.P. Morray, a former US diplomat and Berkeley law professor, was now also assisting Che.

I spent two and a half, maybe three hours, talking with Che that morning, 14 September 1961. He spoke softly. You had to lean over to hear him. He was self-effacing. Here he was, one of the two major leaders of the revolution, and he sat and listened and talked, man to man, as an equal, with this young student radical from Berkeley. He had suffered from asthma since childhood, and often during our talk he'd take his medicine from his pocket and inhale it. (He had immense physical courage. As a student, despite the asthma that plagued him, he had played soccer and rugby; and later, after getting his medical degree, traveled in the Amazon as a doctor.) He looked like a movie star, incredibly handsome.

I was able to sit nose to nose with him and argue about the revolutionary government's policies. Here I am, a kid, and I'm lecturing him about "dangerous tendencies in the revolution." I'm warning him about Cuba's growing dependence on the Soviet Union. This in itself, his willingness to engage in a genuine political debate with a young American compañero, was an example of Che's lack of dogmatism and his openness as a revolutionary leader. I had a copy with me of Che's little book *La Guerra de Guerrillas* (Guerrilla Warfare) and, when we were done talking, I asked him to inscribe it. He wrote (in Spanish): "The lessons in this book are not intended to apply to the Rocky Mountains."

Outside his office, some huge woodcut murals were hanging on the walls. I remarked on how powerful they were and wished I were able to exhibit them in the United States. Only minutes before my plane was scheduled to take off for Miami, a set of the four murals—among which was the 14 x 4 ft. "Patria o Muerte," which *The New York Times* called "the largest woodcut print in the world"—was delivered to me. The Princeton University Library put them on display a couple of months later. This was, as the *Times* (10 December 1961) said, "the first exhibition of post-revolutionary art in the United States.... All the prints level strong criticism at the United States."

(The formal interview with Che was published in the winter of 1962 in *Root & Branch*, a magazine that Scheer, I, and other students were editing. We also published it as an appendix to our book, *Cuba: An American Tragedy*. The interview was supposed to have been published in *Look* magazine but, without photos of Che and myself, the editor decided against using it.)

I returned to Cuba in the summer of 1962, again with permission from the State Department. I was now a research associate of the Center of International Studies at Princeton University, which gave me a small grant for my research. I had joined Princeton's sociology faculty in the fall of 1961, right after returning from my first trip to Cuba. So, being in the heart of the Eastern Establishment defending Fidel and the revolution drew the media to me like a magnet. I appeared on television in debates about US-Cuba policy.

Although I was a member of the Princeton faculty, I was still technically a graduate student at UC Berkeley, as I hadn't yet completed my dissertation. Research on the dissertation gave me a practical reason for returning to Cuba, and for wanting to meet with Che again. I planned to carry out a countrywide survey of workers. I needed Che's authorization, as Minister of Industries, to get into factories, mines, sugar mills, refineries, and plants, and to have workers released from work to be interviewed. I had mentioned my project to him when I met him in 1961, and he was interested in my doing it: he wanted an objective report on what the workers were saying about their work, their lives, and the revolution.

So I like to say that Che was on my doctoral committee! In July 1962, he went over my interview schedule and suggested changes in language for clarity and to include idiomatic Cuban Spanish. He did not interfere with the content of the questions nor did he put any restrictions on what I could discuss. His only condition was that I provide him with a report on what I learned, especially about workers' thoughts on the unions and the new Workers Committees. Che arranged for me to receive credentials—a few of which stated specifically that my research was "approved

From *Che Vive, Viva Che!* (Berkeley, CA: Berkeley Bonaparte, c. 1970).

by Comandante Guevara" and were signed by him—authorizing me and my wife Marilyn (who grew up in a Puerto Rican neighborhood and was fluent in Spanish) to interview workers in twenty-three different workplaces.

Over that summer, during twelve-hour workdays in high heat and humidity, I and my pregnant wife crisscrossed Cuba in an open jeep; we were guarded, when we were in remote mountainous places where anti-Castro guerrillas were still active, by a burly bearded fellow armed with an Uzi. We completed interviews with 210 workers in twenty-one plants scattered around the island. I wrote a preliminary report of my findings and delivered it to the Ministerio de Industrias. Sometime in the late summer, Che met with me to discuss the report. (In my 1967 book, *Revolutionary Politics and the Cuban Working Class*, reporting the results of this survey, I acknowledged Che's cooperation.)

Marilyn hadn't yet met Che. Then, on the night before our flight back to the US, on 12 September 1962, our phone rang: a car was on its way to pick us up and take us to Che.

This is how Marilyn remembers our meeting with Che:

"When we got to Che's office, I walked in and there was Che sitting at a huge desk. He stood when we came in. Two armed guards stood on either side of him. (After an hour or so, they left, and we were alone with Che.) There I was with my big belly and the first thing I thought of was, 'Jesus Christ, this guy is absolutely gorgeous.' I kept thinking, 'Why in the world do I have to be pregnant now?' They say eyes are the windows of the soul—he had eyes that seemed to go right through you. When I spoke with Che, I told him that there were rumors that, while so many people had inadequate housing, he had three houses—including a *dacha* (villa) in the countryside and an apartment on the sea in Varadero. 'How do you have the nerve to have three houses,' I asked, 'when people don't have adequate housing?' (Maurice looked like he was going to faint.) Che was very honest. He said it was not true, just a rumor, that there were many rumors on the island.

"He was a doctor, you know. So we talked about his asthma. We talked about my pregnancy. I was in the second trimester of my pregnancy in a place that had everything counter to what I was supposed to have at that time, like milk and cheese. So I asked for medical advice. It was almost like I was talking with someone I'd known for a very long time. I felt that way. It was one of the highlights of my life, meeting this man. I was with Che Guevara for six hours, and we were just talking. Try talking to somebody for six hours! (I'm a journalist now and have been for many years, and I've interviewed all sorts of famous people, from Ben Gurion to Bob Dylan. But no one has ever made an impression on me like Che did.) Back in the US, I had no idea what was going on in Cuba. I wasn't a political person like Maurice. I'm a person who doesn't like politicians. But there was something about Che. I don't know what—there was something Christlike about him. I really felt that when he was talking to me, he was telling the truth."

Years later, after a long court battle under the Freedom of Information Act, the FBI and CIA released some heavily censored parts of their surveillance files on me. Our travels to Cuba hadn't gone unnoticed by either agency. An undated document, released to me by the CIA on 9 September 1977, reminded us that "Guevara was at the airport in Cuba to see the Zeitlins off for the US." An FBI document (4 October 1962) "loaned" to the CIA, noted that, according to its source, "Mrs. Zeitlin was seen at the airport in Havana before they took off talking to 'Che' Guevara." In November 1980, a federal judge in Milwaukee refused to order the release of further possibly illegal surveillance documents on the grounds, as *The Milwaukee Journal* reported (6 November 1980), that this "would damage the national security." But the *Journal* somehow got its hands on one of the CIA documents: "The CIA....," according to the newspaper, "[noted] that in Cuba in 1961 Zeitlin became 'very friendly' with the late Che Guevara."

These remarks were adapted from a transcript of a discussion about Che by Maurice and Marilyn Zeitlin, held in David Kunzle's art history seminar at UCLA on 2 December 1996.

Corrales (Raúl Corral Fornos). Photograph, 1959. From *Barbudos* (Havana: Visual América, 1996).

Che and Latin America

Che was never content that Cuba's revolution should remain isolated, but intended for it to ignite movements all over the continent, indeed the world. He hoped that the example of his Bolivian campaign would spread to the five adjacent countries: Argentina, his native land, Chile, Peru, Brazil, and Paraguay. Although he was defeated, it is certain that revolutionaries and dissidents in virtually all Latin American countries—especially and most effectively in Central America in recent decades—were inspired by Che.

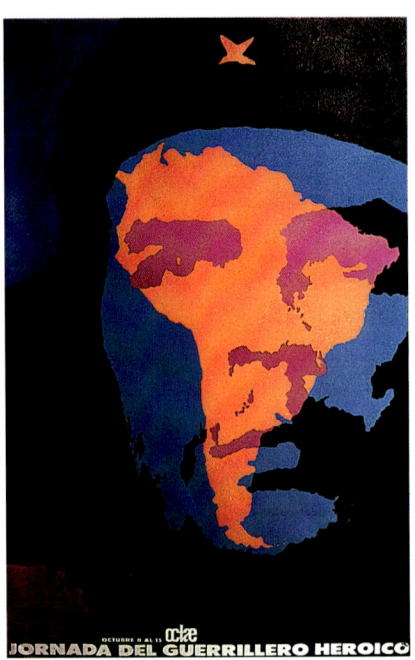

Figure A.1. Balaguer, *Days of the Heroic Guerrilla, 8–15 October*, Continental Latin American Student Organization (OCLAE), 75 x 48 cm.

Figure A.2. *Days of the Heroic Guerrilla, 8–15 October*, OCLAE, 57.5 x 38 cm.

Figure A.3. Latin America to the stake. Troops of Augusto Pinochet burn "subversive" literature and pictures at the coup of 13 September 1973 (international wire photograph). The readily identifiable "Korda matrix" of Che over Bolivia was sufficient to condemn the design.

Figure A.4. Alberto Pérez and Patricia Israel (Chile), *America Awaken(s)*, silkscreen, 1972, 144 x 110 cm (composite of two sheets).

Ernesto Che Guevara: A Brief Chronology

1928 Born in Rosario, Santa Fe, Argentina, of upper-middle class family. From age two suffered from asthma which plagued him for the rest of his life. Devoted to his paternal grandmother, who was born and lived her first years in California. Much affected by her death, he switched his studies from engineering to medicine.

1945 Began medical studies. Wide reading in French and Latin American literature.

1949 First extensive trips through Argentina on motorbike.

1951 Traveled through Latin America, on motorbike, then hitchhiking; penniless, living rough, doing odd jobs along the way, enjoying beauties of nature and archaeological sites; experiencing the misery of the people and working in leprosaria.

1952 Rejected for military service because of asthma.

1953 Awarded MD in Buenos Aires, with a thesis on allergies. Travels, via Bolivia, to Peru and Ecuador and to Guatemala. Meets, later marries, and has one daughter by Hilda Gadea, a Peruvian exile. Tries to organize resistance to US invasion of Guatemala, which overthrows popular Jacob Arbenz regime. His political lesson: the need to mobilize and arm people and resist US interference everywhere.

1954 Takes refuge in Mexico, meets Fidel Castro, thus determining his revolutionary future. Briefly jailed. As physician to the expedition, he departs with eighty-two others for Cuba, where they arrive 2 December 1956.

1956 Guerrilla campaign (2 December 1956 to 1 January 1959), organized and led by Fidel Castro and Che Guevara, culminating in capture by Che of Santa Clara, 29 December 1958, and triumphal entry into Havana on New Year's Day.

1959 Land reform, the first major reform of Revolution, is enacted by Che. Appointed head of National Bank. Divorces first wife, and marries guerrillera comrade Aleida March, with whom he has four children. Travels as diplomat seeking economic aid and trade to Europe, Africa, and Asia.

1960 US refineries refuse to process oil in Cuba; US cuts sugar quota. US-Cuban relations turn sour, revolution radicalizes, and Fidel declares Cuba socialist, in the face of US economic blockade (which continues to this day). More travels by Che around the world seeking trade agreements and aid. As Minister of Industries, he prepares plans for industrialization. Ascetic and disciplined, his typical work day runs from 1 PM to 6 AM. He pays himself 250 pesos (dollars) a month. A typical ministerial salary was 750–1,000 pesos.

1961 Bay of Pigs (Playa Girón). US mercenary invasion is defeated. Che continues to develop theory of New Man (including Woman) imbued with the spirit of sacrifice. Economic progress and human happiness are to be attained by moral, not material incentives. All Che's economic and social theories are, in essence, ethical theories.

1962 Missile crisis. An agreement between Khrushchev and Kennedy to remove Soviet missiles in exchange for promise not to invade island, made over the heads of Cuban leaders, angers them, especially Che, who grows progressively disillusioned with Soviet Union.

1963–1964 More worldwide travels. Formulates theories on unity of Third World (southern hemisphere) against superpower and northern hegemony. Speaks at the United Nations, denouncing US imperialism, registering 1,323 provocations of all kinds against Cuba. His speeches also attack the Soviet Union.

1965 March 21: last public address in Cuba. Disappears; rumored alive, dead, murdered, jailed, mad in various parts of the world. Later revealed to have been many months in Africa, organizing, in vain, resistance to neocolonialism in newly and nominally independent Belgian Congo (Zaire).

1966 Returning to Cuba in spring, trains for new revolutionary adventure, started in Bolivia, 7 November. The country is chosen in the hope that a "guerrilla focus" there will eventually ignite the whole Latin American continent.

1967 Fails to win support of demoralized and indifferent Bolivian peasantry or the Bolivian Communist Party, which influences the potentially revolutionary mineworkers, and urban dissidents. Government responds to Cuban-Bolivian-Peruvian (50–60 strong) guerrilla presence with massive repression of population. After initial successes against a poorly motivated and equipped Bolivian army, rebels in dire condition and cut off from outside help, are hemmed in by forces hastily injected with sophisticated weapons and training by the CIA.

1967 8–9 October: Wounded and captured, Che and two comrades are taken to village of La Higuera, and shot the next day. Bolivian army at first announces he was killed in combat, but his body, exhibited in Vallegrande to journalists and photographers who sent their photos by wire to the world, belies the claim. After fingerprints were taken and the hands severed (and later sent to Cuba), the body disappears, and despite recent excavations (1996–1997) in Vallegrande, remains missing.

1968 *The Bolivian Diaries* published. Legend becomes myth.

Figure B.1. Walter Fröhlich (Switzerland), created in Paris, May 1968.

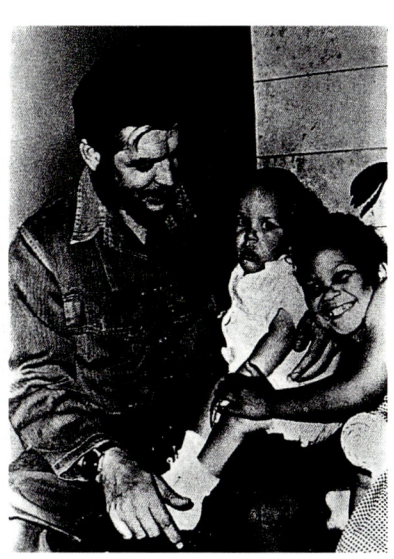

Figure B.2. Che with children, posterized photograph, 73 x 57.5 cm. Courtesy of Michael Rossman/The AOUON Archive.

Figure B.3. Rupert Garcia (US): Ho Chi Minh, Frantz Fanon, and Che, silkscreen, 1972, 66 x 20 cm. Courtesy of the Fine Arts Museums of San Francisco. Achenbach Foundation for Graphic Arts. Museum purchase, Graphic Arts Council Funds.

Che and Cuba

The Cuban revolution was fought from the start—beginning in 1953 when Fidel led the attack on the Moncada barracks—under the aegis of the War of Independence (1868–1895) and specifically José Martí, who was cited by Fidel as the "intellectual author" of his revolutionary aims. The bracketing and mingling of Independence and Revolution heroes shows that Cuba's was a nationalist revolution, rooted in the quest for an independence which had been thwarted by the US when it "confiscated" the victory against the colonial power Spain.

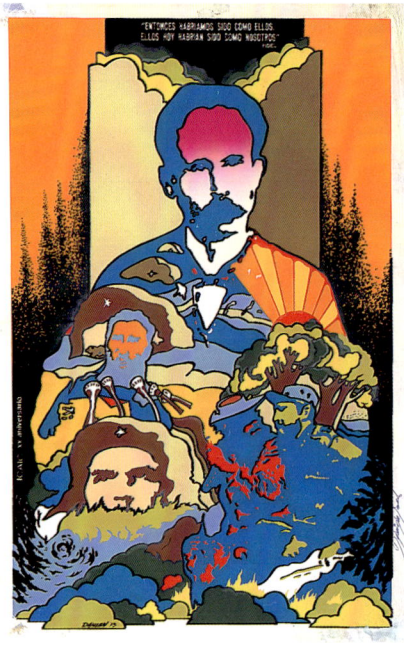 

Figure C.1. Damián: José Martí, Fidel, and Che. *"So if we had been like them, they today would have been like us."—Fidel*, ICAIC (Cuban Film Institute) Twentieth anniversary, 1973, 75.5 x 51 cm.

Figure C.2. Raúl Martínez. *Cuba*, with portraits of Fidel, Che, Camilo Cienfuegos, and Cuban types, 150 x 92.5 cm.

Figure C.3. René Mederos. Che appears to lead a combination of Independence and Revolution fighters: (from left) Máximo Gómez, José Martí, Eduardo Agramonte, Che, Camilo Cienfuegos, Quintín Bandera. Silkscreen (Cuba). Comisión de Orientacíon Revolucionaria del CC del PCC, 1972, 59 x 67 cm.

Figure C.4. René Mederos. From a twelve-part *valla* (billboard) series of 1973 lining the Avenida Revolución toward Plaza Revolución. In successive phrases, the text reads: "We are heirs of our own traditions, of the nationalist and patriotic tradition of [18]68 and [18]95, we are also heirs of the internationalist traditions of Marx and Engels, heirs of the glorious October Revolution of Lenin, we are part of these traditions and take strength in them" (for series, see Kunzle, *Public Graphics*). The dates are those of the War of Independence, led by (from left) Antonio Maceo, Carlos Manuel de Céspedes, Máximo Gómez, and José Martí. The revolutionaries to their right are (left to right) Camilo Cienfuegos, Fidel Castro, Che, and Raúl Castro.

Impressions

"The most complete man of his age; he lived his words, spoke his own actions, and his story and the story of the world ran parallel."
—Jean-Paul Sartre[1]

"The ideal human being, physically beautiful, morally clean, and politically incorruptible."
—Herbert Read[2]

"He was the world symbol of the possibilities of one man."
—Frantz Fanon[3]

"Apostle of the Immaculate Revolution"
—Richard Bourne[4]

"I tell you, his thought was in space before the Russians, before the Americans walked on the moon."
—Benigno
(Dariel Alarcón Ramírez)[5]

"His life is a shining example for youth whose struggles are moved by the desire to build a new world."
—Graham Greene[6]

"He had eyes that went on forever. Truly windows to the soul."
—Marilyn Zeitlin

"The struggle of Guevara against the US was the struggle of the Spirit against Matter."
—Ernesto Sábato[7]

"The word that first came to mind on meeting Che Guevara was simplicity...he was the first man I had ever met whom I thought not just handsome but beautiful. With his curly reddish beard, he looked like a cross between a faun and a Sunday-school print of Jesus."
—I.F. Stone[8]

"He seemed and was very young. His image fixed itself on the retina, lucid intelligence, ascetic pallor, asthmatic breathing, protuberant forehead, thick hair, dry disposition, energetic chin, serene demeanor, inquisitive look, sharp thinking, restful speech, vibrant senses, clear laugh, and face aureoled as it were with a radiation of magical dreams."
—Raúl Roa[9]

"The myth, the legend, the romance, the tradition passed from mouth to mouth, carried the name of Che over the breadth of the land, the ridges of the mountain, the length of the rivers."
—Alejo Carpentier[10]

"The most accomplished human being I have ever met. Throughout my time in prison (fifteen years) a little photograph of Che dead, naked, thin, pierced with bullets, his face illuminated by its internal light, a photograph I had cut out of a magazine, gave me hope when it was cold in my life."
—Ben Bella, independence leader of Algeria[11]

"You were always an apostolic and evangelical condottiere, and a courageous child athlete who knew how to throw a triple somersault and always land in place."
—León Felipe[12]

"His ideas, his portrait, and his name are banners in the struggle against injustice by the oppressed and exploited and they arouse passionate enthusiasm in students and intellectuals everywhere.... Che stood for the spirit of internationalism in its purest and most disinterested form...."
—Fidel Castro[13]

"There was something extraordinarily calm and gentle about Che; his voice was very low, slightly hoarse. I think he was a bit shy himself. What was odd was the contrast between his athletic, muscular frame, and his excessively delicate, aristocratic features, his pale, almost sickly complexion. He was as handsome and attractive as people have made him out to be, but it was not so much his good looks as his expression, so intelligent, kind, and humorous, which gave him such charm."
—Ania Francos[14]

"I just want to say that my mind is richer for your thoughts,
My humanity prouder for your actions,
My life less acceptable for your death,
My death more acceptable for your life."
—John McGrath[15]

"The death of Che Guevara brought a sense of grief and disappointment to people who had no Marxist sympathies. He represented the idea of gallantry, chivalry, and adventure in a world more and more given up to business arrangements between the great world powers; he expressed for us the hope that victory did not always go to the big battalions.... They were afraid to bring [Che] to trial; afraid of the echoes his voice would have aroused in the courtroom; afraid to prove that the man they hated was loved by the world outside. This fear will help to perpetuate his legend, and legend is impervious to bullets."
—Graham Greene[16]

"Everything you created was perfect, but you created a unique being, you created yourself; you demonstrated how the new man is truly possible. All of us then saw that this new man is a reality, because he exists: you are he."
—Haydée Santamaría[17]

"Che's life has had the unique virtue of impressing even his worst ideological enemies and making them admire him.... Che did not die defending any interest or cause other than that of the exploited and downtrodden of this continent. Che died defending that cause alone, and even his worst enemies have not dared to suggest otherwise."
—Fidel Castro[18]

Introduction *David Kunzle*

Icon, myth, and message—and commercialization?

It was my original intent to do a book and exhibition for the thirtieth anniversary of Che's death which would combine in about equal proportions posters of Che—which I had been collecting since 1968 and existed in abundance already—and a survey of posters (those of OSPAAAL, etc.) relating to his ideas, to the Cuban revolution, and its culture (notably film). We would thus be celebrating not only Che as an icon (and myth) but also illustrating his message, the Cuban revolution, and broadly Cuban poster art, which has still to receive the major exhibition and monograph it deserves.

After the idea of a Che exhibition was accepted by a museum with limited space available, more Che posters and iconography flowed in from many sources, and it soon became apparent that there would simply be no room for a full component of non-Che posters if we wished to present as wide and international a variety as possible of Che material. I had, therefore, to sacrifice the bigger display of Cuban posters, keeping only a small sample of posters from OSPAAAL (Organization of Solidarity with the Peoples of Africa, Asia, and Latin America) and silkscreens from ICAIC (Instituto Cubano de las Artes y Industrias Cinematográficas, the Cuban Film Institute). These must now stand for the incomparable aesthetic and political graphic riches generated by Cuban revolutionary culture.

The sacrifice of so many non-Che posters meant that the primary focus on Che, under the banner of *Che Guevara: Icon, Myth, and Message*, leaves us open to the charge of iconicizing and mythicizing Che to the detriment of the message. Our intention here is to illustrate and analyze icon and myth, and extract some essentials of the message, without engaging Che's ideology in detail or as a whole.

The commercialization of Che, which we are told everywhere is rampant on this thirtieth anniversary, is another problem. Ideally we would have minimized the price of this book to make it easy for all to buy and not charged for admission to the exhibition (Thursdays are free). This would have been especially appropriate in the case of a figure like Che who stood against monetary rewards and even the very idea of money. A scholarly museum exhibition and book are not, however, the forms of commercialization (the term may not be appropriate anyway) against which the critics rail; truly commercial forms of exploitation usually involve consumer objects. How do we stand in relation to the "Cult of Che"? Corporate media like to deride the very process in which they are engaged, which is to reduce the revolutionary to the role of "leftist pop star," as a recent *Spiegel* feature article did in a headline, in the hope presented as fact, that "the more he (Che) is reproduced, the further he gets from reality." The reality of Che is, of course, still threatening. The *Spiegel* (a sort of German *Time* magazine) lines Che up with "the likes of John F. Kennedy, Humphrey Bogart or Mickey Mouse, of Jesus or Tarzan."[1] This flattening and homogenizing of totally different phenomena is of course standard mass media practice (fig. 8.3).

Is putting Che on anything from a T-shirt to a lapel pin just another instance of business (mostly, I think at the moment, small business) capitalizing on our nostalgia for revolution? It would take too long to argue here whether such exploitation ultimately serves the preservation of Che's ideas or not; the motives for making and buying a Che artifact would vary widely from case to case. Of course, wearing Che on your chest does not necessarily mean bearing him in your heart. The habit does not make the monk, nor the Che necklace the revolutionary, any more than a statuette of Jesus makes the Christian. A symbol should be the outward and bodily sign of an inward and spiritual grace but often is not; religious and political reformers alike have long been disturbed by the dissonance between outward show and inner substance.

Political posters, obviously in the forefront of commercialization insofar as they are sold (as they are now, mostly, even in Cuba), themselves raise the cry against a process in which they are inevitably implicated. In this example, the harshness of the complaint is, in one respect, not exaggerated: pictures of Che *are* honored in the very US military schools where "murderers"—Latin American death

Figure D.2. Market stall, Havana, 1996.

Figure D.3. Che on key chains, pins, and other memorabilia, Cuba, 1996.

Figure D.1. Alfredo Rostgaard, OSPAAAL. 66 x 39.5 cm.

squads— are trained. Thus a Mexican Zapatista poster:

> In an attempt to conceal your example and
>   your ideas
> your portrait was placed in the windows
> the murderer usurped your quixotic sphinx
> made you into a T-shirt, profit, folklore
> thinking that this would put the brakes
>   on you.
>
> The reactionary too claimed your image
> turning it into something superficial,
>   banal, insignificant.
> Copied the outer shell concealing the
>   ideology
> and for years you were passed off
>   as a "new wave" personality
> usable by the bourgeoisie as well...[2]

Gerardo Mosquera, a leading Cuban critic of contemporary art, has taken a no less jaundiced view, derived from observation of the burgeoning Cuban tourist handicrafts market, and shaped by the broader concern which is shared by many Cubans and friends of Cuba, namely that the pell-mell promotion of tourism as a form of economic salvation carries a deadly price.[3] Citing Cuba's sun, unfairly, as the country's "most efficient economic force," Mosquera complains that Cuba—and its icons—are being sold off dirt cheap, and that Havana, in suffering a novel plague of prostitution caused by tourism, is becoming the "Bangkok of the Caribbean." In this unflattering context, Che (along with *santería* icons of Ochun and Chango) is the victim of a "complete commercial banalization" carried out by the Cuban revolution itself, a process as it happens that is constantly being critiqued and ironized by contemporary Cuban art itself. "The official rhetoric belies the desperation of a country that is forced to sell even its symbols." In fact, all countries visited by tourists sell their symbols; the real problem is when they sell— cheaply—their basic resources along with them.

A small, socialist island-nation, isolated in a capitalist world, suffering from a thirty-seven-year-old trade embargo with the US, may be pardoned for "acts of desperation" to survive, and for engaging in tactics which the rich countries of Western Europe, selling far more than Cuba's one million dollars annually of tourist artifacts, have applied for centuries. Michelangelo's *David* miniaturized in plastic or printed on a T-shirt or coffee mug seems an innocent enough contribution to the Italian economy, and indeed to the artist's popularity.

Che: a new kind of Cuban portraiture

A primary function of portraiture has always been to reinforce the sense of individuality, to set the sitter above and apart from others by emphasizing either his or her uniqueness or social superiority, or both at once. Portraiture of the political hero, moreover, has often pushed this function to an extreme, dignifying the idea that certain individuals are called upon to transcend the norms of humanity and that they possess superhuman (that is, supersocial) will.

In the present century, as capitalism has suffered one crisis after another and the artist has become alienated from the social system, portraiture has fallen into decline; "official" and "public" portraiture is neglected in practice and derided in concept. To be sure, photographic portraiture survives, but almost apologetically so in official contexts. Public political portraiture has, however, been revived in socialist countries, which have tried to blend into the tradition of hero imagery the idea of the individual as representative of, rather than transcending, the mass, as standing for doctrine rather than for individual will. Formally, the results of this effort have little appeal to Europeans and North Americans, who tend to dislike the Soviet or Chinese modes of "heroic" portraiture (which are often heroic in scale as well as in content). We are struck by the uniformity, as well as the ubiquity, of portraits of Marx and Lenin. Those of Mao are even more uniform and fixed in their idealization. In socialist countries, an aesthetic form of bureaucratic centralism and a massive collectivization of individual artistic will have eradicated personal interpretation in order to stamp the outlines of universality, permanence, and facility of recognition upon the image of the "revolutionary hero." This approach has a certain ahistoricity, and tends to contradict the Marxist precept that all social phenomena flow from particular material conditions and must change along with those conditions.

In Ernesto Che Guevara, Cuba, too, has its "universal" and "permanent" revolutionary hero, but the iconography which has emerged around him is anything but uniform or ahistorical in a formal sense. True, there is the stereotyped Che image, a very high-contrast "photographic" simplification of a kind much prized in Western graphic art for its powers of immediate visual impact and symbolization. But the existence of the stereotype is less important than the fact of innumerable variations upon and departures from it. In Cuba, there are, it seems, as many ways of seeing Che as there are artists. It is a striking fact that this tiny country, within a few years, produced a hero iconography far more varied—as well as far more exciting— than the socialist countries of Eastern Europe produced in decades. This may be because of the special geographical-historical circumstances which tied pre-revolutionary Cuba so umbilically to the US and thereby to a US-European artistic tradition characterized by the unremitting search for formal novelty.

Immediately upon the death of Che, on 9 October 1967, a myth sprang to life. In the US, his image quickly became a commercial commodity, a poster to be sold along with posters of Humphrey Bogart and Mick Jagger; simultaneously, it offered fresh revolutionary inspiration internationally to protest movements from Washington to Paris, from Berlin to Tokyo, as it was used in posters at demonstrations for peace and against US imperialism, which escalated so radically in 1968.

In Cuba, the production of Che imagery quickly exceeded that for any other contemporary Cuban leader, including Fidel, who discourages fetishization of his person,[4] and rivals that of José Martí, the Cuban national hero from the Independence era, small busts of whom are ubiquitous in the island nation. In Cuba, 1968 was declared the Year of the Heroic Guerrilla, and, before it was over, the Cuban critic Edmundo Desnoes was suggesting that the

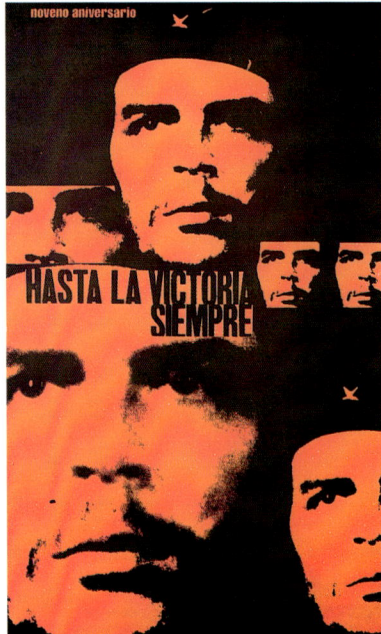

Figure D.4. Ñiko (Antonio Pérez González), *Ever Onward Unto Victory*. The first public poster of Che (October 1967), ninth anniversary version, 98 x 54.5 cm.

imagery of Che might be reaching saturation point.[5] Desnoes also pointed to a danger confronting the Cuban poster in general: that it could become repetitive, dogmatic, and a purely mechanical stimulus productive of unilateral thinking. Desnoes's fears were not realized, as he himself attested a few years later, in an article dedicated exclusively to Che iconography.[6] The continuing vitality of this iconography flows from the vitality of the legend itself and shares the vitality of all Cuban poster art, of which it is a central component.

The permanent presence of Che in the home, at work, and in community centers is publicly augmented and focused during October, the anniversary month of his death. At this time Che looks down (and up) from a multitude of highway billboards (*vallas*) and street posters. The ubiquity of his portrait (often joined to that of Camilo Cienfuegos) avoids monotony through the policy of constantly changing the vallas and posters (fig. D.5). The urban context for these bright billboards is, like the background of Che's own way of life, austere and even drab, for the Revolution has given low priority to the renovation of the big cities; the posters provide special psychological focus, sudden moments of beauty. As visually sophisticated and splendid as they are, they are not intended simply to intrigue or dazzle the eye but primarily to form a revolutionary consciousness in the mold of Che—a consciousness which is morally motivated and internationally dedicated.

The poster is probably the most widely known and admired outside Cuba of all that country's cultural manifestations. Too little literature is available in translation, and to this day too few Cuban films (for all the prizes they have won at European film festivals) have managed to evade the US economic blockade, but the posters have become known in this country as well as all over the world, at first through the best-selling collection of facsimiles published by McGraw-Hill in 1970.[7] Small public exhibitions of originals have been staged by several major European museums. There is now a reverse flow of influence: deriving from their formal language, largely from the bourgeois world, the posters are presently exerting a direct formal and political influence on graphic artists of the bourgeois world.

Before the Revolution there was no such thing as a "Cuban poster." It has sprung into being since 1965. If there is now a "Cuban school" of poster art (an idea Cubans tend to reject), it is characterized by far-ranging but discriminating eclecticism of style combined with great centrality of purpose. Its sources are avant-garde graphics from all over the world—North America, Europe (especially Eastern Europe), and Japan—and its products embrace styles which have emerged over the last fifteen years—Pop, Op, psychedelic, neo-Surrealist, neo-Art Nouveau (fig. D.6). They also sometimes incorporate indigenous Third World art, but they exclude both Soviet and Chinese Socialist Realism. The development of an aesthetic appropriate to the Cuban poster began around 1965, spurred by Raúl Martínez's adaptation of a Pop Art style. Before the Revolution, it was retrograde in style as well as debased in its commercial content, and between the Revolution and 1965, a pro-Socialist Realism faction struggled with the contemporary style proponents. The visual language of a certain artistic elite suddenly found in Cuba a true meaning and the vehicle for popular expansion.

The formal idealizations of Che portraiture enrich the ideas the Che image represents in a complex way: as simplifications of line and contour tend to uniformity and deindividualization, the free and very diverse coloristic embellishments and tonal contrasts contribute notions of spontaneity, flexibility, and plurality. Diversity of form here points to diversity of appeal, and the formal sophistication of the Cuban poster suggests a high respect on the part of cultural professionals for the artistic literacy of the Cuban people and for their capacity to interpret new systems of symbolism.

The process by which Cuban artists absorbed and activated styles formulated by the giant to the north may be likened to the tactic emphasized by Che of the guerrilla fighter who captures arms from the enemy and turns them against him. Cuban eclecticism represents a truly Cuban fusion of national purpose with international visual styles. At the same time, it appears more internationalistic in purpose than, for

Figure D.5. *The best homage is daily effort. Ideological Day of Camilo [Cienfuegos] and Che*, billboard, 1973.

Figure D.6. Raúl Martínez, *El Che y Camilo [Cienfuegos]*, ICAIC (Cuban Film Institute).

example, the Mexican mural renaissance (which was less stylistically eclectic and more nationalistic). The image of Che, who incarnates the much controverted principle of international revolution, is, fittingly, couched in a truly international visual language.

The Cuban poster has gone extensively into the world, often through OSPAAAL (see Chapter 1). Thus, it challenges the isolation threatened by the US economic and cultural blockade. The idea of "exporting revolution" may have long since been abandoned, but the Cubans continue, through Che, to export the *idea* of revolution. At the same time, internally, the image of Che challenges social isolation and elitism, embodying an egalitarian ideal, and an ever-present reproach to certain trends of the 1990s: dollarization of the economy, "tourist apartheid," and other compromises with capitalism. The Cubans see in Che not only the guerrilla hero, the government minister, the revolutionary diplomat, and intellectual, but also the man who systematically engaged in voluntary manual labor—a worker like themselves.

The Cubans see themselves in Che. So often, hero imagery is imposed unilaterally upon indifferent, divided, or even wholly hostile popular opinion. In Cuba, people have always felt a very real affection for Che (as they do for Fidel and other leaders), and the outpouring of posters after his martyrdom represents a spontaneous expression of popular feeling. This is not to conceal, of course, the fact that many—even the majority—of Cuba's posters were issued by agencies and institutions operating under carefully controlled ideological and political programs. But here there is no incompatibility between the "spontaneous" and the "official." It is not merely rhetorical to suggest that, for most Cubans, Che is the very *Hombre Nuevo*—the selfless New Man and Woman, at once ideal man and Everyman—that he desired the Revolution would bring into existence.

The richness, the completeness of Che imagery, reflects a feeling that also exists widely outside of Cuba. Che has inspired tributes from writers not given to hyperbole, such as Herbert Read and Jean-Paul Sartre. The unique combination he represents of revolutionary theory and concrete action, of myth and reality, is an admonition, too, that Che is not just an image.

And yet, is Che not perhaps the most imaged of all twentieth-century political heroes? The Che poster is now part of his historic definition. In Jean Cau's *A Passion for Che Guevara* (1979), he is "defined," on the back cover, as a "guerrillero, saint, adventurer, hero, martyr, and poster." Films revert again and again to the poster image: Roberto Massari's video *Ernesto Che Guevara* (Rome: Erre Emme, 1996) ends on a review of the posters. Notably, Santiago Alvarez' *Always Unto Victory*, passes the posters in a swirling sequence as if to say: this is the vortex of the man's effect on us. Pedro Chaskel's documentary film *A Photo Traverses the World* is entirely about the posters. A screenplay by English novelist Alan Sillitoe called *Che* (a film never made, unfortunately) starts with the film director in a meeting with the scriptwriter and others. The writer, asked what Che means to people, says that although he has read all there is, he needs to meditate upon a poster he has just bought before he can answer, or start work. There follows a series of shots of Che posters. It is the Che poster, rather than any great sculpture to the individual, to which Cubans are not given on principle, that is his enduring and ever renewable public monument.

Unique example, single image, multiplication

The posters' almost exclusive focus on Che's face or bust both personalizes and universalizes the hero, and tends, no doubt, to that kind of "personality cult" all too familiar in the mass culture of capitalism. It does so in a way that pictures of Che full-length, engaged in some recognizable activity, placed in a social or military context, would not. The posters in this book and exhibition (the hundreds of others not illustrated or exhibited are no different in this respect) do not pictorialize the life of a man who was many things: doctor, soldier, government minister, orator, writer, family man, worker, poet, chess player. To do so would be the task of the innumerable press photographs (another book, another exhibition).

Why do the artists return again and again to the face, and so often the same, single "matrix photograph" of the face (see Chapter 5)? Is it the sense that Korda's version was the result of a unique and (one is tempted to say loosely) divine inspiration? Che certainly looks inspired at this moment. And that such a moment of inspiration, which is twofold, Che's and the photographer's, cannot by its very nature, recur? Or is it the "copycat" instinct of artists today, who feel that art is at its most modern (postmodern) when it adapts rather than invents?

There is some validity to these considerations, but the root, I believe, of our satisfaction in the one (or very few) matrix images of Che lies deeper, in our perception of Che as a unique historical moment, an unrepeatable example, as the most perfect single realization of our accumulated desires (call them mythic or not), for which a single image, or very few images among the thousands taken, is most appropriate. Che was a singular man. So we seek out a single most "authentic" rendition of him. This image may be repeated and varied, while the original man himself remains somehow essentially fixed (as popularly imagined); in reality the meaning of Che is constantly evolving. The Che image, moreover, is repeated within itself, so that the favorite modernist tactic, commonplace in graphic and other art since Pop Art and Warhol, of internal as well as external multiplication of identical or similar images, may be applied, with a modernist irony, to one human example that cannot be duplicated, to one image that can never again be captured at its origins.

Not Mars, but Adonis: not war but love

We leave here many questions by the way: how far does the conformity of Che's face to current ideals of male beauty—we know from photographs that Che was at least as good looking as Omar Sharif or Antonio Banderas, to cite only his best known impersonators—contribute to his romantic (not to say sexual) appeal? What if Che had been less handsome, what if he had been clean-shaven? What if he had not been personally charming, photogenic, charismatic? Idle questions perhaps, but it is noteworthy that historically artists have always made it their task or been set the task of beautifying power, giving aesthetic substance to ideals. Nature, in Che's case, made it easy for them.

The most remarkable example of Che's beauty inspiring an instant kind of love in a stranger is recounted by Jon Lee Anderson. A Russian assigned to discuss Che's reputed pro-Chinese stance with him confessed to falling in love with him.

> I told him: "You know, I'm a little older than you, but I like you, I like above all your looks"...and I confessed my love for him because he was a very attractive young man.... I felt attracted to him, do you understand? It was as if I wanted to get away to separate myself, but he attracted me, you see.... He had very beautiful eyes. Magnificent eyes, so deep, so generous, so honest, a stare that was so honest that somehow one could not help but feel it...and he spoke very well, he became inwardly excited, and his speech was like that, with all of this impetus, as if his words were squeezing you.[8]

Artists have not disputed the general assumption that Christ was physically as well as morally beautiful. For Petrarch (with no more historical evidence than exists for Christ), Scipio Africanus the Elder had to be physically as well as morally perfect. Significantly, the great Roman warrior became in the hands of artists, not only handsome, but magnanimous and pacific—cleansed, like Che, of an essential aspect of his life and character: that of the soldier given perforce to killing.

It seems that the need to detach Che, Scipio-like, from the immediacy of death and war, is paramount among the poster designers, and remarkably so in Mederos's painting series of Che's life (see Chapter 6). The posters, all Cuban, showing a gun (on its own, with Che present only in a text, fig. M.25) are in a very small minority. It is love, not war that he represents, hence the popularity, now in Cuba as well as outside, of Che's phrase about a revolutionary being motivated by feelings of great love (figs. M.49, M.50).

Che the writer

The use of citations from Che's writings is another characteristic feature of the posters. Che is acknowledged as a master of prose style: elegant, laconic, moving easily from polemic denunciation to careful analysis, unrivaled in the sober, self-effacing chronicle of the day-by-day guerrilla experience. The latter, immortalized in the *Episodes of the Revolutionary War* and the *Bolivian Diary*, points to a characteristic rare among men of action, who tend to relegate autobiographical reconstruction from often faulty memories to their declining years. Che kept diaries rigorously, with a regularity only now becoming known since the publication of the youthful *Motorcycle Diaries*, and the African diary; there is apparently more to come. Che's self-discipline and self-critical sobriety are extraordinary in a warrior: no Caesarian, or Napoleonic or Pattonish posturing or self-glorification here. Pithy citations from Che in murals, billboards, posters, and on buildings are as ubiquitous as those from Martí. Che's writings and speeches are a gospel from which exhortations, guidance and inspiration flow. And the phenomenon of false attribution of sayings, which is the lot of many great men, holds for Che as well: the phrase "let us be realistic, demand the impossible," popularized by the posters and on the walls of Paris, May 1968, is attributed to Che (fig. 5.5), to the point of figuring as the epigraph of a book about him.

Che as a source of literary inspiration to others is a distinct phenomenon dealt with in Fabian Wagmister's chapter here. We need add only that Che's face has been constituted by the very words of texts about him, notably the famous poem by Nicolás Guillén (figs. 3.2, 3.7).

"Posterization"

The adaptability of Korda's "matrix" photograph has much to do with the ease and clarity with which it can be "posterized." This Che photograph has indeed been used in a recent book on how we see images as a test-case for "posterization," that simplifying process, photographic in origin, essential not only to graphic art, but also contemporary visual art

Figure D.8. Ernesto Che Guevara, *Writings and Speeches, Edition in Commemoration of the 10th Anniversary of His Death in Combat*, Social Science Publishing, 1977, 76.5 x 51 cm. Courtesy of the Center for Cuban Studies Art Space.

Figure D.7. Don Honeyman, published by Big O Posters, c. 1970, 106 x 88 cm.

Introduction

The Volatile Face: Two, Three, Many Ches

and film. There are now also electronic screening methods which mechanically reduce the tonal structure of a photograph, "replacing smooth tonal gradients by sequences of distinct levels separated by contours—much like a landscape architect might transform a sloping hill into a sequence of flat terraces separated by abrupt level changes."[9] Apart from gratifying and often surprising aesthetic enhancements, there is an economic advantage to the silkscreen maker, in that s/he needs fewer masks to realize the portrait.

The erasure of graphic tones to arrive at an essence of form and contour may be analogized to the process of heroization and myth-making: the historic figure becomes simplified, essentialized, easily recognized, remembered, reusable. S/he becomes like a familiar friend recognizable from a distance. Given minimal data, likeness is preserved even under the distortions of a clumsy, untrained hand. Posterization operates like cartoon shorthand with "tabs of identity" and synecdoche: star, beret, beard. The process can be studied in other heroes, of course: in Zapata with his characteristic mustache and piercing eyes, who also depends very much on a single, matrix photograph, that taken in full-length by Agustín Casasola; and in the Nicaraguan hero Augusto Sandino, with his Stetson hat, the crudest graffito of which suffices, in his homeland, to conjure him up. José Martí, in Cuba an icon even more ubiquitous than Che Guevara, is often reduced to the full, ovoid mustache and receding hairline (cf. figs. 1.15, 1.18).

An icon, activated, becomes a banner, a rallying point. Fidel Castro himself has bannered Che, in his "Necessary Introduction" to the *Bolivian Diary*: "His ideas, his portrait, and his name are banners in a struggle against injustice by the oppressed and the exploited and they arouse passionate enthusiasm in students and intellectuals everywhere."[10] Fidel goes on to speak, approvingly, of the adoption of Che's image in demonstrations in the United States. What, then is a Che T-shirt but an individual banner worn in the social parade?

Portions of this section previously appeared in "Uses of the Portrait: The Che Poster" in *Art in America* 63:66-73, September 1975. Reproduced with permission.

The photographic record reveals a range of expressions that one associates with professional actors rather than political figures. Artists, playing variations upon and subtly adapting photographs, expand this range further. Here we see many different moods, all characteristic of Che, who was always remarkably spontaneous in public, had no "official face," and was highly sensitive to people and surroundings.

Sweetness and gaiety (figs. E.1, E.2) shift, via sudden turning of the head, to sudden concern (fig. E.3) and an outright worried look (fig. E.4), to a brooding sadness (fig. E.5), and in a version painted in New York, "the belly of the beast," anguish or anger (fig. E.6). The *Time* artist, in the early days of the revolution, captures a faunlike mixture of cunning and charm (fig. E.9) which seems very percipient, given the ideological blinkers of the magazine toward anyone labeled a "communist stooge."

In two posters based on a photograph by the Swiss René Burri (figs. E.7, E.8), Che is seen slightly from below, giving him a touch of debonair arrogance, which in the recent OSPAAAL version curdles to a suspicious look. The Burri photograph, one of the best known of Che, was used by Swatch watch (p. 106) and by the Bern-based Cuba-Switzerland solidarity organization. Burri rephotographed the latter poster—hanging tattered on a wall—and used this image for an independent photograph and poster.

Figure E.1. Nicaragua: Che with part of Guillén poem *Che Comandante* printed below (see also figs. 3.2–3.6). The red and black border refers to the colors of Sandinismo.

Figure E.2. Rafael Enríquez, OSPAAAL, 1982, 53 x 33 cm.

Figure E.3. Rafael Enríquez, OSPAAAL, 1986, 68 x 48 cm.

Figure E.4. Alberto Blanco, OSPAAAL, 1989, 58 x 47 cm.

Figure E.5. Modesto Braulio, with citation from José Martí, *10th Anniversary of the Death of Comdte Che Guevara, Day of the Heroic Guerrilla*, 1977, 70 x 44 cm.

Figure E.6. Ricardo Carpani (Argentina). Detail from a mural (now covered) on the Pathfinder Press building in New York, 1989 (see fig. M.44).

Figure E.7. OSPAAAL, *This great humanity has said, "Enough." 8 October, Day of the Heroic Guerrilla*, based on photograph by Swiss René Burri, 72 x 53 cm.

Figure E.8. O. Molina, Luis Miguel, and S. Puga, *Forever Comandante*, OCLAE 20th Anniversary, 1987, based on a photograph by René Burri.

Figure E.9. Bernard Safran, Cover of *Time*, 8 August 1960.

Figure E.10. Oswaldo Guaysamín. *Homenaje a Che Guevara*, lithograph, 1975, 45 x 34 cm. This startling transformation by Ecuador's international celebrity is obviously unrelated to any photograph, but combines some of Che's known features with those traditional to Don Quixote. The physiognomic fusion is as far as I know unique, but the association of Cervantes's fictional hero with Latin American revolution is not uncommon. Che himself, in his farewell letter to his parents (mid-1966) before departing on his Bolivian campaign, spoke of his feeling the ribs of Rocinante, Don Quixote's horse, beneath his legs: "And once more I hit the road with my shield upon my arm." The statue of Don Quixote in the center of Havana (23 and K streets) stands as a symbol of resistance and idealism, likewise that of the same character in the Palace of Pioneers in Parque Lenin. A book for juveniles on Che, *Con la Adarga al Brazo* (With My Shield upon My Arm, 1974) by Mariano Rodríguez Herrera, is illustrated with pictures of the don. Quixote is central to the work of Walter Solón Romero, creator of *The Christ of La Higuera* (fig. 8.16), who avows a "fifty year complicity" with the Cervantes hero. Solón went to jail in the 1970s for representing the military as enemies of Quixote, and sees him still as a persecuted would-be liberator, for all that Quixote's vision is anchored in the past. Does Guayasamín's Quixote-Guevara fix his eyes, each a different color, upon a noble vision of the future—or does he hallucinate an impossible vision of the past?

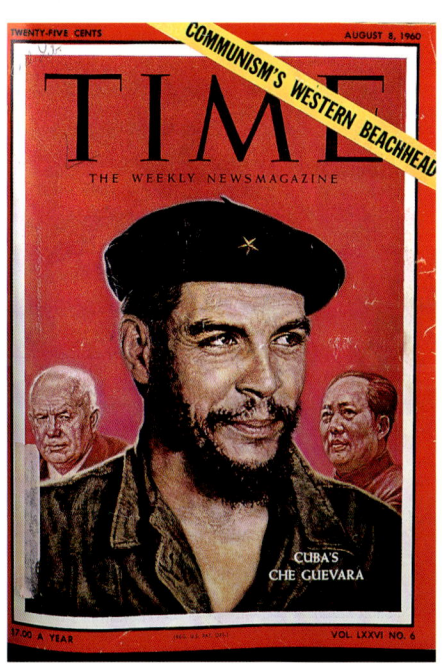

Chapter 1.

Che's Ideals in the Cuban Poster: OSPAAAL, Frémez, ICAIC

Internationalism of theme and style

We may credit the inspiration of Che with a critical development in the Cuban political poster: those published by OSPAAAL (Organization of Solidarity with the Peoples of Africa, Asia, and Latin America). Following Che's globetrotting in the early 1960s, and the sense he fostered for the necessity of Third World unity in the face of First World (American and Russian) imperialism, the first conference on Solidarity with the Peoples of Africa, Asia, and Latin America was held in Havana, 3–15 January 1966. Che himself was at this time in Dar Es Salaam, recuperating from the failed campaign in Africa, and planning the next, in Latin America. Out of this conference came a magazine called *Revista Tricontinental* (fig. 1.1), to which Che sent from Bolivia his famous "Message to the Tricontinental."

The magazine was soon printing fifty thousand copies (by 1989, thirty thousand), a large edition for so small an originating country. At first the posters were kept small and uniform in size (53 x 33 cm), so that they could be folded into the magazine; later they were issued physically separate, and from the mid-1970s, in larger formats (but less frequently), reaching on occasion 51 x 72 cm. Published in editions of 2,000–2,500, a remarkable proportion reached the US, despite the embargo, where they were eagerly sought and still constitute a small point of sale for progressive bookstores. The posters, like the magazine, were aimed at the world at large—a pictorial declaration of Cuban foreign policy. *Tricontinental* magazine was originally published in Spanish, French, English, and Arabic (the latter edition was soon dropped), and reached eighty-seven different countries; the distribution of the posters with their multilingual texts must have been comparable.

The overarching concept behind the posters is to create a "Day of Solidarity" with the many peoples of the world oppressed by and struggling against (US) imperialism. Since so many of the thirty-eight countries commemorated in the OSPAAAL posters are given such a day (or week) of solidarity, based on some recent historic event (for African American people, for instance, the Watts uprising of 11 August 1965), the number of commemorative days rivals that of the Catholic calendar with all its saints' days. The total production figures of different OSPAAAL posters over thirty years are impressive: over 350, reaching a numerical crescendo around 1970, and tapering off in the 1980s, as Cuba's support for armed popular struggles became muted,[1] declining to a mere trickle today and employing only two artists, where before the team was much larger.[2]

The quantitative decline in a once-glorious and proliferating field of public graphics is unfortunately widespread, whether it be the billboards, or the Cuban Film Institute (ICAIC) posters; both were once ubiquitous in the streets. The latter, like OSPAAAL's, are assured of a place in the history of world graphics in this century.[3] The billboards, large, colorful, splendidly variable in composition, and often designed to be read as series (some of the best from the 1970s are by René Mederos), constitute like the OSPAAAL graphics a valuable record of Cuba's stance in the world; like the OSPAAAL posters, the billboards have paid continuous (annual, in October) homage to Che (fig. D.5, p. 23).

The general decline of public sector and political art in Cuba has been accompanied by an ever-expanding sector of private, gallery art, which is partly driven by a lucrative export market. This art is, like the public art, consciously modernistic, aware of international trends, and able to exercise a limited critical function denied to the officialist public art of OSPAAAL and the billboards.[4] This can be seen in the private, ironic, self-indulgent manipulations of the Che image (e.g., figs. K.1–K.4, p. 94), among other places.

Like Che, like the Revolution, Cuba's public art has been internationalist. This is true in regard to styles, as well as themes, to a degree that makes the art of other revolutions seem insular, concerned as it has been in modern times primarily with internal issues, with fostering revolutionary spirit in order to create unity from within. "Internationalist" revolutionary art connotes, in Cuban practice, a remarkable degree of eclecticism flowing from a receptivity to modern (and postmodern) "vanguard" art currents on the one hand, and traditional Third World cultures on the other, the latter particularly evident in the OSPAAAL posters. Euro-American "vanguard" art has itself been eclectic, in a highly experimental way—so, too, Cuban art.

Given the real restrictions on oppositional political expression, cultural expression in Cuba has always been relatively open and free, experimental. The right to be a bit crazy has been cherished. Was not the very idea of trying to make revolution in the face of the US touched with craziness? So why not crazy art? There is an anecdote about Fidel Castro's own artistic tolerance which is more enlightening, I think, than his much repeated (and probably deliberately vague and ambiguous) dictum about the limits on freedom of expression: "Within the revolution, everything, without it, nothing." Confronted with a large, abstract mural by René Portocarro in the presidential palace, some delegates from the Eastern bloc asked Fidel, "What does this mean?" Fidel replied, "It doesn't mean anything. It's just some crazy thing painted for some people who like crazy things of this kind, by a crazy person who was commissioned by the crazy men who made this revolution." And elsewhere, famously, he said, "Our enemy is imperialism, not abstract art."[5]

Neither Fidel nor Che was given to aesthetic theorizing, but both are/were very literate, if not particularly so in the visual arts. In a rare excursion into art theory, published in his well-known essay "Man and Socialism in Cuba" (1965), Che expressed his doubts about the traditional modernist mania for experiment for its own sake, for the celebration of "artistic freedom" which ended up as indulgence in "meaningless anguish and vulgar amusement," although it offered "convenient safety valves for anxiety." For "meaningless," read "useless": useless in terms of the liberation of consciousness—artistic and otherwise—to embrace new social visions. But as one who was very well read in French and Latin American literature, Guevara appreciated the value of new forms of expression which the bourgeoisie found in the nineteenth century, and which must be sought, in different historical conditions, by the proletarian classes taking power in the later twentieth century. At least two prominent writers, Susan Sontag and Herbert Read, have made Che personally responsible for the considerable degree of artistic freedom prevailing in Cuba.[6]

In a precious insight into some still undisclosed in-fighting involving Soviet-inspired cultural "commissars," perhaps old Cuban Communist Party hacks who favored Soviet-style socialist realism, Che warned against the style that had been imposed in the Soviet Union of Stalin, survived under Khrushchev (who was famous for his hostility to abstract art), and adopted in the China of Mao. It was a style which

Figure 1.1. Alfredo Rostgaard, Ho Chi Minh and Che, cover of *Tricontinental* 14, Sept.–Oct. 1969, 23 x 15 cm.

Chapter 1.

threatened to "put a strait-jacket on the artistic expression of humanity which is being born and which is in the process of making itself anew through revolution." This was written, be it noted, while public art was still in the doldrums before Cuban artists discovered that "liberated" style of graphics that found such a receptive audience.

Fittingly, it is in the multitudinously varied portraits of Che himself that we can gauge the extent of the victory over the socialist realist threat. Compare our polychrome dream-coated Ches with the drab monotony of all the official portraits of Lenin, Stalin, Mao, or Kim Il Sung, beholden to an outdated concept of physiognomic verisimilitude and gravity. Ironically, as Che perceived, the socialist realist art of anti-capitalist twentieth century revolutions was based on an essentially bourgeois academic realism of the nineteenth century, which was "also a class art, more purely capitalist perhaps than the decadent art of the twentieth century, which at least reveals the anguish of alienated humanity. Why then should we try to find the only valid prescription for revolutionary art in the frozen academicism of Socialist realism?"

The 1971 Congress on Education and Culture emphasized in one of its resolutions, what Cuban artists had been practicing for years:

> The art of the Revolution will be internationalist, at the same time as it will be tightly bound to the national roots. We shall encourage the legitimate and combative cultural expressions of Latin America, Asia, and Africa, which imperialism tries to destroy. Our cultural institutions shall be vehicles of the true artists of these continents, of the neglected, of the persecuted, of those who do not allow themselves to be domesticated by cultural colonialism and who fight together with their people in the struggle against imperialism.[7]

Taken as a whole, the OSPAAAL posters constitute something of a museum of world cultural symbols, and a great diversity of ethnic representation. They systematically incorporate, as it were, a stamp of any given struggle's indigenous legitimacy, the style and/or an artifact typical of that country's native tradition, accompanied, often enough, by a symbol of modern armed resistance which defends or tries to recover that tradition. Thus the poster of the Angolan liberation struggle shows the statue of a local deity stamped on the forehead with a grenade, like a "third eye" of revolutionary wisdom (fig. 1.2); a poster of solidarity with the Arab peoples uses a pharaohlike figure surrounded by a frieze of cartridges and grenades in lieu of the ancient hieroglyphics (fig. 1.3): the language of pharaonic power transmuted into that of popular struggle. It should be noted that Cuban symbology of armed popular struggle includes only small arms; when the indiscriminate weapons of planes and bombs appear in posters, they are invariably those of the cowardly imperial aggressor (fig. M.2).

The poster for the African American people, commemorating the Watts rebellion (fig. 1.4), reproduces an entire design by Black Panther artist Emory Douglas, showing an American black bearing a rifle, originally published in the *Black Panther* newspaper (c. 1970) at the time when the party stood for militant self-defense. But a caution here: the use by OSPAAAL of Black Panther imagery does not connote a political endorsement of that improvised, chaotic, savagely repressed movement, but rather recognition of a Black liberation movement in the broadest sense. With the OSPAAAL poster for Angela Davis (cf. fig. 1.5), a Communist, on the other hand, one may infer an ideological endorsement, as well as a demand for justice for her; she and George Jackson are the only US individuals so honored in the OSPAAAL series.

Use of the local idiom is not binding however, and some of the best OSPAAAL posters employ an appropriate modernistic means to convey the idea of oppression, suffering, and resistance. A poster for Japan (fig. 1.6) uses a very simple but macabre effect by burning the paper, as if it were the skin of the Japanese child, to express the terrible mass incineration of 8 August 1945.

The magazine *Tricontinental*, of which Alfredo Rostgaard was for many years director, is itself of great graphic interest and often closely related to the poster styles (magazine and book illustration, in fact, blazed the stylistic trail). The illustration of the magazine is midway between documentation and cartoon, and indulges in

Figure 1.2. Daisy García, *Angola, Day of Solidarity, 4 February 1971*, OSPAAAL, 56 x 33 cm.

Figure 1.3. Bertha Abelenda, *Day of Solidarity with the Arab Peoples—5 June*, pre-1973, 54 x 33 cm.

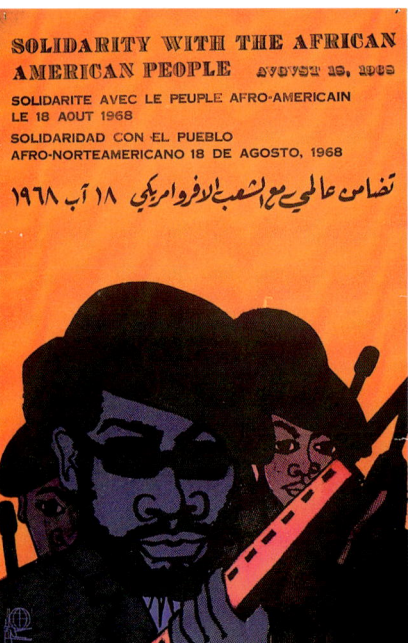

Figure 1.4. *Solidarity with the African American People, 18 August 1968*, OSPAAAL, 36 x 54 cm. The design is based on a drawing by Black Panther artist Emory Douglas for the *Black Panther* newspaper.

ironic, sleight-of-hand photocollage, which re-uses fragments of US political, commercial, and industrial iconography as a means of incrimination. In this respect *Tricontinental* magazine, the posters of OSPAAAL, and OCLAE (Continental Latin American Student Organization), another major internationalist political magazine, together with the magazine's often OSPAAAL-like posters, remind one of the "underground" or "counterculture" press in the United States, and the satirical US posters of protest of the late 1960s and 1970s.

Tricontinental and the OSPAAAL posters are eloquent testimony to Cuba's unremitting and vigorous ideological support for the Third World liberation, which most other socialist countries, in the interests of conciliation with the United States, tended to mute. Even over Viet Nam, the Soviet Union observed resounding silences. *Tricontinental* roundly condemned that country, and China, for putting their quarrel above succor to Southeast Asia.[8] Cuba's fraternal identification with Viet Nam, by contrast, was complete: the twenty-two to twenty-four posters for Viet Nam (fourteen of them before the 1975 victory) are the largest group for any single country.[9] Viet Nam has also been the subject of the most beautiful silkscreen posters to come out of Cuba, by René Mederos, the major artist of the Department of Revolutionary Orientation and author of several OSPAAAL designs (he died, sadly, in September 1996). Much of Che's famous "Message to the Tricontinental" is devoted to Viet Nam, with its final appeal to create "two, three, many Viet Nams" throughout the world.

René Mederos's exquisite silkscreens about Viet Nam, although done in 1970 when the war was at its height, project a future of beauty, tranquillity, and peace. The OSPAAAL posters on behalf of Viet Nam since 1975, during a period of postwar reconstruction hindered by the active hostility of the US, are also optimistic, but one can detect a change in stylistic preferences which accompanied the shift to a larger format poster. The earlier, smaller poster of c. 1970 (fig. M.2) uses a strong and simple graphic symbolism to convey the network (literally) of solidarity, led by Cuba itself, which would eventually help stop the bombing, and the war. By contrast, a later, larger poster (fig. 1.7)—featuring the famous phrase of Ho Chi Minh, "For a Viet Nam ten times more beautiful"—shows the Vietnamese leader, now dead, presiding over happy, smiling people engaged in peaceful work and play (note particularly the relaxed, friendly look of the female militia woman). The mood of the poster differs from earlier OSPAAAL posters, which were usually tightly controlled, artful, and strident.

This image may also be usefully compared with a recent poster for El Salvador, which was designated by the US protest movement as "Spanish for Viet Nam" (fig. 1.8). While the stage reached by the popular struggle was never comparable and it is now "on hold," the suffering in El Salvador was also acute; but rather than show one of many massacres perpetrated (and photographed), the OSPAAAL poster uses the motif of a smiling, "liberated" young woman, holding, of necessity, a gun. Smile and gun stand in evident, superficial contradiction, explained in the slogan: "We make war to win peace." (The word "peace" seldom appears on the earlier posters which are, arguably, open to the charge of promoting the idea of armed revolution for its own sake.) Here, as on comparable US posters, the smile on the face of the revolutionary seems to invite the medical and other aid which has been offered so widely by sympathetic organizations and persons abroad.

The smile is new in the OSPAAAL posters, as it is in the US solidarity poster movement. The guilt-ridden Poster of Protest of the Viet Nam era has passed to the concept of the Poster of Liberation,[10] emphasizing the positive and hopeful aspect of the struggles in Central America against which the US has committed so many atrocities. The guns of armed revolution are now matched with and ready for supersession by the images of peaceful postwar development, as in the Ho Chi Minh poster (fig. 1.7). In his mural on Cuba-US solidarity for the UCLA exhibitions of art about and from Viet Nam in 1990,[11] René Mederos took motifs from the 1969 and 1971 posters series mentioned, and demilitarized them with flowers and doves replacing war and weaponry. The imagery of Che has undergone a comparable

Figure 1.5. Félix Beltrán (Cuba), *Liberty for Angela Davis*, Committee for the Liberty of Angela Davis, silkscreen, 1970/1971, 56.5 x 36 cm. Angela Davis was a UCLA professor of philosophy fired by the University regents.

Figure 1.6. Daniel García, *Hiroshima, Solidarity with the Japanese People*, OSPAAAL, 1969, 53 x 33 cm.

Figure 1.7. Alberto Blanco, *For a Viet Nam Ten Times More Beautiful*, OSPAAAL, 1983, 71 x 47 cm.

Chapter 1.

development, associating him relatively less with armed struggle than with a better, more peaceful future symbolized by flower and dove (figs. M.53, M.54).

Compare the facial expressions of the earlier OSPAAAL posters: the grim or impassive look of the Pharaoh figure (fig. 1.3); the impassive but menacing Angolan ancestral deity (fig. 1.2); or a figure perceived in reality as truly threatening by the US government which responded so murderously—the tight-lipped, heavily armed Black Panther masked in black eyeshades and beard (fig. 1.4). Add to this range of expression the serene but questioning glance of Jesus Christ, armed, in a notorious poster by Alfredo Rostgaard that was banned in the Catholic countries of Brazil and Poland (fig. 8.1); the vision of Che Guevara radiating over Latin America (p. 20); and, not least, the suffering faces of the poor (figs. M.3, M.4, M.8, M.9, p. 113); and a poster against Nixon's atrocities in Viet Nam (fig. M.4). These posters represent the range of our perceptions of and responses to Third World conditions and struggles. I say "our" for Cuba speaks for all of us.

There is the world of difference between defense of the concept of armed liberation struggle, Cuban style, and the "mere" condemnation of oppression. The OSPAAAL posters have, to a degree, moved from an emphasis on the one, which climaxed in the immediate aftermath of the death of Che Guevara in Bolivia in 1967 and is figured in the idea of all Latin America as a gun-holding fist (fig. 1.9), to the other, broadly acceptable to many liberal as well as left opinions in the capitalist world, and current in its poster art. To underline this shift, we can make a striking comparison between two posters for the Palestinian people: the highly stylized Arab head whose vision is symbolized by the barrel of a gun, the mouth of which serves as his eye (fig. M.6, p. 113); and Alberto Blanco's realistically drawn Palestinian or Lebanese child whose head is filled with screams of pain, but also shouts of (unarmed) defiance, to commemorate Sabra and Chatila in 1982, in which four thousand civilians were massacred (fig. 1.10).

OSPAAAL and Africa

The island Cuba, continuously besieged and aggressed by the US, artificially cut off from its natural commercial and cultural relations with Latin America, had to reach out globally for survival—to socialist Europe, of course, for economic help, but also to Africa and Asia, where materially it has given more than it has received back.

As an actor on the world stage Cuba has been described as more important than any other Latin American country, not excepting Brazil.[12] Cuba has been a leader, often the leader of the group of Non-Aligned Nations (NAN), which held their first conference in Belgrade, Yugoslavia in 1961; Cuba was the only Latin American country represented. In 1979 the sixth meeting of the NAN was held in Havana with Fidel Castro as president. To Cuba goes the historic credit of linking Africa and Latin America. The catalyst was Che's campaign in Africa, and the Tricontinental Conference which followed it.

Carlos Fuentes has said that Cuba is the only country in the history of the world which has gone to Africa and brought back nothing save the coffins of its soldiers—including some of Che's companions, a decade before the larger Cuban troop commitment to Angola. It has only recently become known, through the partial publication and availability of the African diaries of Che and testimonies of his comrades, what Che was doing in Africa, in 1965, "the year in which we were nowhere,"[13] trying in vain to unify the various anti-colonial Lumumbista forces in and around the Congo. Che was training and leading them in guerrilla warfare and setting, in vain, an example to those Africans who preferred to fight for personal or factional advantage and live parasitically off the people. Che failed to ignite the spark of continental fire in Africa, as he failed shortly afterward in Latin America; but in South Africa at least his efforts were crowned (indirectly), a generation later, with the resulting ouster of the apartheid regime, and the installation of Nelson Mandela as president. Mandela, the man reviled by Western leaders as a terrorist yesterday, is now hailed as a savior. He would do even better if he would forswear his friendship with Cuba. As this book goes to press, an associate of Che, Laurent Kabila, seems poised to oust the Zairian dictator Mobutu.

Figure 1.8. Rafael Enríquez, El Salvador, *We make war to win peace*, 1982, 69 x 48 cm.

Figure 1.9. Asela M. Pérez, *International Week of Solidarity with Latin America (18–25 April)*, OSPAAAL, 54 x 33 cm.

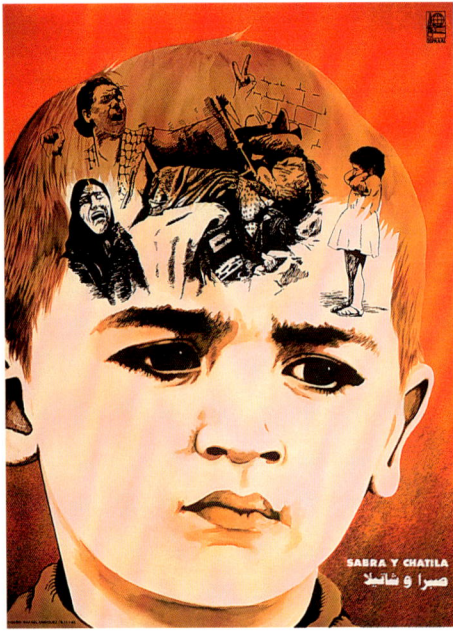

Figure 1.10. Rafael Henríquez, *Sabra and Chatila*, 1983, 50 x 37 cm.

In Africa, specifically Angola, Namibia, and even South Africa, Cuba has changed history. Black Cuban troops defended the Angolan revolution (fig. 1.2) against its US-supported enemies, and fought off white South African troops attacking from Namibia; as a result, Angola remains free, Namibia became independent, and South African apartheid (fig. M.4, p. 113) was weakened. Cuba gave essential political support to the anti-colonial independence movements in Mozambique, Guinea-Bissau, and Zimbabwe (ex-Rhodesia). All this shows up powerfully in the OSPAAAL posters. The military aid given to the self-styled "revolutionary" regime in Ethiopia, which was generally regarded as extremely repressive, did not, significantly I believe, leave its mark in the OSPAAAL posters. Cuba and OSPAAAL posters repeatedly condemned US interference in the Congo, now Zaire, (fig. M.3, p. 113) and honored Patrice Lumumba, probably murdered by or on behalf of the CIA, as a great patriot and would-be liberator of Africa from US imperialism. They also remember Ben Barka, a Moroccan revolutionary who disappeared in the mid-1960s, presumed assassinated, and has now faded from our political memory. In the late 1960s, aligning with the liberation movements in Africa and the Third World, Cuba earned the hostility of all the major powers. At odds with China, the Soviet Union (and its satellite Latin American communist parties) and, of course, the US, "it seemed that Fidel Castro had decided to take on the whole world."[14]

Cuba has its own foreign policy agenda and its emphasis on Africa, so clearly reflected in the OSPAAAL poster (where, with seventy-eight items for eleven different countries, it represents the largest continental group), may also be explained in terms of Cuba's sense of its own negritude, and the historic origins of a third or a half of its population in the African continent. OSPAAAL posters accompanied the thousands of workers who volunteered for duty there, as well as in Southeast Asia and the Middle East. The growth of Cuban military and economic aid programs in Africa measured in terms of personnel (which is the proper measurement, for it is not technology nor material resources that Cuba is exporting) was phenomenal: an estimated 750–1,000 military advisors and troops in Africa in 1966 had become close to forty thousand a dozen years later. In 1977 there were about 5,400 Cuban civilians in that continent, and six hundred in the rest of the world; by the early 1980s, there were about twenty thousand civilians spread about the globe, mostly in medical, construction, and educational cadres. Thirty-five hundred Cubans were teaching overseas in 1980, or two percent of all teachers in Cuba; about nine thousand foreign students, mainly from Africa, were studying in Cuba at this time. Nicaragua had two thousand Cuban teachers in 1983; some of them died in contra attacks. Seven to thirteen percent of Cuba's doctors were working abroad at any given time, together with dentists, nurses, technicians, and support personnel. There were more doctors in Africa from Cuba than from the US.[15] This is, truly, in the legacy of Che.

In terms of gallery art, the level and distribution of artistic exchange between Cuba and the Third World may be judged by the Bienal held in Havana in November 1989, with participation by artists from about fifty-five Third World countries (the exhibition was deliberately limited to such countries): six from the Middle East, ten from Asia, nineteen from Latin America and the Caribbean, and twenty from Africa. The high African profile need not surprise us; but the impressive contingent from Latin America is a victory for Cuban persistence, and forbearance, vis-à-vis anti-socialist, anti-Soviet, pro-US regimes, in the face of the US-imposed quarantine. There is a growing acceptance of Cuba in the Latin American, Caribbean, and Canadian "family" of nations, all of whom now have diplomatic relations with Cuba.

But all in all, in a broad overview of thirty years' production, and allowing for a numerical decline over the second half of the period due to a waning of revolutionary adventurism on the one hand and diminishing resources and help from the old Socialist bloc on the other, OSPAAAL upholds its original faith in the vision of Che. New portraits of him appear regularly (totaling now twenty), even if there are far fewer new images of liberation struggles. Is there an inverse relationship here? Che—the dream—endures, even if the world he fought for seems, in some ways, concretely more distant.

Chapter 1.

First World illusions, Third World realities: the lithographs of Frémez

The occasional OSPAAAL poster and *Tricontinental* magazine illustrations used contrasting images of indigenous poverty and imperialist oppression. The latter, to take a poster for the Congo (fig. M.3, p. 113) as an example, is coded as an abstract agglomerate of multinational logos. Capitalism, the enemy, is never seen as actively seductive, although that is obviously how it presents itself to and is seen by many in the Third World: the "good life" it promises is attractive for its luxuries, glamour, artiness, and sexiness, as is dismally familiar in the most visible and ubiquitous form of capitalist art: commercial advertising.

One Cuban artist par excellence (who also did many portraits of Che)—José Gómez Fresquet, signing Frémez—has specialized in juxtaposing or superimposing capitalist seductions and Third World reality in a pictorial dialectic which incriminates the rich nations for their illusions of self-sufficiency. His series of prints on this theme, called *Burgueses* (Bourgeois), which is extensive but not uniform, and was executed mainly by 1973, was never intended for the kind of massive distribution given to OSPAAAL posters. They are "art prints," printed in small editions mostly given away by the artist as gifts.

The symbol and vehicle of the capitalist dream is a fashion model, usually female, occasionally male. In the best known print, much circulated and copied in the US, and admired for what may be termed its "sensational simplicity," we see a Western, white beauty, against a yellow ground, applying bright red lipstick, while her counterpart, shown yellow and facing the other way but joined graphically so that their hair is one, bleeds from the nose (fig. 1.11). She is obviously Vietnamese. (The print was done c. 1970.) Is there a cause and effect sequence here? Does the one vision of humanity necessitate the inhumanity? Or could these simply be unrelated worlds? Yes, and no.

A similar tactic was also used by the US poster of protest, in taking an advertisement showing a beautiful woman luxuriating in a bath, the perfumed waters of which seem to merge with the raging flood unleashed by US bombing of the dikes in Viet Nam, sweeping away a desperate Vietnamese woman.[16] There is an important graphic difference however, between Frémez's work and the US photomontage of this type, where the photographs are reproduced as such (as in the grandfather of this hardy satirical tool, Johnny Heartfield). The Cuban manipulates both kinds of photograph to accord graphically, by means of a coarse screen which gives a grainy, photographically reduced or "impoverished" look to the fashion model, as well as to the Third World person to whom such a look might seem a priori appropriate.

In one print she sits, legs asprawl, with the blankly "come-hither-if-you-dare" look cultivated by the fashion magazines, against a background of skeletons (she may be recognized, ironically, as one of the many anorexic-looking professional models). In another print, she kneels, one arm laid tenderly along her thigh, dancelike, trancelike, in her perfect self-absorption oblivious to the face of the anguished boy, much larger than hers, looming behind, hands thrust through the barbed wire as if he were trying to touch the pitiless, sacred body just beyond (fig. 1.12). The glaring color contrasts, green woman, magenta boy, orange "sky" above, point up the incongruity with a certain artistic seductiveness.

Other lithographs reverse the foreground/background relationship. Against a background of pretty pink dolls, a little girl holds in her lap a starved—dying?—infant body, sitting on a bed of green dollar bills (fig. M.8). These are generally in Frémez's work symbols of prostitution, or the ill-gotten gambling win. The starved child reappears with that quietly morose look of the scarcely alive, an orange spook before the huge, grinning American actress who is grotesquely sucking her own toe (fig. 1.13). This is Goya updated. In another print, the poor African child, from his crouching position, gazes up curiously at the beautifully stockinged legs which stride past him (fig. M.10); in yet another, the famished Indian mother with her children stands like a brittle ancient statue before a dull gold wallpaper into which a sleek beauty with rich hair seated on a rich sofa is flattened (fig. M.9).

Figure 1.11. Frémez, from the series "Burgueses," lithograph, c. 1970, 46 x 61 cm.

Figure 1.12. Frémez, from the series "Burgueses," lithograph, 1969, 62 x 43 cm.

The question is insistent: what is the relationship between the two colliding worlds: immediate and necessary, or distant and fortuitous?

Rich tourists whose presence and money are transforming the domains of poverty as surely as industrial "progress," should be uncomfortable, caught in Frémez's eye. The rich, of course, have learned—or chosen, for comfort's sake—to "dress down" when circulating among the really poor. But are they not represented by governments which regard the growing gap as a matter to be fixed by The Gap?

Film Institute posters

The Cuban Film Institute (ICAIC), created three months after the victory, was dedicated to that art which was the most immediately appreciated and actively fostered by the revolutionary leadership (fig. 1.14). It was placed under the directorship of Alfredo Guevara (no relation to Che), a close personal and political friend of Fidel's from the Sierra Maestra campaign. Many ICAIC films have become internationally renowned and, with the posters made especially for them, were the midwives of a tremendous artistic explosion. Film became a most powerful force in the collective memory, and a tool for the raising of consciousness in ways both affirmative and critical of the revolution. Before the revolution there was no native film industry; since, it has reached extraordinary heights in quality and quantity for so small a country, reaching a climax of 130 feature films a year. The film audience, which always showed a preference for Cuban films over foreign imports, rose to 120 million per annum, falling by the mid-1980s to 86.5 million.

It is said that Haydée Santamaría, head of Casa de las Américas (an important Cuban cultural outreach institution), on seeing the ICAIC film posters demanded that the political posters be as imaginative; and they became so. From the start, ICAIC insisted on the utmost aesthetic pluralism in both films and posters. The posters, whether for Cuban or foreign films, did not aim, graphically, to "sell" the film in the US manner; rather, they were visual embroideries, imaginative adjuncts to films people could be expected to go and see anyway. They were placed in cinemas, but most visibly in the streets on the *paraguas*, the umbrellalike posts marking bus stops, which carried four vanes on which posters (before the revolution, consumer ads) were fixed. Unfortunately, few of these paraguas now survive, and none carry the ICAIC posters, the production of which has radically diminished, along with that of the films themselves. Down to a few per annum for lack of internal resources, the films are now mostly made in association with companies outside. Larger in size than the typical early OSPAAAL posters which were done in large, offset editions, the ICAIC posters were made in small editions and in silkscreen, which is labor-intensive, but renders great intensity of color in rich, palpably pigmented surfaces, similar to a painting.

With a selection favoring posters made for politically-oriented Cuban films, we start logically with the "Apostle" and "Intellectual Author" of the revolution, José Martí, at once cultural and political hero, poet, essayist, independence leader, and martyr, whose collection of lush, deceptively simple, and very personal poems, *Versos Sencillos*, is commemorated in a film by Enrique Pineda Barnet (fig. 1.18) . The hairline of the semi-bald Martí, in its own way a "tag of identity" as famous and reducible as the profile of Che's starred beret or beard, sprouts multicolored hair which flickers into a luxuriance of tropical, polychrome plants. In two other posters, celebrating the twentieth anniversary of the Film Institute, Martí's face is a red and orange dawn glowing inspirationally over the insurrection of the guerrillas (fig. 1.15) and appears as a blue- and pink-flushed bust arising over portraits of his heirs, Che and Fidel, each depicted twice, embedded in a turbulent landscape (fig. C.1, p. 18).

Of the five short documentaries made in Cuba about Che (no feature length documentary film has ever—as yet —been attempted), two stand out: Santiago Alvarez's *Hasta la Victoria Siempre* (Ever Onwards Unto Victory), whose poster (fig. 1.16) uses the Korda matrix, was put together in forty-eight hours of nonstop work immediately after the news of Che's death arrived. The first showing was not in a cinema, but projected at a mass demonstration in the Plaza de la Revolución, preceding Fidel's eulogy.[17]

Figure 1.13. Frémez, from the series "Burgueses," lithograph, c. 1970, 58 x 44 cm.

Figure 1.14. Alfredo Rostgaard, *Cuban Film Week*, ICAIC tenth anniversary, silkscreen, 1969, 76 x 50.5 cm.

Chapter 1.

Another memorable film on Che uses the same material as this book: Chilean Pedro Chaskel's *Una Foto Recorre el Mundo* (A Photograph Traverses the World), a "film of great beauty and poetry,"[18] shows how the Korda photograph has been posterized in so many ways and carried in demonstrations around the world.

Santiago Alvarez is considered the master of the short news documentary in an age where its function has been long since taken over by television. His extensive production has elicited some of the very best posters: *79 Primaveras* (79 Springtimes) of 1969, honoring Vietnamese leader Ho Chi Minh, which won many prizes at international film festivals; Ho's enemy LBJ, in the film of that name, shown glowering in a medieval helmet and being carted off (to the rubbish bin of history?); and *Cómo, Porqué y Para qué se Asesina a un General* (How, Why and for What Purpose a General Gets Assassinated) about the killing of Allende's defense minister in 1970, where the design of the poster incriminates US money interests.

The newsreel, the *noticiero*, like the OSPAAAL posters (and there is a technical and aesthetic overlap in the intercutting/collaging of incongruous elements) represents Cuban foreign policy, so one would expect to meet Uncle Sam: as an angry eagle nesting in corporate detritus (*Viva la República*, feature film by Pastor Vega), or as a caricatural old man from the past, bound helpless in the bonds of film stock (twentieth anniversary poster by Muñoz Bachs, 1980).

In the "Cuban cultural heroes" category we may place Charlie Chaplin, who was rejected as subversive by the US government in the McCarthy era, but is hailed by Cuba as a liberator. It was under his aegis, with silent films by him and a poster of him by Muñoz Bachs, Cuba's premier humorous poster designer (fig. M.11), that ICAIC introduced "mobile cinema" to remote parts of the country, and to peasants who had hitherto lacked not only any form of schooling, but had never seen a movie.

All foreign films shown in Cuba were donated, and came from a variety of countries: European, Eastern bloc, Japan. The Soviet film *The Brothers Karamazov* uses a style both symbolic and reminiscent of German renaissance woodcuts (poster by Luis Vega, 1972); posters for certain Japanese films such as *A Bloody Search for Peace* and *Kansuke the Strategist* engage in extreme simplifications. ICAIC designs came in a variety of styles by many different artists, some of great sophistication, often both sensuous and subtle, others of stunning simplicity, and of the most exquisite coloring. These are, of course, also the qualities of the Che poster.

In the poster for Cuban Film Week 1969, it is as if the colors belching forth from the movie projector are aimed at the poster paper itself, rather than a viewing screen (fig. 1.14). Music and song, in which revolutionary Cuba has staked out a vanguard position, have elicited important designs: Rostgaard's starkly painful *Canción Protesta*, featured on the cover of the McGraw Hill 1970 facsimile collection (Sontag and Stermer) has achieved its own celebrity.

Posters celebrating Women's Day (fig. M.12) remind us of the efforts the revolution has made to advance the cause of woman in her multiplicity of roles. As the posters graphically imply, the revolution owed very much to women fighting and helping in every way, as Che recognized; and the support for Fidel among women of all ages is strong. Che acknowledged, "Liberation of women is not complete, and one of the tasks of our Party is to obtain their total freedom, their internal freedom." In 1989 women were 40 percent of the labor force, 48 percent of labor leaders, 57 percent of technical and professional workers, and 37.6 percent of deputies. In 1995, 55 percent of all scientific professionals were women. In the Che Guevara Technical High School in Havana, of over five hundred students, three hundred are female.[19]

Figure 1.15. Damián, *"And this is the age in which the hills will top the mountains."—Martí*, ICAIC twentieth anniversary, silkscreen, 1973, 76 x 50.5 cm. José Martí dawns over revolutionaries.

Figure 1.16. Alfredo Rostgaard, *Ever Onwards Unto Victory*, Cuban documentary by Santiago Alvarez, ICAIC, silkscreen, 1968, 76 x 51 cm.

Figure 1.17. Ñiko, *Che, Today and Forever*, Cuban documentary by Pedro Chaskel, ICAIC, 1983, 76 x 54.5 cm.

Figure 1.18. Luis Vega, *Simple Verses*, Cuban documentary on Marti by Miguel Pineda Barnet, silkscreen, ICAIC, 1973, 76 x 50.6 cm.

Chapter 2.
Che as Landscape
"*The revolutionary is not a portrait, he is a landscape.*"[1]

Land, guerrilla, peasant

Mythic heroes have always been assigned a special relationship to the land. They arise magically from the earth, they often travel great distances over it, they command or appear to command natural phenomena, and may even appear as such. Nature in the wild—forests and jungles—are the habitat of the guerrilla, as Sherwood Forest was for Robin Hood. They are home, refuge, protection. Fidel and Che made the Cuban revolution in the countryside, in the Sierra Maestra mountain jungles, absorbing or neutralizing the urban insurrection. Che, to the end, as his Bolivian campaign shows, believed that the countryside was the foyer of revolution: in this respect he was always more Maoist than Leninist.

The guerrillas' familiarity with the countryside—they learned every nook and cranny with the help of local peasantry—was their strength; the regular army's foreignness to it was their weakness. The peasants who belonged to the land as the land did (rightfully) to them were the natural allies of the guerrillas, and in large numbers became guerrillas themselves; indeed many passed into leadership positions after the victory.

In this situation it was logical and necessary for Che to initiate agrarian reform from the very beginning; it started even in the Sierra, together with literacy programs and schooling which he spearheaded and conducted personally; afterward, Che found himself in charge of agrarian reform as institutionalized under INRA (National Institute of Agrarian Reform). Even today, when there is much discontent in the towns, the countryside represents a backbone of support for the revolution.

The posters see Che as an emanation of the landscape. He emerges victoriously from it, multiplying himself, as identical and commonplace as trees (fig. M.13); his face is ensconced, from different angles and with different expressions, in the very substance of the trees, plants, fronds; less camouflage than potent fruit of nature (fig. 2.2). The familiar silhouette is filled with colored mosses, as in a cavern, but flat, with a glimpse of daylight above and beyond, and springs of water, one rainbow striped, gushing from within (fig. 2.3). In a German woodcut-style print by Luis Miguel Valdéz, Che's face is composed of a swirling thicket of line, a slightly spooky effect enhanced by the presence of a figure on horseback half cut off at the left and reminiscent of Albrecht Dürer's *Knight, Death and the Devil*.

In the colored ink drawings of Serón (fig. 2.4), sold in the little tourist jungle of a marketplace in Havana's Cathedral Square, the Cuban Sierra or Bolivian jungle takes on a utopic-mythic quality. Che's face mingles magically with a delicate network of fronds and leaves, and the dripping ink suggests a melting of form in unrelenting rainstorms.

Ramón comes from the wind,
   the rain
from where sadness begins
(In his face there seems to lie
a continent of melancholy).

Constellated with clay, he is
   already known to be
a bit of the history of the earth...

Seasons sleep in his hands
Like unpublished daughters of
   time.
All in him is dark and luminous:
The dawn bursts forth from his
   body.

Root, leaf, grain dream of him...

Ramón is a garden on the move.[2]

Che erupting as a force of nature is the theme of one of Havana's least known murals, hidden from the general public in the presidential offices of the national bank, executed by Lebanese Cuban Fayad Jamís in 1968–1969 to commemorate Che's presidency, November 1959 to February 1961 (fig. 2.5). It is large, filling a whole wall (about 4 x 8 m), and shows Che's head as a fistlike apparition bursting out of the soil, rooted by his beard, and with the hair of his head licking off into a cosmic whirl of miniaturized industrial processes, and the profile of his features filled with graffiti and assorted elements of posters and murals: Che as Nature, and as Popular Art. Walter

Figure 2.2. Many Ches, 56 x 41 cm.

Figure 2.3. Rafael Morante. *Ernesto CHE Guevara*. OSPAAAL, 1983, 61 x 41 cm.

Figure 2.4. Séron (Sergio Padillia García), ink drawing, 1996, 45.5 x 33 cm.

Figure 2.1. Elena Serrano. *Day of the Heroic Guerrilla, 8 October*. 1968, 50 x 33 cm.

Solón's *The Christ of La Higuera*, also arboreal and apparitional, fits in here, but will be discussed more extensively in Chapter 8.

Then there are the portraits where the lineaments of Che's features take on a cartographic quality. The shadow boundaries of the eyes, the frontiers of mustache and beard, are drawn with arbitrary-looking, continuous squiggles like those of a map, tracing borders which follow the accidents of nature and history (fig. 2.6). Each indentation and protrusion on the much reduced scale of a map responds to some great geographical feature, a river, lake, mountain, ocean, like the comparable metaphors in the poetry for the great nature-given qualities of the hero. Che is also the pathway and refuge of the guerrillas, who crouch in the protective shadows of his beard and hair which sprout weaponry (fig. 2.7).

It is an age-old graphic trick to transpose an emblematic animal or personage onto a map of the country to which they relate. The map of Che's face is, however, never that of Cuba as we know it, but of a new Cuba, a new country, or rather a new continent—unified Latin America. Che's face is superimposed on the single landmass of the subcontinent, his features obliterating the artificial divisions by country, unifying it (figs. A.1, A.2, p. 16). The process is analyzed, in a poster divided into nine compartments. Che rising from the left and gradually, cinematically, advancing bigger and bigger, closer and closer, so as to obliterate those frontiers which lead to and are the product of internal wars, divisions and weakness—advancing so big and close that he actually seems to pass by and through us, transubstantiating us, transcending himself, leaving behind only his spirit symbolized in the comandante star. Such designs seem to illustrate Che's own prescient words, spoken in Peru, in his youth: "Latin America's division into illusory and uncertain nationalities is completely fictitious."[3]

In a poster by Elena Serrano which has become celebrated, and was used on the cover of Max Gallo's *Poster in History*,[4] Che radiates and reverberates chromatically and luministically, a single pulse over a unified landmass which both frames him and is reconstituted by him (p. 38). This is the ideal; the present reality is conjured up by the Chilean designers of a giant, double-sized silkscreen, called *America Awaken(s)*, who pose—literally—as the new geographers of the Latin American continent, which is seen as a mosaic not so much of countries, which are not geographically profiled as such, but of interests, viewpoints, prejudices, stereotypes, sufferings. Economic, natural, touristic, and political symbols jostle each other restlessly with Che at the heart of the continent over Bolivia: the instant recognizability of the famous icon is sufficient to doom the whole print to the bonfire of revolutionary vanities made by troops of the Chilean fascism at the coup of September 1973 (figs. A.3, A.4, p.16).

The legacy of Che: to defend biodiversity as well as sociodiversity

The history of landscape depiction is the history of imagined utopias. Every revolution imagines a land, in Ho Chi Minh's phrase, "ten times more beautiful." Che insisted that his men, even as they respected peasant property, respect nature, not cutting and destroying where not militarily a necessity or a matter of survival. Without wishing to rank Che Guevara as a precocious ecologist, which would be anachronistic in the 1950s and 1960s, we may be permitted a brief digression into one little known Cuban legacy of Che as the defender of all vulnerable life forms. For Cuba today, deprived by the blockade of chemical fertilizers and high-tech agriculture, is a laboratory of a new kind of low-tech, organic farming. A Nicaraguan agronomist speaks of Cuba's "new revolution: it's not making much noise and not very many people are aware of it. It's an ecological revolution, still full of contradictions, still very fragile, but...."[5]

At the triumph of the revolution eight percent of the property owners, including many Americans, owned eighty percent of Cuban agricultural land, mostly used for sugarcane and cattle. The agrarian reform promoted by Che which redistributed the land was also an ecological boon. After Independence in 1902, sugar and greed went axe in hand: by 1959, only fourteen percent of Cuba's original forests remained. The revolution's first environmental step was to

Figure 2.5. Fayad Jamis (finished by Julio Pérez Medina), left side of mural in presidential office of Cuban national bank, Havana, 30 January 1969, full mural c. 4 x 8 m.

Figure 2.6. Olivio Martínez, *8 October, Day of the Heroic Guerrilla*, OSPAAAL, 1973, 68 x 49 cm.

reforest with massive help from the military so as to cover, at present, twenty-five to thirty percent of Cuban territory, although this is now under threat as the fuel shortage forces Cubans to use firewood for cooking. The efflorescence of plants from José Martí's head in the poster (fig. 1.18, p. 37) points to a remarkable statistic: Cuba has the richest plant biodiversity of all the islands in America—6,200 higher plant species compared with four thousand in all of Central Europe. In Cuba, 2,340 species of mollusk have been identified, compared with four hundred in all of France. Six percent of Cuban territory has been declared "protected areas of natural significance;" other kinds of protection cover twenty-two percent of the island. Cuba has over thirty-seven thousand scientists working in biotechnology or related activities. "With only 2% of the Latin American population, Cuba currently has 11% of the continent's scientists."[6]

Bandido on horseback

Che learned to ride as a child, and there are a remarkable number of photographs and much film footage of him on horseback, most of them taken in the Sierra Maestra, where a horse or a mule was often the most practical means of transport. Among the artists who showed Che on horseback, Mederos stands out: Che solo, in profile, statuesque like a renaissance condottiere, against a background of mountains in various shades of romantic purple (fig. 2.8); and again Che heading a group of horsemen including Camilo (both are in green) and independence leaders (fig. C.3, p. 18). A presumed last photograph of Che before capture shows him holding the head of a horse by the reins.[7]

The hero on horseback, not so readily associated with the twentieth century which developed mechanical means of transport, summons up an agrarian world and that favorite character of myth, legend, and folk tale: the social bandit.[8] Is Che Guevara, the redresser of social wrongs, a kind of leftist Robin Hood, an outlaw who takes from the rich to give to the poor? If so, he fits into an old Cuban and Latin American tradition. In Cuba in the nineteenth century, numerous peasant outlaws, solo and in bands, fought the landowners in the Sierras; some joined in the independence war, where they "earned the right to be called patriots."[9] Like the Fidelistas later, the old Cuban *bandidos* expropriated the rich sugar plantation owner and cattle rancher; they also engaged in kidnapping, not a practice of the later revolutionaries. They were both fierce and charitable, in the classic mold. The most famous Cuban nineteenth-century bandit was called Manuel García. Known for his humanity, he was politically educated and a friend of independence leader Antonio Maceo.

There were bandidos in the Sierra at the time of revolutionary war "who stepped into the tradition of rebellion, however vague and ill-defined."[10] They were either incorporated into the guerrilla bands, or suppressed by them. Che had some bandidos executed who were found guilty of crimes against peasants. In general Che respected the bandidos, for they "have all the characteristics of a guerrilla army: homogeneity, respect for the leader, bravery, knowledge of the terrain, and even a complete understanding of the tactics."[11] Crescenzio Pérez, with his large band of loyal peasant followers, was apparently the first to give effective help to Castro in the Sierra. He was to be sanctified by the revolution, although he was originally a brigand, living hidden as an outlaw and smuggler of illegal drugs.[12]

The iconography of the old Cuban bandido is scarce or nonexistent: his exploits are recorded in ballads. There are innumerable songs and poems in praise of Che, composed after his death, which may be placed in the ancient tradition of the bandit ballad. At the time, the revolutionary war itself was celebrated in ballads and became the stuff of legends, with the help of the publicity-conscious guerrillas themselves.[13] Che recalled a peasant named Crucito: "This magnificent comrade had written the whole history of the revolution in ballads which he composed at every rest stop as he puffed on his pipe."[14] Calixto Morales, veteran of the Granma expedition, called himself the "nightingale of the plains" as the writer and singer of ballads which passed into the opposition press at the time.

The most famous bandido-like persecuted rebel (who did not rob) in Latin American literature is probably Martín Fierro, hero of the eponymous classic by the Argentine José Hernández (1872). This epic poem was a favorite of Che, who gave a copy of it to his fiancée in Mexico. He knew much of it by heart, and used to read or recite passages of it to his horse, whom he named after the fictional hero. As so often happens, animal and human were closely bonded, and "Martín Fierro's" stuffed outer remains are to be seen today, together with Camilo's favorite steed, in Havana's Museo de la Revolución. Martín Fierro was also the nom de guerre given to Che himself as honorary chief of the Argentinean guerrilla group preparing for his arrival in Bolivia, organized by his friend Jorge Masetti, who took the name of another outlaw called Segundo Sombra.

Figure 2.8. René Mederos, Che on horseback, silkscreen, 1971, 58.5 x 72.5 cm.

Chapter 3.

Che-Man ↔ Che-Project: A Collective Poetic Articulation *Fabian Wagmister*

Figure 3.1. Fayad Jamis. Preparatory Drawing for the National Bank Mural of Che. The drawing reveals the surreal, Boschian combination of mechanoid, vegetablelike forms around Che's face, with plantlike stalks, flamelike shoots, directional arrows, and tentacular trumpets sprouting from his crown and name. As in Hieronymus Bosch's work, there is a touch of the sinister, in an arboreal fungus where the right ear should be and wartlike bullets or warheads protruding from the temple above it. The right side of the head dissolves into a cacophony of jumbled graffiti and slogans arising from mountains, the profiles of which match the lines of Che's facial hair. From Fayad Jamis, *Tintas* (Mexico DF: Premia, 1980).

No es que yo quiera darte
pluma por pistola
pero el poeta eres tú.
—Miguel Barnet[1]

I would not give you
pen in place of gun
but it is you who are the poet

Ernesto "Che" Guevara, his journey, his work, and his life itself have inspired an extraordinary amount of creative work by artists, artisans, and people in general from all over our world, possibly more so than any other twentieth-century personality. Countless poems, paintings, murals, songs, installations, films, and every imaginable creative representation have been and continue to be produced by individuals, groups, and communities from the most diverse geographical, historical, and political contexts. The quantity and quality of the work, its international nature, and the preeminence of many of the authors constitute a major creative phenomenon in the history of political art.

This significant collective international body of work identifies Che Guevara as representative of both a set of human ideals and the model of being necessary to accomplish them. Through this multitonal, dynamic, creative voice a broad and profound articulation of the concept of new man (and woman), which he so vigorously promoted, has and continues to reverberate throughout our world.

Songwriting and poetry are particularly interesting within this collective body of work because of the metaphoric freedom and richness of the written and spoken word. A wide range of expression permits both internal (form and content) and external (authoring context) diversity. The remarkable variety of poetic voices joining in this creative stream is indicative of the symbolic power of Che's image and ideas and their capacity to transcend preestablished dividers.

While the poetry about Che probably presents the deepest and most sophisticated articulation of his aspirations for future generations, the songwriting is the most directly political and unapologetically emotional. Combined, these two modes of expression give us the most comprehensive understanding of Che Guevara's phenomenal impact on the creative representation of the aspirations of the left and the revolutionary movement. Reading and listening to these works makes one aware of the profound inspirational power Che has had over the men and women of his generation and beyond.

As part of "Che Vive," a self-organizing multimedia digital database, I have compiled and analyzed over 350 poems and 120 songs from more than forty countries. And more works keep emerging every day. This collection represents many points of departure and approaches, from the personal intimate confession through the collective utopian dream to the ideological proclamation, all unified by Che's thought and action as a central theme.

The guiding motifs can be said to belong to two distinct categories. On the one hand there is a constant effort to distill the essential characteristics of his personality, his particular way of being and engaging the world. In this category, which we will call "Che-Man," a rich and very complex array of concepts and metaphors are used to characterize him emotionally, intellectually, and physically. Within "Che-Man," some major sub-groupings can be identified: "Che as Nature," "Che as Compañero," "Che Warrior-Poet," and "Che Constructor of Himself."

On the other hand there is the intent to reveal the connections between Che and his sociopolitical context, to place him within history, and to project him and his influence into the future. This implies the belief that Che is a part, and usually a major one, of a larger project initiated well before his time, and destined to continue after his death. Of this second category, best described as "Che-Project," we will focus on three dominant subgroupings: "Che Model," "Che Historicized," and "Che Demystified."

Che-Man

Che as Nature

Che is constantly interconnected and equated with the elements and the forces of nature. Che is an intrinsic part of the land. Nelson Osorio sings of "El Gigante" (Che) as having "bits of jungle scattered in his blood."[2] Thomas Merton describes his clothing as made of "leaves and moons."[3] And Efraín Huerta metamorphoses Che's

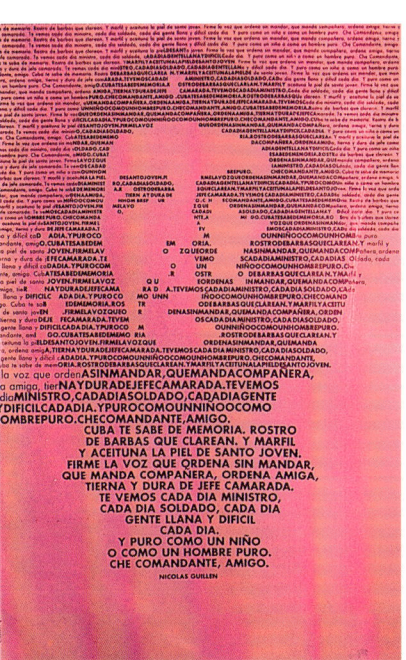

Figure 3.2. Ideocarteles. This pre-1973 poster shows Che's face composed of lines from a poem to him by Nicolás Guillén. The Afro-Cuban Guillén (1904–1989) is one of Cuba's, indeed Latin America's, greatest poets and is considered the Cuban "Laureate" for the national themes he undertook. He was a close friend of Che and his family; Che revered Guillén's poetry, a volume of which, together with one by Pablo Neruda, was found in his knapsack when he was captured in Bolivia. The poster uses the fourth stanza of *Che Comandante*, the most popular of the four poems Guillén wrote in honor of his friend. It was written 15 October 1967 and first read to the public three days later at the memorial ceremony held in La Plaza de la Revolución. The same poem was used as voice-over in the Cuban film *Che Comandante, Amigo*.

Cuba te sabe de memoria. Rostro
de barbas que clarean. Y marfil
y aceituna en la piel de santo joven.
Firme la voz que ordena sin mandar,
que manda compañera, ordena amiga
tierna y dura de jefe camarada.
Te vemos cada día ministro,
cada día soldado, cada día
gente llana y difícil
cada día.
Y puro como un niño
o como un hombre puro,
Che Comandante,
amigo.

Cuba knows you in all by heart,
The bearded face of radiance,
Young saint painted in ivory and olive.
Firm the voice which commands
But never overbears;
Orders given by a friend, a companion,
Tender and hard the comrade commander.
Every day we still can see you,
Minister, soldier still, every day
Intransigent and frank, every day
Pure as a child
And as a man, still pure,
Che commander
Friend and brother.[4]

Chapter 3.

"words of love" into "orchids and butterflies."[5] Che is also a natural force affecting the very condition of the land. He does so by becoming volcano, earthquake, storm, hurricane, torrent.

Nature and the land are seen as Che's permanent allies. For Eduardo Escobar, Che's "love hid in subterranean rivers and found refuge in the wilds,"[6] and in Félix Pita Rodríguez's *Cantata para el Guerrillero Heroico*, he "descends with rivers, emerges with minerals, and establishes his transparent light with the dew."[7] Through this metaphor (nature), Che is revealed as an organic, vital, unstoppable force.

> *y al imperioso llamado de tus pasos*
> *te seguirían*
> *los montes, los ríos, los árboles, formando ejércitos*
> *que levantarían fusiles y banderas en lo alto.*
>
> and to the imperious call of your steps,
> mountains, rivers, trees would follow,
> forming armies who would raise on high
> guns and flags.
> —Marcelo Arduz Ruíz[8]

But of all the elements of nature, water is the one which is most often used to characterize Che. As water, he is pure, essential, and flowing. Like water he courses through diverse terrain, adaptable, flexible, unrestrainable. Like water he can be at once life-giving and deadly.

Enid Vian best celebrates the comparison in his poem *El Río* (The River)[9]:

> *Sus aguas en alarma*
> *corren entre las piedrecillas o los riscos,*
> *murmuran, tras las algas y los musgos,*
> *fluídos proféticos y coros fascinantes,*
> *se deslizan sobre el flanco de la tierra,*
> *en busca de su cauce o de su asilo*
> *y suben la marea en ristre,*
> *cuando al desembocar en sendas anchas,*
> *se trueca en ras de mar*
> *su hymno de guerra.*
>
> Its alarmed waters
> course between pebbles and cliffs,
> murmur, passing weeds and mosses,
> prophetic fluids and fascinating choirs,
> slipping over the flank of the earth
> in search of its bed and asylum
> and raise the ready tide
> when flowing into broad streams
> it finds the sea and mingles with
> his song of war.

This conjuration of the transformative power of Che-Water epitomizes the body of creative work inspired by him, at once a passionate celebration and a continuation of the flow. In this way the artist and artwork both describe water and become water.

The relationship between Che and water has, moreover, important historical references. Bodies of water figure prominently in two major projects of his life: the Cuban Revolution and his Bolivian campaign. Matilde Bianqui summons up the Granma expeditionaries and the role of the sea in the start of the island's revolution in her poem *Cantar del Che*[10]:

> *y surgieron del mar como los dioses*
>
> and they rose from the sea like gods

Alberto Guerra Gutiérrez connects the Ñancahuazú river and Che's Bolivian guerrillas in *El Vado del Yeso*[11]:

> *se abrieron, cantando sus aguas*
> *los ríos de Ñancahuazú*
>
> The rivers of Ñancahuazú opened up,
> these waters singing

These examples also acknowledge religious connotations which bind Che and water.

Che's power, like that of mountain rivers, overflows, surprises, and takes command. This makes him emotional, abrupt, aggressive.

> *Elegiste, Comandante*
> *el corazón de Latinoamérica*
> *para desbordarte*
> *por sus abiertas venas...*
> —Marcelo Arduz Ruíz[12]
>
> You chose, Comandante,
> the heart of Latin America
> to overflow
> by her open veins...
>
> *es la lluvia que llega con la música del viento.*
> *Los ríos que se desbordan para fecundar campos*
> —Marcelo Arduz Ruíz[13]
>
> He is the rain that comes with music of the wind.
> The rivers that overflow so as to fertilize the fields.

Finally, like mountain water, Che is transparent, he hides nothing, he is direct, sharp, strong, and clear. Héctor Miranda describes him as "crystalline as a water

Figures 3.3–3.6. Heriberto Echevarría, series of four prints, published 1987 by Editora Política for the 20th anniversary of Che's death, each 52 × 43 cm. In each case the first text is taken from the poem *Che Comandante* by Nicolás Guillén (see also fig. 3.2); the second text is from Fidel Castro's commemorative speech of 18 October 1967.

Figure 3.3
Che knows you in all by heart
The bearded face of radiance.
Young saint painted in ivory and olive...

...Without any doubt, the most extraordinary of our revolutionary comrades.

Figure 3.4
Firm the voice which commands
But never overbears:
Orders given by a friend, a companion,
Tender and hard the comrade commander.

Che was unsurpassed both as a leader and as a soldier; militarily speaking he was extraordinarily able, a courageous and warlike guerrilla...

spring."[14] He had a transparency, says Laurette Sejourné, made possible and accessible only by the breaking of all chains and the opening of all doors.[15]

Carlos Puebla, in the most famous of the songs about Che, highlights transparency as the key element of Guevara's personality.[16]

*Aquí se queda la clara,
la entrañable transparencia
de tu querida presencia,
Comandante Che Guevara.*

Here lingers the bright
precious transparency
of your beloved presence
Comandante Che Guevara.

Che as Compañero

Puebla's verses describe Che in terms that seem to indicate friendship and familiarity. Many other artists also suggest that our relationship to Che Guevara, like the one we have with water, can be intimate, personal, and ever present.

*pido hablar del agua, del aire,
de su presencia cotidiana
como el aire y como el agua.*
—Jaime Valdivieso[17]

Let me speak of water, air,
of his daily presence
like air and like water.

To Julio Cortázar, Thomas Merton, and Matilde Bianqui, Che was their "brother," to Víctor Jara and David Viñas their "older brother," to Nicolás Guillén and Atahualpa Yupanqui their "friend."[18] Thus, Che is brought closer to one's own life, made approachable, reachable. For greater intimacy, many address their verses directly to him. "I write you letters," Merton says, and Claudia Beck simply titles her poem *Hola Che* as if talking to an old friend.[19]

Che Warrior-Poet

War and poetry, constantly surfacing as two predominant activities in Che's life, are represented as sides of the same triangle. With the revolution as its third and base side, these two forces join in a unified upward vortex which in itself defines the essence of the Latin American revolutionary. This capacity to simultaneously destroy and create signifies the most profound potential for change and the making of a new and better society, a dignified human, a just future.

*Te debatías unánime
entre las exigencias de dos brujas feroces:
la poesía y la guerra.*
—Pablo Armando Fernández[20]

You were unanimously debating
between the demands of two ferocious witches:
poetry and war.

*Semidesnudo
el poderoso pecho de fusil y palabra,
de ardiente vendaval y lenta rosa.
No hay descanso*
—Nicolás Guillén[21]

Half naked
the powerful breast of a gun and word
of a burning storm and slow rose
There is no rest.

*Si el que asomó al futuro su perfil
y lo estrenó con roces de fusil
fuiste tú,
guerrero, para siempre, tiempo eterno...
Si el poeta eres tú...*
—Pablo Milanés[22]

If it were you who showed his profile to
    the future
and celebrated it with voices of a gun
warrior forever, in eternity...
For sure you are the poet...

Che Warrior-Poet is driven by intense feelings of love and hatred unified.

*Tu corazón de música y acero
tan sólo latía
al compás del son de la libertad
y al ritmo milagroso del amor.*
—Manuel María[23]

Your heart of music and steel
only beats
to the measure of the sound of liberty
and to the miraculous rhythm of love.

*el asma boca arriba, tu amor que
    nos sustenta,
tu ser violento, tu odio indispensable,
tu garganta de tiernas palabrotas*
—Antonio Conte[24]

asthma face up, your love that sustains us,
your violent being, your indispensable
    hatred,
your throat of tender curses

*Artífice de soldado,
grito de amor hecho guerra*
—Andrés Machin Barrios[25]

Craftsman in soldiery
cry of love made war.

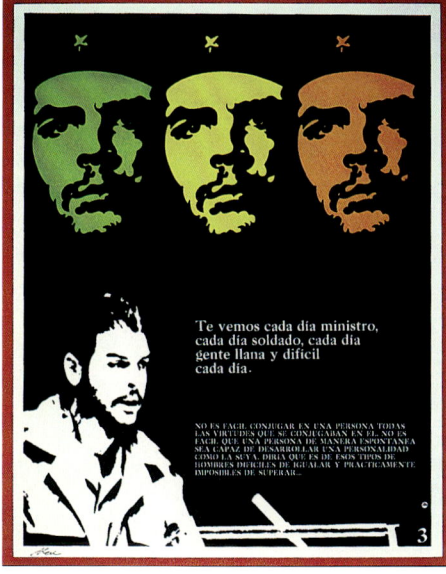 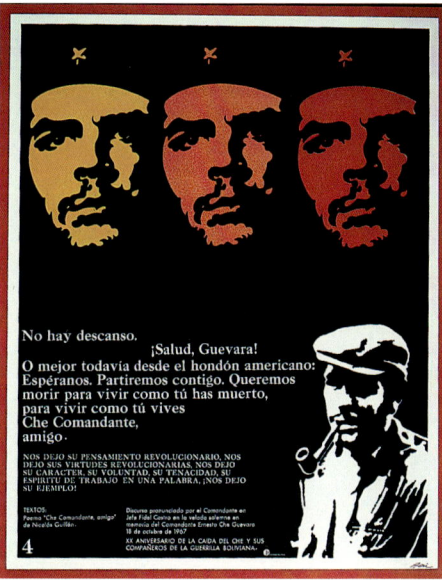

Figure 3.5
Every day we still can see you,
Minister, soldier still, every day
Instransigent and frank, every day

It is not easy to combine in one person all the virtues which were combined in him. It is not easy for a person to be spontaneously capable of developing a personality like his. I would say he is one of those kinds of men difficult to equal and practically impossible to surpass...

Figure 3.6
There is no rest for you, Good heart, Guevara!
Or better yet, from the deep heart
Of America: Wait for us!
We will set off with you.
We would die, then, to live
As you have died, as you still live.
Che commander
Friend and brother.

He left us his revolutionary thought, he left us his revolutionary virtues, he left us his character, his willpower, his tenacity, his capacity for work. In a word, he left us his example!

Inspired by love and driven by hate the revolutionary becomes a formidable weapon-man:

> ¡Che afilado instrumento de constructivo y amoroso odio!
> —Francisco Fernández-Santos[26]

> Che sharp instrument of constructive and loving hatred!

> como un rayo de amor
> destruyendo y creando
> —Idea Vilariño[27]

> Like a ray of love
> destroying and creating

> ...su amor rodaba entre sus enemigos,
> aplastándolos
> —Eduardo Escobar[28]

> ...his love moved among his enemies,
> crushing them.

Che Constructor of Himself

Of all the characteristics of Che-Man, the one which particularly separates him from the other man, alienated man, is his conscious effort to define and construct himself on the model of an ideal, better person. Che is constantly represented on a journey of self-determination and self-realization. Laurette Séjourné asks him, "[When] were you stricken by the bold vision of man as maker of his own destiny?", a vision that confers upon him the "sovereignty to choose one's own life."[29] "You are what you wanted to be," writes David Fernandes.[30] Matilde Bianqui beautifully describes him as "bird of chosen feathers."[31]

Jaime Valdivieso, in a most inspired fragment of his biographical poem *Presencia del Che Guevara*, articulates this self-conscious process and the initial and target states[32]:

> Naciste Ernesto Guevara de la Serna
> último eslabón del lobo,
> primero del hombre verdadero
> que tú mismo comenzaste
> arrancándote la piel a
> espinas y a barro y con el
> pan y el agua diarios.

> You were born Ernesto Guevara
>   de la Serna
> last link with the wolf
> first of the true man
> whom you yourself started
> pulling off the prickly
> and muddy skin and with
> daily bread and water.

Che-Project

Che-Model

The process of personal self-determination, and in relation to life and society, implies a guiding model. This model is for Che and the artists inspired by him where the realm of the personal and the contextual merge. In this context, Che ceases to be a man and becomes a project. Che in his time and the artists since then were well aware of the historical relevance and practical impact of this model. As the creative definition of Che, it is the single most important thematic force in poetry and songs about him.

> a guiding hand is Che Guevara
> to lead us past the place at which he fell
> —Peggy Seeger[33]

> Proclamo que nunca es tarde
> para crecer hasta tí
> —Ernesto Agüero[34]

> I proclaim that is never too late
> to grow up to you

> No, el Che no ha muerto
> porque el Che es más que el Che.
> El Che es el mundo que late y espera
>   y lucha,
> es la vida que alienta por más vida,
> es nuestra razón de ser lo que
>   queremos ser,
> es nuestra estatura moral de hombres...
> —Francisco Fernández-Santos[35]

> No, Che did not die
> for Che is more than Che.
> Che is a world that throbs and
>   hopes and fights,
> is the life that emboldens more life,
> is our reason for being what we wish to be,
> is our moral stature as men...

> Cuán vivo estás comandando la Historia
> y se impone tu ejemplo a quemarropa
> —Coco Manto[36]

> In life you are commanding History
> and your example imposes itself
>   point-blank.

For Carlos Puebla, it is in becoming this model that Che dies victorious defeating the machine of the empire.[37]

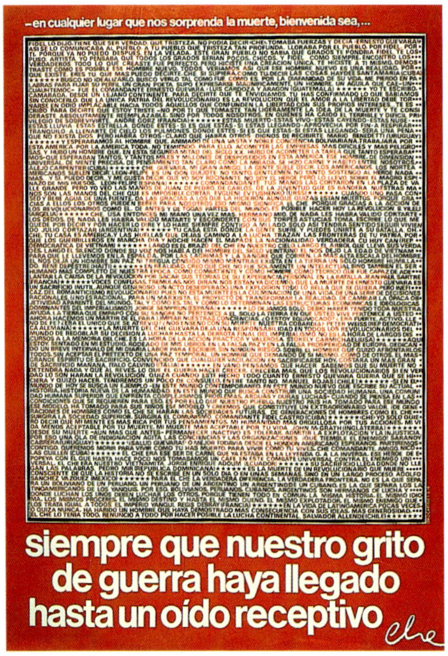

Figure 3.7. *"Wherever death may surprise us, let it be welcome as long as this, our war cry, reaches a receptive ear"*—Che. These words are taken from Che's *Message to Tricontinental* (1967). The face of Che is composed of twenty-five homages from writers around the world. 98.5 x 52 cm.

> Puede que tu carne humana
> no resistiera el acero,
> pero el acero tampoco
> puede resistir tu ejemplo

> It may be that your human flesh
> could not resist steel
> but neither can steel
> resist your example

In the poetic representation of this model, three metaphoric stages of development are revealed: Che-*Espejo* (mirror), Che-*Estrella* (star), Che-*Camino* (path).

Che-Espejo (mirror)

The concept of Che-Espejo (mirror) presents him as a vehicle for self-reflection and criticism, as an inspirational force to break static, mechanistic notions of the self. The rigorously exact reflection indicates at once the urgent need and the concrete possibility of change.

> Las astillas filosas de tu espejo
> empiezan a enconarse en pies desnudos
> —Claribel Alegría[38]

> The sharp splinters of your mirror
> begin to fester in naked feet.

> Miradlo entrar, como jamás tan vivo
> en espejo del hombre
> convertido
> —Félix Pita Rodríguez[39]

> Behold him enter, never so alive
> in the mirror of man
> transformed

> Lo buscaré en las estrellas
> y en mi propio espejo.
> —Matilde Casazola[40]

> I will look for him in the stars
> and in my own mirror.

Che-Estrella (star)

The star, the most important visual symbol associated with Che Guevara, functions as a guiding beacon, indicating the proper goal for our efforts; it represents the new person, the dignified person, the empowered person.

> Mi hermano mostrándome
> detrás de la noche
> su estrella elegida.
> —Julio Cortázar[41]

> My brother showing me
> behind the night
> his chosen star.

> ...hasta que supe un día
> que eras luz ensangrentada, el norte,
> esa estrella
> que hay que mirar a cada instante
> para saber en donde nos hallamos
> —Rafael Alberti[42]

> ...until I discovered one day
> that you are bloodied light, the north,
> that star
> we have to look at every moment
> to know where we are.

*...pero no se apaga
la estrella de tu mística viable*
—Coco Manto[43]

...but it does not grow dim
the star of your viable mysticism.

*y la estrella que corona tu frente
alumbrará como un radiante sol
    de libertad*
—Marcelo Arduz Ruíz[44]

And the star that crowns your brow
will shine like a radiant sun of liberty

Che-Camino (path)

Finally and most important, Che guides us on the path from the critical self-analysis of the mirror to the righteous fulfillment of the star. The Che-model proposed by the artists transcends intellectual questioning and a theoretical ideal. It actually presents, through his action and attitude, the means for self-transformation and social change.

*¡Era rojo faro de camino
y ahora es el camino...!*
—Eduardo Ibarra[45]

It was the red beacon on the road
and now it is the road...!

*la senda está trazada
nos la mostró el Che.*
—Jorge Salerno[46]

the path is traced
Che showed it to us.

*tu camino
repartido
aquí
para siempre*
—Jaime Nisttahuz[47]

your path
shared
here
forever

*abre sendas por los cerros
deja huellas en los vientos*
—Victor Jara[48]

he opens pathways in the hills
he leaves tracks in the winds

From where we stand, at the edge of our
    foothills
the steep heights seem much more easily
    reachable.
Ever since your last journey down into the
    ravine,
we knew we must climb it, tomorrow,
    because of you.
—Andrew Salkey[49]

*dicen que incineraron
toda tu vocación
menos un dedo
basta para mostrarnos el camino...*
—Mario Benedetti[50]

They say they burned
your whole purpose
save one finger,
enough to show us the way

*Ay, Che camino, patria o muerte es
    mi destino*
—Alfredo De Robertis[51]

Ay, Che pathway, fatherland or death is my
    destiny.

Che-Historicized

In the work of poets and songwriters there is a constant effort to define Che and the new man (woman) as part of a historical continuum, as members of a long and ongoing lineage of righteous individuals. As project, Che is not a historical exception but the realization of the historical aspirations of the continent and the world. In him are expressed the struggles of the past and victories of the future.

*Che Guevara cargado de la muerte
    de los siglos,
Che Guevara padre e hijo de la
    independencia
nieto de todas las libertades de todo
    el mundo*
—Efraín Huerta[52]

Che Guevara laden with the death
    of centuries
Che Guevara father and son
    of independence
grandson of all the liberties of all the world

*este gran Capitán que ha parido
    la historia*
—Leoncio Bueno[53]

this great captain who gave birth to history

*Su sangre vendrá
de todas las sangres,
borrando los siglos
del miedo y del hambre.*
—Daniel Viglietti[54]

His blood will come
of all bloods
eliminating the centuries
of fear and of hunger.

As one of the key historical figures in this struggle for liberation, Che stands in the company of Guauhtémoc, Túpac Amaru, Bolívar, Martí, Sandino, Zapata, and Lumumba. *El Libro de la Historia del Che*, a poem by the Nicaraguan revolutionary martyr Leonel Rugama, delineates a genealogy of American liberators from the indigenous resistance to the European conquerors through the wars of independence, ending with Che Guevara and a prophetic last segment on the poet's own participation in the Nicaraguan revolution.

Che-Demystified

The historical contextualization of Che, his ideas, and struggle serves to counter the mystification and/or commodification to which his image has been so susceptible. Political artists in general and poets and songwriters in particular have been very aware of the danger of contributing to the process of alienating the memory of Che Guevara from its deepest revolutionary message, the potential of people to transform themselves and reality. Poets have incorporated warnings to themselves and their readers and listeners on two related fronts: oversimplification and glorification. First they warn us and themselves against the Che-poster syndrome and the decontextualizing tendency of the iconographic:

*No quisiera invocar al héroe
pegado a las murallas,
ni al guerrillero
detenido a la distancia*
—Jaime Valdivieso[55]

I would not wish to invoke the hero
stuck on the walls
nor the guerrilla
kept at a distance

*Mañana, comandante,
de grabado en grabado, de estatua
    en busto,
de relato en relato,
tú ya lejos de tí.*

*¡Pero contigo, no!
Que no te alejen de tí,
que no te miren mañana como se mira a
    las estatuas.*
—Félix Pita Rodríguez[56]

Tomorrow, comandante,
From poster to poster, from statue to bust,
from story to story,
you now far from you.

But with you, no!
Let them not take you from you
Let them not look at you tomorrow as one
    looks at statues.

Second and more poignantly, the poets and songwriters are aware of the dangers of glorification of Che's personality to the point where he no longer functions as an example of what every revolutionary can be, but on the contrary becomes mythologized so that his model is longer reachable.

*Pero nunca falta alguien que te alce
en un altar;
y haga leyenda de tu imagen formadora
y haga imposible el sueño de alcanzarte*

*Para que nunca seas
pasto sólo del rito y las palabras*
—José Angel Valente[57]

But there is always someone to raise you
    on an altar:
and turn your formative image into legend
and turn the dream of attaining you into
    an impossibility

So that you may never be
merely the stuff of ritual and words

Che

Here we come full circle to the cohesive unifying force underpinning the creative representations of Che, the dialectical interweaving of both categories: Che-Man and Che-Project as a one multidimensional symbiotic unity. The threads of the self, context, and history become a tight weaving of interdependency: his flowing as water is his flowing in history; his camaraderie allows for his demystifying; his self-construction makes the model viable. Che's embodiment of this dialectical conception of existence is expressed through the multitude of organic metaphors associating him with nature that portray him at once as environment, agent, and process. The power of this remarkable creative articulation of Che Guevara's legacy resides in the revolutionary becoming the revolution, the individual becoming history, becoming struggle, becoming victory.

Chapter 4.

Symbols: Hair and Beard, Cigar, Uniform, Beret, Star, the Name

Figure 4.1. Raúl Martínez, painting, private collection, Havana.

Hair and beard

> So the hairs of your beard are turned into gunshot
> Your sad gaze inspires thirst for justice
> Your agitated hair bespeaks hope.[1]
>
> America takes form, becomes concrete: America, which means Cuba; Cuba which means Fidel Castro (a man representing a continent, whose only pedestal is his guerrillero beard).[2]

Che's long, flowing hair and curly, chestnut-colored beard, the famous frame to a famous face, become in the posters not only marks of instant recognition, unique individualizing features which immediately set him off from other heroes, but also vehicles of aesthetic and metaphoric exploration in their own right. In reality, the beard was relatively sparse and discontinuous (there is a marked break midway in the jawline, often preserved by artists), compared with Fidel's denser and Camilo Cienfuegos's much longer thicket. Che's beard becomes in the art a deep, resonant shadow below, while joining with the copious head hair to fan out in decorative, electric, wanton wisps: a map, a landscape, the contour of amazing revolutionary itinerary (fig. M.14). Nowhere does the beard spark more brilliant coloristic fireworks than in the many portrait paintings and silkscreens of Raúl Martínez, where it functions as a shamanic aura and a power explosion (figs. 4.1, 4.2). Children have also seen the beard as an arresting feature to be tugged and splashed at with a crayon (fig. 4.3) "His hair is black, or blue: almost steel."[3] For *Granma* caricaturist René de la Nuéz, the flaming (red) beard of the revolutionary becomes a great torch of defiance and liberation.

There can be no doubt that the extent and flamboyant beauty of Che's hair was a special factor in his physical appeal outside Cuba, at a timely conjunction with an important change in male youth fashions of the mid-1960s. Flowing hair and beards, with their ancient associations with unleashed power and sexuality, and more recently with political liberation (à la Byron, Marx, or Garibaldi) became potent signs of separation from a mainstream culture still under the discipline of the conformist crew-cut and clean-shaven look of the postwar era, required by the military and imitated in business and on campus, and still or again more or less the rule. With the protest movement against the Viet Nam war, "hippie" (inherited, one might say, from beatnik) hirsuteness became a vogue for the dissident young, who wanted to "let it all hang out." Celebrations of hippie and "flower-child" locks in posters (and a musical called *Hair*) coincided with admiration for the Cuban barbudos (bearded ones) and the Cuban revolution.

In the US counterculture of the sixties and seventies, long hair (on women, too) and beards signified an aesthetic affirmation of peace and a protest against a business and war ethic. There were also connotations of love, vulnerability, even Christlike sacrifice. The "long-hair freaks," as the politicians and media chose to call them, were in fact reviving a fashion condemned by Cromwell in his army and for good military reasons, as the modern long-hairs discovered in close encounters with the police, who reacted to flowing locks as a natural target and provocation and made them a convenient point of purchase for the wielding of the billy club against the enemy head. But the conscious motivation for dissidents wearing long hair was, above all, individualistic, for hair has a strongly individualizing effect, which is the principal reason why it is prohibited by today's professional armies and discouraged in the business world.

Barbudos became synonymous, inside and outside Cuba, with the Cuban and generally Latin American guerrillas. A series of photo albums featuring Fidel, Che, and Camilo bears this title. One Cuban magazine is called *El Caimán Barbudo* (The Bearded Alligator). Beards were a natural outgrowth of guerrilla life in the Sierra Maestra, where time, razor blades, and often even soap and water were at a premium. They were also a form of camouflage, and served to impede infiltration by army spies, since beards take time to grow. After the triumph, in order to preserve their special revolutionary identity, the guerrillas chose not to shave, wearing their beards with pride and at the behest of Fidel who proclaimed, "Your beard does not belong to you. It belongs to the Revolution."[4]

It was also a badge of honor, denied to those too young to have fought in the

Figure 4.2. Raúl Martínez, private collection, Havana.

Figure 4.3. Alejandro Medina (six years old), drawing, 1973, c. 20 x 30 cm. Collection of the National Library, Havana.

insurrection. When I visited Cuba in 1973, I found a number of young Cubans annoyed at the strictures against long hair, despite the example, now frozen in time, of Che, whom they were summoned to imitate in all but appearance. This, in turn, has changed: hairstyles are free again, although Fidel's example remains constant: full beard (now gray), hair relatively short on top.

The barbudos were feared by all the Latin American dictatorships. In the Dominican Republic, Trujillo offered a thousand dollars per bearded head which would be, supposedly, that of a Cuban guerrilla. The number of bearded decapitated heads brought in by the peasants exceeded the number of possible invaders. It was a serious handicap for the real guerrilleros in Bolivia that the Indians learned to see beards as the mark of the foreigner, and were apt to obey orders to denounce their wearers to the authorities.

The magical aura attached to Che's beard is shared by Fidel's beard, the latter becoming a natural target, with the cigar, for some of the CIA's more exotic assassination attempts on him (little is known about US plots against the life of Che). These included putting a chemical in Fidel's cigars so as to make his beard fall off, and thus expose the Cuban Samson to ridicule and political impotence; and fabricating attractive fish which would explode in Fidel's face when pursuing his favorite hobby of spearfishing. The threat of killing him via his cigars was real, and just as he had (has) bodyguards taste his food and drink, so he had a taster for each cigar he smoked.[5]

At the end of a famous interview with the Cuban leader, with that forthrightness the media have always shown towards Cuba, Barbara Walters asked, "Will you ever shave your beard?" Fidel replied, "In exchange for what? The ceasing of the blockade?" and went on, patiently, to explain the function of the beard in Cuba, and the not irrelevant savings on the importation of imperialist razor blades. In a public address in Nicaragua to celebrate the first anniversary of the Revolution there (1980), Castro remarked, "It is said that the tyrant Somoza [overthrown by the Nicaraguans] in bidding farewell to the troops [embarking for the Bay of Pigs invasion] asked them to bring back at least one hair from Castro's beard. I have come with my entire head, to offer it, if only symbolically, to the victorious people of Nicaragua."[6]

So much are the capillary curlicues of Che's facial frame a part of his identity, it is hard to imagine him without them; and photographs of him clean shaven and short-haired are rare. In the best known, the Bolivian passport photo, where his whole head is shaved down to tufts at the side, as if he were naturally bald, he is unrecognizable, as he is meant to be. The most commonly reproduced version of this photograph has the frontal lobes above the eyebrows subsequently circled by hand, as if they constituted a decisive proof of identity; and indeed, the few photographs of him taken in lost profile show these lobes to be exceptionally developed, which one does not expect in a face otherwise noted for its regularity (the pronounced frontal lobes have been connected with his asthma, see fig. G.3, p. 61).[7]

Che's hair was sacrificed, like Achilles' on the pyre of Patroclus, for the sake of the Bolivian campaign. Che took a photograph of himself in the mirror in the Hotel Copacabana in La Paz, shaving off what had grown since he arrived a few days before. A similar photograph was published in *Granma*, 17 April 1967, with the text of his *Message to Tricontinental*. Together, photograph and text announced that Che was indeed engaged in a new campaign, although the exact location was still to be kept secret. A pamphlet probably of the same date, with the same text and photograph, features the phrase, "Like the Phoenix BIRD, he was born again from the ashes, guerrilla-war-hardened," as if the shaving marked a resurgence from a long deathlike disappearance.

Disguise by taking off rather than putting on is rare, when one thinks about it. Spies put on false mustaches and beards; Che's disguise was "merely" to shave off his luxuriant facial hair, add spectacles and a maxillary prosthesis to thrust out his jaw. He deceived Bolivian immigration officials, who had been provided only with an artist's imagining of Che shaved, for lack of a photograph of him thus, a process in which, curiously, the CIA agent-turned-anti-imperialist Philip Agee was involved. But Che also deceived his closest friends, co-workers, and family, showing up incognito

Figure 4.4. Su Negrin (US), "...*the true revolutionary is guided by great feelings of love*," Times Change Press, 1970, 43 x 56 cm.

at meetings and even his own home. Fidel gave a farewell dinner with government members for a distinguished "visitor"—whom none recognized.[8] A vivid account by Aleidita, daughter by Aleida March, five years old at the time (in the spring of 1966), and remembered twenty years later, tells how she was introduced at her home to this bespectacled, clean-shaven and almost completely bald gentleman called Ramón, supposedly a close friend of her father. Amused, he observed her dispute his place at the head of the table and show him how her father mixed mineral water with his wine; he charmed her by inviting her to sit on his lap after she hurt her head on a table, comforting her and giving her some sweets. He parted from her without her knowing who he was. She had, to be sure, not seen him for a year.[9]

One imagines Che, whose affection for his children shines through in his letters, happily letting them play with his beard, as small children like to, which would enhance its significance in his own eyes. His first wife Hilda Gadea tells how their daughter Hildita liked to pull on Camilo Cienfuegos's beautiful mane, and asked, "How is it you have such a long beard?" "Because I tug on it a little every day. Like this." (A few days later he disappeared and was presumed dead). If Che's beard was part of his graceful image, that of Camilo inspired awe: in Che's own words, "Asked about the Russian submarines, Camilo replied seriously that they had only one, a submarine with feet. The man did not dare to doubt the terrible beard of Camilo."[10]

The only known surviving part of Che's body, apart from the hands, are locks of hair cut secretly from his publicly exhibited corpse.

The cigar

The cigar so often seen in the iconography in the mouth or hand of Guevara, as in that of Castro and other Cuban leaders, stands forth as the essence of *cubanidad*, as much an assertion of national identity and the right to simple pleasures as the drinking of rum and the dancing of the conga. Ironically, because of its relatively high cost outside Cuba, and historic association with the rich, the cigar has always served cartoonists in the West as the emblem of the bloated capitalist plutocrat. In Cuba, meanwhile, the cigar has always been seen as democratic, affordable by the worker, prized for its world-renowned superior quality, a source of national pride.

Early forms of resistance to Spain revolved around the tobacco industry. In the eighteenth century, Spain established a monopoly over the product, as had Britain over tea in her colonies; this monopoly was broken in 1817. In the War of Independence, patriotic leaders had ownership interests in the cigar factories and the workers, unionized early on, formed a proletariat naturally opposed to Spanish rule. Victorious strikes of the Federation of Tobacco Workers in 1889 and 1890, under the influence of José Martí, helped impel the Independence movement. Cigar box labels were used to propagandize the successes against Spain, and then the new friendship with the United States. Later, tobacco workers sympathetic to socialism formed a much persecuted core of the National Labor Confederation. Castro's revolution found receptive ground among them, which facilitated nationalization. Che Guevara was appointed head of a task force for the promotion of the Cuban cigar abroad, to earn exchange needed to finance agrarian and industrial reform.[11]

Guevara himself had not smoked until he arrived in Cuba in 1956. He noted the novelty—with a sense of its wider significance in turning him into a Cuban guerrilla fighter—in a letter to his mother written early (28 January 1957) in the Sierra Maestra campaign days. "As if I were really a soldier (I'm dirty and ragged at least), I am writing this letter over a tin plate with a gun at my side and something new, a cigar in my mouth."[12]

It may be that Che took to the cigar in public because he wanted to appear as Cuban as the rest; he personally preferred a pipe, which he deemed better in guerrilla operations, since the light was less visible. Tobacco was the solace and companion of the guerrillero; it was, said Che, along with reading, his only "vice." It served also a practical purpose. Either cigar or pipe smoke may act as an insect repellent, as does tobacco macerated in water and spread as an ointment on the skin.

Cigar smoke, unlike that of the cigarette, is not inhaled into the lungs and is, therefore, less dangerous. Still, it is hard

Chapter 4.

to square the asthmatic and ascetic Che putting this pleasure above his health; as a doctor, he knew it to be a health hazard before smoking was conclusively linked by science to cancer and emphysema. At the end of February 1959, prostrated by exhaustion from overwork and "smoking like a chimney," he was diagnosed with double and diffused pulmonary emphysema in the right lung. At first prohibited from smoking at all, he was then told to cut down his cigar habit to one a day. He responded by showing up with a cigar half a meter long.[13] In the Che iconography (photographs more than posters) the omnipresence of the cigar in the mouth, or more often perhaps passively in the hand, seems to constitute a triumph of a national symbol.

Che's pipes (there were two of them, each for a different tobacco) became, at the end in Bolivia, relics to be eagerly competed for. According to the (suspect) account of the CIA agent Félix Rodríguez, Che remained uncooperative and silent until Rodríguez gave him some tobacco for his pipe. Among his last words were his blunt refusal to give his pipe to one of his guards, before he surrendered it to Rodríguez, who had asked for it more politely.[14]

When Fidel Castro, who had smoked cigars since he was fifteen years old, announced in 1985 that he was quitting, on grounds of his personal health and in order to set an example to the Cuban people, it became a big media event, "one last sacrifice I must make for the public health."[15] There had been an anti-smoking campaign in Cuba for some years: the prevalence of photographs and posters of Che smoking cannot have helped.

Unlike cigarette advertisements which make smoking sexy and purely pleasurable, photographs of intellectuals smoking are imbued with a thoughtful air, as they seem to ingest and expel the smoke in the process of mental digestion, or as a necessary fumigation of overtaxed brain cells. The cigar in the Che iconography reinforces his role as an intellectual. The cigarette, and *a fortiori* the cigar, also serves to emphasize gestures. The currently widespread recognition of the harmful, indeed lethal effects of tobacco tends to reduce the pool of acceptable images of Che as the ideal man, and the man of the future, and the preference today is for the nonsmoking Che, which is yet another reason for the triumph of the Korda image. It is noteworthy that a poster derived from a photograph of Che with a cigar butt dangling from his mouth, intact in one version (fig. 4.4), has the butt removed in another (US) version.

Uniform

In virtually all photographs of Che Guevara he wears a loose kind of uniform, unironed fatigues; in the Korda matrix picture, exceptionally, he is wearing a leather zipper jacket. Che, unlike Fidel, was wholly uninterested in clothes, and generally wore his uniform fatigues on formal and diplomatic occasions as for daily work, because it was convenient, economical, saved having to think about what to wear and match, and because it retained associations of revolutionary combat. Che was notoriously disinclined to change his clothes—in this, his habit was more Argentinean than Cuban.

Even his manner of wearing the uniform was idiosyncratic and militarily incorrect. "Ever the iconoclast, Che steadfastly wore the shirt-jacket of his olive-green uniform outside his trousers, with his belt on top—the only Cuban *comandante* who refused to conform to the military dress code. More often than not, he wore his trousers hanging loose, outside his boots, instead of tucking them in. No one dared reproach him, of course. 'Che es como es,' his colleagues would say, with a shrug of their shoulders, 'Che is the way he is.'" According to Che's wife Aleida, who checked on his appearance before he left for the office each morning, his preference for the shirt hanging outside his trousers had to do with his asthma.[16]

The Cuban olive-green guerrilla uniform, worn on state occasions, naturally offends US dignitaries, who prefer to see their own client military dictators disguised as civilians. Vice President Dan Quayle voiced his concern at the inauguration of a new Brazilian president on March 1990. Castro's response was to refer the symbolism to the revolutionary ideas it embodied. The Cuban comandantes have become used to "wearing uniforms in civilian life, as the monk gets used to his habit and the nurse to her hat."[17] As Che said, the uniform is to the body like the bark is to the tree.

Beret

Berets have been worn widely in this century by military and civilians, workers and intellectuals alike, although not important businessmen or politicians, so that the association is broadly that of the active but not upper-class man. The beret is traditional French military headgear, adopted by Montgomery for the British during World War II, and by the US for their special forces, the Green Berets, and for the Boinas Verdes, their Bolivian equivalent. The choice of the beret, in black, by the Black Panthers was probably designed to enhance their militaristic self-defense posture. But the choice of the beret by Guevara, against the more common type of headgear favored by the other guerrillas (e.g., the wide-brimmed sombrero, worn by Camilo Cienfuegos, baseball or other kind of cap as worn by

Figure 4.5. René Mederos. Final billboard in a series of eleven lining Avenida Revolución in August 1973 that spelled out—word by word and phrase by phrase—the exhortation, "We are all one people in revolution, we accelerate our victorious step, we advance toward new victories." The flags are those of Cuba and socialism.

Fidel), is not easily explained.

The beret is not as convenient in combat as the cap, which can be put on and off with one hand, and offers better protection from sun and rain. Photographically, however, the cap confers an aesthetic disadvantage, for it tends to cast unwanted shadow over the eyes and upper part of the face, and at certain angles interferes with the facial silhouette. The beret forms a clean line over the brow, forming a "semi-halo." While these cannot have been conscious factors in Che's choice, it was the right one from the point of view of effective portraiture. But Che's preference for the beret, usually in black, was conscious, and it was part of his disguise in Bolivia to wear, at first, a modest Bolivian-style cap (*cachuca*) which he declared, according to Ciro Bustos, he was glad to exchange for his usual beret once the secret of his presence in Bolivia was out.[18]

Star

> You brought the force of truth, and its light gleamed like a sun in your most pure star, clearer than the other stars…the light of your star, won the hard way, with humanity and love, lit for all eternity, can never be extinguished. It is our guide, the north pole of all our yearnings, the compass that marks the pathway of our heart, the fire which warms our blood, the torch that lights our way in the struggle in which we are engaged.[19]

The star pinned to Che's beret designates his military rank, the highest accorded under the relatively unhierarchical guerrilla system, that of comandante, weakly translated as major, better as commander (the other ranks were captain and lieutenant). The simple, single star, the only insignia worn by a man of such proven valor, seems to shame all the generals who have never been in combat, whose valor consists of ordering the slaughter of defenseless civilians but who appear in public bedecked with medals all over their chests. The rule seems to be, the less glorious the military exploit, the more need for medals and decorations.

The story of how Guevara was raised to the highest rank (second only to Fidel, as comandante en jefe) is told in his *Episodes from the Revolutionary War*: at the moment when he was required to add his name to the list of those signing a letter of condolence, and hesitating (since he was still technically the army doctor) over a title, Fidel simply said, "Put comandante." The actual star was given to him, together with the gift of a wristwatch, by Celia Sánchez, a guerrillera and long-time intimate friend of Fidel.[20]

Like the hair and beard, the star is an aesthetic magnet, a source of light, of power. It is, of course, also the star of socialism and as such appears blended with the personal one of comandante in the splendid billboard (*valla*) series by Mederos, passing from Cuban and socialist flag to the heavens where it radiates orange and yellow light like a sun, until it is subsumed in the star on Che's beret (fig. 4.5). It also appears alone, synecdochically with the outline of the beret; it continues to burn even when (the face of) Che is gone. It is the guiding star, even (says Alfredo Rostgaard, on a "second reading" of his very popular poster, fig. D.1, p. 20; cf. M.16, p. 13) the Star of Bethlehem that led the shepherds to the baby Jesus. In the great Rebeldía mural at the university in La Paz (fig. H.10, p. 72), the star on Che's beret is the spark detonating an explosion of flames around his head.

In Raúl Martínez's posters, among the wondrous variations worked by so many artists, stars rise from the beret in a celestial, protective spray and as the sparks of ideas which travel the globe and reach out toward us (figs. 4.6, 4.7). An experienced Cuban designer, Alberto Blanco, took the challenge of letting the chromatic gradations of the star dictate the design as a whole to the point that, unintentionally, Che looks like he has his head imprisoned by his own symbol (fig. M.16). This is another aspect of myth-making. The ultimate use of the star, combined with the signature, appears in a mythic connection as the leitmotiv in an atlas on Che,[21] where—against a firmament veined with cosmic energies—the "e" of the name launches a meteor on a path which strikes a star onto the forehead of a Leonardo da Vinci figure popularly known as "Man the measure of all things" (a naked man with limbs outstretched, inscribed in a square and a circle based on Vitruvian proportions). The image suggests Che sparking, out of primordial time, universal human intelligence.

Figure 4.7. Raúl Martínez, silkscreen, 61 x 55.5 cm. Private collection.

Figure 4.6. Raúl Martínez, silkscreen, 1968, 81 x 39 cm.

Figure 4.8. José Villa (sculptor) and Rómulo Fernández (architect), *Che and the Children*, 1982–1983, approximately 3 m high. The design, chosen by children, consists of nine concentric stars into the heart of which is cut a silhouette of Che. The idea is that Cuban children should project themselves like stars, see themselves reflected in the polished steel, and feel a connection with Che. The motto of Pioneros, the Cuban children's organization, is "We will be like Che" (see fig. M.18).

Generally averse to realistic monuments, the Cubans have erected as perhaps their best three-dimensional commemoration of their hero a strictly symbolic one, a great star made in shining aluminum sculpture, the centerpiece of the entrance patio to the great Palace of Pioneers, a children's organization. This institution is dedicated to Che, whose familiar (Korda) silhouette is cut into each of the nine plates of increasing, then decreasing size, radiating their light in space (figs. 4.8, M.18, p, 114). The design was chosen as the result of a competition, by the children themselves.

The (holy) name of Che

> To me, "Che" represents what's most important, what I'm most fond of in my life. How could I not like it? Everything that comes before, my first name and surname, are small, personal, insignificant. On the contrary, I like very much to be called Che.[22]

Three single letters, initially a nickname but standing perfectly for the man and capable of encapsulating the myth, have been iconicized and revered in a manner comparable to IHS, the holy name of Jesus as glorified in the sixteenth and seventeenth centuries. The accent on the "e" (Ché), commonly used outside Cuba and especially by writers in English, should be regarded as superfluous; as Che found occasion to remind the schoolteacher of La Higuera just before his death, single syllable words in Spanish do not normally take an accent.[23] Quotation marks around the name, defensible only when the full name is spelled out (Ernesto "Che" Guevara), are also normally superfluous.

Che is a nickname commonly given by Latin Americans to Argentineans outside Argentina, where the syllable is thrown casually into speech as a filler or punctuation, possibly deriving from the Italian (Italian immigration into Argentina has always been preponderant): "cioé"[24] meaning "that is" and functioning as filler like our "right" or "so," or the American English "man" and British vernacular "mate." Significantly, the nickname that Guevara accepted without reservation and that he used on official documents is of the kind which does not personalize, but generalizes, which makes him everyman from Argentina. Coincidentally, "che" means "man" and "my" in Indian languages.

The very simplicity of the name is one of the reasons that it stuck, to the point that Che used it when he signed the banknotes, as director of the National Bank, as it were in mockery of the florid signatures commonly appended to what capitalism regards as sacred, and what Che regarded as trivial or obsolete (fig. 4.9). Simplicity is the key to Che's character, as Edmundo Desnoes has observed: Che "rejected the glorification of external attributes, from dress to signature, to restore authority to moral conduct."[25]

The name, formed as a signature and in various kinds of lettering, dominates many posters, as if it were imbued with a magical power of its own (figs. M.19–M.25, p. 114). In a poster by Julio Eloy (ICAIC, 1970), it bursts forth in rays of light emanating from the star.[26] It is the only means of identifying the author on the cover of an Argentine edition of his *Relatos de la Guerra Revolucionaria* (Omnia, 1986). In a Chago cartoon, used in a mural, it also becomes the combative path we follow into the future (mural version fig. H.13, p. 73). Over the great Palacio de los Pioneros in Parque Lenin, near Havana, which is dedicated to Che, the name is monumentally enthroned (figs. M.24, M.25, p. 114).

Invocations of a name tend to arouse associations with religious hymns ("at the name of Jesus, every knee shall bow") or love poetry. "Let your name ring forth, Che, like a friendly bell, let your name roll out, Che, like the sharp staccato of bullets."[27]

Figure 4.9. Che banknotes: three pesos with portrait of Che, 1984 (top); ten pesos with Che's signature in the lower left (1960).

Felix Beltrán, 4 Ches

U.S.-trained Cuban graphic designer Félix Beltrán, now working in Mexico, has made close to fifty different versions of Che for posters and magazines, all marked by his tendency to reduce form to autonomous systems of contours—typically blobbed and splashed in a tight, very precise, intricate rhythm or, alternatively, faceted and fractured in a semi-cubistic manner. See also Beltrán's depiction of Angela Davis (fig. 1.5) and other posters of Che (figs. M.27, M.28, p. 115).

Figure. F.1. Félix Beltrán, silkscreen, 47 x 38 cm.

Figure. F.2. Félix Beltrán, *"Other hands will take up the weapons,"* ICAP (Cuban Institute for Friendship with Other Peoples), silkscreen, 53 x 33 cm.

Figure.F.3. Félix Beltrán, ICAP, silkscreen, 56 x 43 cm.

Figure F.4. Félix Beltrán, silkscreen, 1971. Courtesy of the Center for Cuban Studies Art Space.

Chapter 5.
The Korda Matrix

The role of photography in Che's life

Photography has been so ubiquitous in twentieth-century life, events and celebrities have been so intertwined with the photographic images made of them, and the very idea of "celebrity" having become virtually a photographic (or electronic) construct, the existence of a great photographic gallery of the Cuban leadership may seem unsurprising. The Cuban revolution has cherished the photographic arts, as it has the cinematic arts; and elements of Che's biography establish a curiously close relationship to photography. Che was born to a shutterbug of a father, to judge by the hundreds of childhood photographs of him: eighty-four from the first five years alone were published in a book for children about the boy Che.[1] Guevara earned his living for several months as a street photographer in Mexico, taking pictures of families and then tracking the subjects to their homes in the hope of persuading them to buy the usually indifferent results as priceless likenesses of the children. Che then became a photographer for a news agency, "reporting on the ches [Argentineans] who show up here."[2]

This, as the photographer was too well aware, was the art practiced at its most trivial and innocent level. At the same time, no Cuban at the time of the revolution can have been unaware of the great political and propaganda value of news photographs: those taken after Fidel's attack on the Moncada barracks of the atrocities committed by Batista's soldiers, which roused public opinion against the dictator, and in favor of the Fidelistas; those taken by Herbert Matthews of Fidel and his comrades in the Sierra 1958, proving the existence of a guerrilla force, which amazed the public in Cuba and the US, and made Batista seem a liar and worthy of ridicule because he refused to believe the evidence. Photography was a potent and dangerous tool; it was used by the US against Cuba most notoriously to prove the presence of Soviet missiles in Cuba in 1962.

Photographs can be used to sign death warrants, as contemporary cinema, notably *Under Fire*, a film about the Nicaraguan revolution, has so often demonstrated. Che in his *Bolivian Diary* upbraids a detachment of guerrillas for leaving behind diaries (and indeed, even writing them in the first place), together with photographs and drawn portraits of comrades, that were confiscated by the enemy. He was particularly concerned about a picture of himself shaven that fell into enemy hands from the guerrillas' camp: how it got where it did was for him and remains today a mystery.[3] Che considered the capture of such photographs bad blows in his campaign, errors of which he himself, with the diary he kept and photographs he took (a dozen rolls were found on him when caught) was most guilty. On the other hand, the publication of the photographs of his collaborators Régis Debray and Ciro Bustos and journalist George Andrew Roth made it hard for the military to kill them quietly, and may have saved their lives.

Che's Mexican biographer Paco Ignacio Taibo II, who lingers again and again over photographs of Che taken at various moments of his life, treating them as primary biographical data, speaks of Che's own use of the camera as a "dangerous habit which accompanied Che the whole length of his life."[4] The full dimension of this habit, which is in accord with Che's unremitting need for self-reflection and self-construction in his diaries, is still unknown to us, since so many of the photographs, like the unpublished diaries, remain in the family archive.[5]

Che's own attitude as to the value of photography as an ongoing record of his role in the revolution was ambivalent. He was always reluctant to see films in which he appeared. He was not, like Fidel, temperamentally a player on the organ of publicity, a seeker of the limelight, or addicted to the cult of personality. Che occasionally showed that he was irked by the omnipresence and pushiness of photographers, and wondered whether their labors justified the cost of time and film, and whether they would not be better employed in really productive work.

Photographer Liborio Noval of *Granma* tells how he was made by Che to join in the real voluntary labor before using his camera. Raúl Corrales recounts how in 1959 when Che was managing the agrarian reform, he was assigned to the INRA (Institute for Agrarian Reform) magazine, for which Che proposed graphic essays on various industrial processes. Corrales took some very expressive photographs of Che doing interviews, and passed them on to him, to which Che responded, "The photographs are fine, what is wrong is your target. Why so many pictures of me? That is a waste of public resources. Take pictures of the people."

The most eloquent insight into Che's impatience with news photographers and their tendency to foster cults of personality comes from an anecdote from Roberto Salas. At an international reception, the lights suddenly went on and the photographers descended, Salas foremost among those seizing upon Che. The latter from his seated position seized Salas's camera, abruptly switched places with him, and clicked off the whole roll of film, saying finally, "Now you know how it gets to you" (*ahora sabes cómo jode*). The US photographer and writer Lee Lockwood told me that when he was covering a rally in Havana, Che would stick his great boot in front of his lens—purely as a joke, says Lockwood, for Che had a great sense of fun—but perhaps a joke with a message.[6]

Roberto Salas, who with his father Osvaldo probably took more photographs of Che than any other single photographer, says that there are at least twenty "incredibly majestic photographs of Che" that really work, "while of the millions taken of Fidel not four or five are really good." Salas remembers Che as melancholy-looking, often brooding, not entirely present. This accords ill with the photographic and poster record, which carries a range of expression unequaled by any, save perhaps professional actors: a myriad small movements flickering about the eyes, eyebrows, and mouth, often shown smiling or laughing. The photographs reveal a joyful Che, irony and humor even present, occasionally a comic one. Noting he had been compared to Cantinflas, the Mexican comic actor, Che deliberately posed with a typical funny Cantinflas expression for the television cameras "as a way of breaking down hierarchies."[7] Is it a coincidence that in a Raúl Martínez painting of fifteen Cuban heroes, Che is the only figure shown smiling or laughing?

Camilo Cienfuegos

Charisma? A cheapened and overworked word, but according to Corrales, Camilo Cienfuegos had more than Che (the "institutionalized charisma" of Fidel is not under discussion here). Camilo was reputed even more photogenic than Che, exuding a "divine" youthful enthusiasm, the emblematic personality of the Cuban revolution, truly Cuban as the Argentine Che, of course, was not. Says Corrales, "People ran after Camilo, they loved him as if they knew him personally, whereas Che was transcendental."

Figure 5.1. José Figueroa, photograph of Alberto Korda surrounded by derivatives of his "Korda matrix" photograph, made March 1990 for the thirtieth anniversary. 35.5 x 28 cm.

Chapter 5.

Long twinned with Che in commemoration of the Heroic Guerrilla in October each year (fig. D.5), "mythic" since 1958, Camilo's star has now dimmed somewhat. He died in circumstances less heroic than Che's, more mysterious and tragically early (he was twenty-seven years old), disappearing on 28 October 1959 in an ancient Cessna helicopter which must have crashed, presumably into the sea, for it was never found. For many years his death was not officially proclaimed. Sabotage (US?) was suspected but never confirmed. Yet Camilo remains among the triumvirate of the most cherished figures in Cuba today, the third barbudo,[8] recognizable by his broad-brimmed hat, long beard, and huge smile. Impetuous and relatively undisciplined in combat but possessed of great military skills, deputy of the army under Raúl Castro, he had a very different temperament from that of Che, who experienced some friction with him before they became really close.

Sursum Korda: the matrix photograph

On 4 March 1960, the French freighter La Coubre docked in Havana's inner harbor with seventy tons of ammunition and explosives acquired in Antwerp. At 5 AM and again at 6 AM there were explosions, killing eighty-one people. Fidel was quick to blame the CIA for sabotage although he did not have proof. The suspicion was reasonable, remembering the explosion of the Maine, believed to have been engineered by the US as an excuse to enter the Spanish-Cuban War of Independence; and, more important, given the fact that the CIA was then, in 1960, fomenting sabotage and counterrevolution all over the island. But the US took offense at the accusation. It was, says Tad Szulc, a milestone in Cuba-US relations, for the Cubans a confirmation of evil US intentions, for the US evidence of Cuba's paranoia and hostility. For an already ill-disposed US government, the accusation "tipped the balance" against Cuba in favor of eliminating Castro by any means possible. But in Cuba the masses rallied round Castro at a time of erosion of his popularity, after he gave an "immensely emotional oration" in Colón cemetery at the funeral of the victims, which used for the first time the great revolutionary slogan "*Patria o Muerte, Venceremos.*"[9] Shortly thereafter, the Cubans requested for the first time weapons from the Soviet Union.

Out of this key moment in Cuban history came the most famous single photograph of Che, which spawned a host of graphic and other derivatives, and innumerable posterized versions. It has exercised an influence aptly termed hegemonic. It was taken by the Cuban photographer Alberto Díaz Gutiérrez, who called himself Korda after the film director Alexander Korda. As he remembers it, while Fidel was speaking Korda aimed his camera at the main stage somewhat above him, ranging along it and searching for the foreign celebrities, notably Jean-Paul Sartre and Simone de Beauvoir. Behind them there was a gap, which was suddenly occupied by Che Guevara. He let his eyes wander over the assembled crowd of mourners for about twenty seconds looking, says Korda, "*encabronado y dolente*" (angry and grieved), then left again. By which time Korda's camera had clicked several times. "I remember it as if it were today: seeing him framed in the viewfinder, with that expression; I am still startled by the impact...(it) shakes me so powerfully."[10] It is ironic that a photograph admired worldwide as personifying Che the serene, even sweet visionary, should have been taken at a moment when Che was feeling not just angry but, according to a close friend, "so furious that if he had met a Yankee he would have eaten him alive."[11]

Revolución, the government magazine which had assigned the freelance Korda to cover the rally, chose not to use the photograph, which lay dormant for seven years. "But I liked it a lot, and I made a 30 x 40 cm print of it." Korda does not know if Che ever saw it. He would have liked to have his opinion, since he (Che) was always curious about cameras, having once earned his living at a photographer in Mexico. In May or June 1967, when Che was already in Bolivia, Korda gave a print to Giangiacomo Feltrinelli, a well-known leftist Italian publisher, who would later print the Italian edition of Che's *Bolivian Diary* (and be assassinated by presumed Italian rightists). Shortly after Che's death, it seems,[12] Feltrinelli decided to use the photograph for a textless poster, of which he printed and sold (according to Korda) "millions" of copies, making more than five million dollars from them.[13] In Cuba, Korda's

Figure 5.2. Frémez, *"Ever onward unto victory"—Che,* October 1967, 59.5 x 44.5 cm.

Figure 5.3. Lesbia Vent Dumois, design for thirtieth anniversary of the Korda photograph, silkscreen, 1990, 76 x 50.5 cm.

Figure 5.4. Paul Davis, *The Spirit of Che lives in the new Evergreen!*, 114 x 175 cm. Designed by Kenneth Dearoff after a painting by Davis and used as a magazine cover for *Evergreen Review* (February 1968). Inspired, says the artist, by

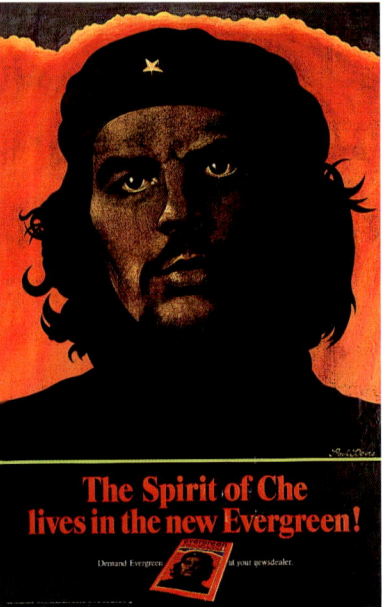

pictures of Italian martyred saints and the resurrected Christ, he has idealized, romanticized, and sensualized his Korda model. The poster, formatted to fit New York subway billboards, was systematically and universally defaced. A bomb was tossed into the *Evergreen Review* offices, and screaming anti-Castro protesters and police surrounded the building, according to interviews with art dealer Jack Rennart and the artist (May

photograph was first used for the first poster designs made in Cuba for use at and immediately after the mass rally 18 October in Plaza Revolución at which Fidel gave his famous eulogy, which confirmed the dreaded fact. Korda's image was enlarged to cover the ten story Ministry of Interior building that dominates the square. The space has been dedicated to changing versions of Che ever since (figs. H.2, H.3, p. 70).[14]

The Cuban printmaker Frémez remembers working all night on his portrait, based on a copy of the photograph given him by Korda, and printing it on the press of the Consejo Nacional de Cultura, not quite believing the awful news, which explains why Che seems to "disappear and reappear" (as the artist put it) among the faint dots of the screen (fig. 5.2). There was no time to use more than one color; red paper happened to be available.[15] As the picture was being printed, the news was confirmed. This was the first poster privately done; the first public poster, by Ñiko (Antonio Pérez González) (fig. D.4), uses multiple images in various sizes, based again on the Korda photograph in a manner virtually prophetic of the subsequent multiplication in different formats of the "Korda matrix." The first use of it I have found, however, dates from before Che's death to July 1967, in posterized form on a billboard placed in the Plaza Revolución for a speech by Fidel where he read a letter from Che to the Organization of Latin American Solidarity conference; another, huge photo-derived image of Che appeared behind the rostrum in the conference hall.[16] In a revolutionary culture which discouraged hero imagery of the living, this homage to Che seems prescient of his imminent death.

Korda remains, naturally, annoyed at the long history of unauthorized borrowing abroad and in Cuba, no permission asked, no payment offered. Not even the National Bank, of which Che had been director, asked his permission or informed him when it used this photograph as the basis for an engraved portrait on a banknote (fig. 4.9), let alone offered a free sample. The situation is, however, changing in commercial seas where Cuba is cut adrift, and Korda was able to sue successfully for $20,000 damages a French pop star who made a T-shirt showing his (Korda's) Che apparently wearing a T-shirt with the pop star's image on it—a not entirely respectful reversal of celebrity hierarchy. Korda also got a fee for the use of his image from the Japanese edition of Vicki Goldberg's book *Power of Photography*, the original American edition of which gave him nothing. Likewise, Cuban photographer Raúl Corrales was able to get a lawyer in France to stop Gallimard, set to print twenty-five thousand copies of a profusely and elegantly illustrated little album called *Che Guevara, Compagnon de la Révolution* by Jean Cormier (1995), at fourteen thousand copies and to make the Italian edition do without the nine Corrales photographs altogether. (Corrales's annoyance is compounded by Gallimard's superimposition of alien images on top of his).[17]

In 1982 Korda's photograph received the singular accolade of having a short documentary film made about it by the Chilean Pedro Chaskel, for the fifteenth anniversary of the "physical disappearance" of the Guerrillero Heroico, under the title *Una Foto Recorre el Mundo* (A Photo Traverses the World). Chaskel was worried about "not reaching cinematographically the minimal level of the photograph," which he shows used on over forty different posters or versions, and in footage of it carried in demonstrations all over the world. The sound track includes ambient noise, fragments of Che speeches, a song by Nacha Guevara called "Liberty," based on a text by Paul Eluard written in Nazi-occupied France, and an account of how Korda took the photo. The film won the Premio Caracol of the UNEAC (Writers' and Artists' Union), and opened the Third International Festival of New Latin American Cinema. A special poster was made to commemorate the twentieth anniversary of the taking of the photograph (fig. 5.3), a limited lithographic edition was made of it by Dermot Begley in the US, and a well-known photograph by José Figueroa shows Korda seated behind a river of the derivatives flowing out before him (fig. 5.1).

The "Korda matrix" was compared in large lithographs by an Italian visiting Havana in 1989, to the Mona Lisa, reproduced in miniature together with Korda's Che, above a text taken from an Italian photographic magazine making this comparison.[18] The lithograph and the text assert that the photograph is "absolutely the

1996). The poster and magazine cover raised magazine sales by twenty-five percent from one hundred thousand. The poster led to a twenty-year long association (producing fifty-one posters) between Davis and theatrical director Joe Papp. The design was resurrected in 1997 on the dust jacket of Jon Lee Anderson's biography of Che.

Figure 5.5. Chilean. "*Let us be realistic, demand the impossible!!!*" (c. 1972). The phrase is widely attributed to Che, but seems to derive from the French Surrealist tradition and/or the French uprising of May 1968.

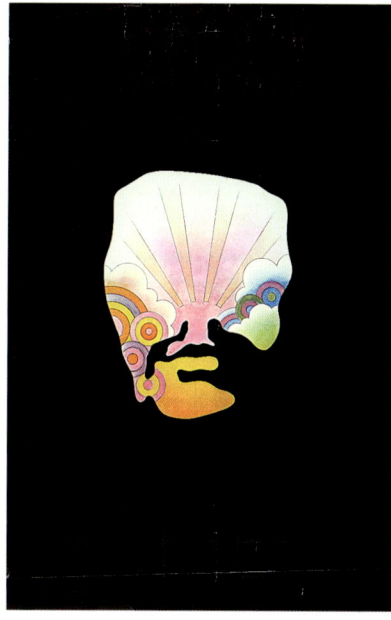

Figure 5.6. Zelek (Poland), published by Verkerke Reprodukties, Netherlands, c. 1971. 93.5 x 62.5 cm.

most famous of history," and captures the "beauty and youth, courage and generosity, aesthetic and moral virtues" of a person who "possessed all the characteristics necessary to be converted into a symbol of an epoch like ours, lacking in historic legends and mythic incarnations." In terms of fame and convertibility to other uses, Leonardo's portrait has a head start of more than 460 years, but as a politically motivating icon, the Korda may well rank, with some atrocity photographs from Viet Nam, among the most enduring of the twentieth century. Given the fact that there is virtually nothing that Mona Lisa has not suffered over the last century or since Marcel Duchamp put a mustache on her, we need not be surprised that she now appears as a painting and T-shirt design by a Cuban artist, wearing Che's starred beret.

The Korda matrix has become both a stereotype in the literal sense (easily adapted to printing on utilitarian objects and sculpting in craft materials, and as stencils), and the template of an astonishing expressive range of artistic variations. The same bittersweet image has been subject to a gamut of psychological interpretations in which much depends on how the eyes, "windows to the soul," are handled—the degree of profiling of shadow, the extent and placement of the highlights on the pupils determining fine shades of feeling and meaning. Yet the conclusion of Vicki Goldberg, a major authority on how certain very famous photographs have changed our lives (*The Power of Photography*, 1991), that "Che's life, ideals, and death seemed to be concentrated within this image" seems exaggerated, as does her further claim that "a portrait of Che accomplished more for his cause that the man himself accomplished in his lifetime," which carries exaggeration to the point of meaninglessness. To elevate the photograph at the expense of the man is to serve neither.

Banknotes, coins, and postage stamps

The most massive form of distribution in Cuba of Korda's Che image must be via banknotes and coins. At first, the "image" was his signature, the almost mockingly simple "Che," added when Che became president of the National Bank, to banknotes which were printed until 1960 by the (US) American Banknote Company. By a law of 4 August 1961, all existing banknotes were withdrawn from circulation, and new ones were printed in Czechoslovakia from designs by a Cuban overseen by Che and also signed by him (fig. 4.9). Opponents of the new alliance with the Soviet Union had only to add a cross before the three-letter signature for it to read "Khrushchev" (Cruz-che).[19]

In 1983 and 1984, for the sixteenth anniversary of Che's death, a three-peso note was launched, the first of this denomination to circulate in Cuba, the obverse a bust of Che based on Korda's, the reverse a scene of his cutting sugarcane, in iridescent red, designed by Jorge Fornes Ramos.[20] This was also made into a valla.

The banknotes with the signatures or image of Che are no longer valid, but the one peso coins, issued in the early 1990s with the (Korda) bust of Che still circulate, not least to tourists who buy them for a dollar (a hefty markup: the Cuban peso exchanges now at twenty to the dollar).

The next in currency of circulation must be the Cuban postage stamps featuring Che, of which there are at least a dozen (fig. 5.9). Most use the Korda image, including one of 1987 which reproduces a 1968 stamp within the stamp. It shows Che, superimposed on Fidel, addressing the masses in Plaza Revolución, as on the banknote. To the side of this image is a reproduction of a Cuban five-peso coin, obverse and reverse, also bearing Che's image—a rare example of philatelic-numismatic self-referentiality. Others (1983, 1988) connect Che with Radio Rebelde and "revolutionary communications." A 1988 stamp commemorating the Battle of Santa Clara shows his statue in that town and a 1971 issue reproduces Raúl Martínez's painting (now in the National Museum) of Che repeated ninefold. A set of five stamps, published October 1968 to launch the day of the Heroic Guerrilla, was given to me in La Paz by Loyola Guzmán, a veteran of the Bolivian campaign. It carries the Korda image with quotes from Che and, curiously, across the top, the Italian words *Solidarietà Internazionale*—in recognition, surely, of Italian solidarity with Cuba, and perhaps as a gift from Italy.

Figure 5.7. Rupert Garcia (US), *Right On!*, silkscreen, 1968, 66 x 51 cm. Courtesy of the Fine Arts Museums of San Francisco, Achenbach Foundation for Graphic Arts. Gift of Mr. and Mrs. Robert Marcus.

Figure 5.8. US (University of California, Berkeley?), *SHUT IT DOWN*, used for UC student strikes, silkscreen, 1969/1970, 51 x 76 cm.

Figure 5.9. Cuban postage stamps.

Che Multiplied

The image of Che divides between the Korda matrix, and a host of the most volatile expressions, roles, moments, and moods. Repetition of the former and combinations of the latter both serve the idea of omnipresence in place and time; they underscore the recurrence of his message.

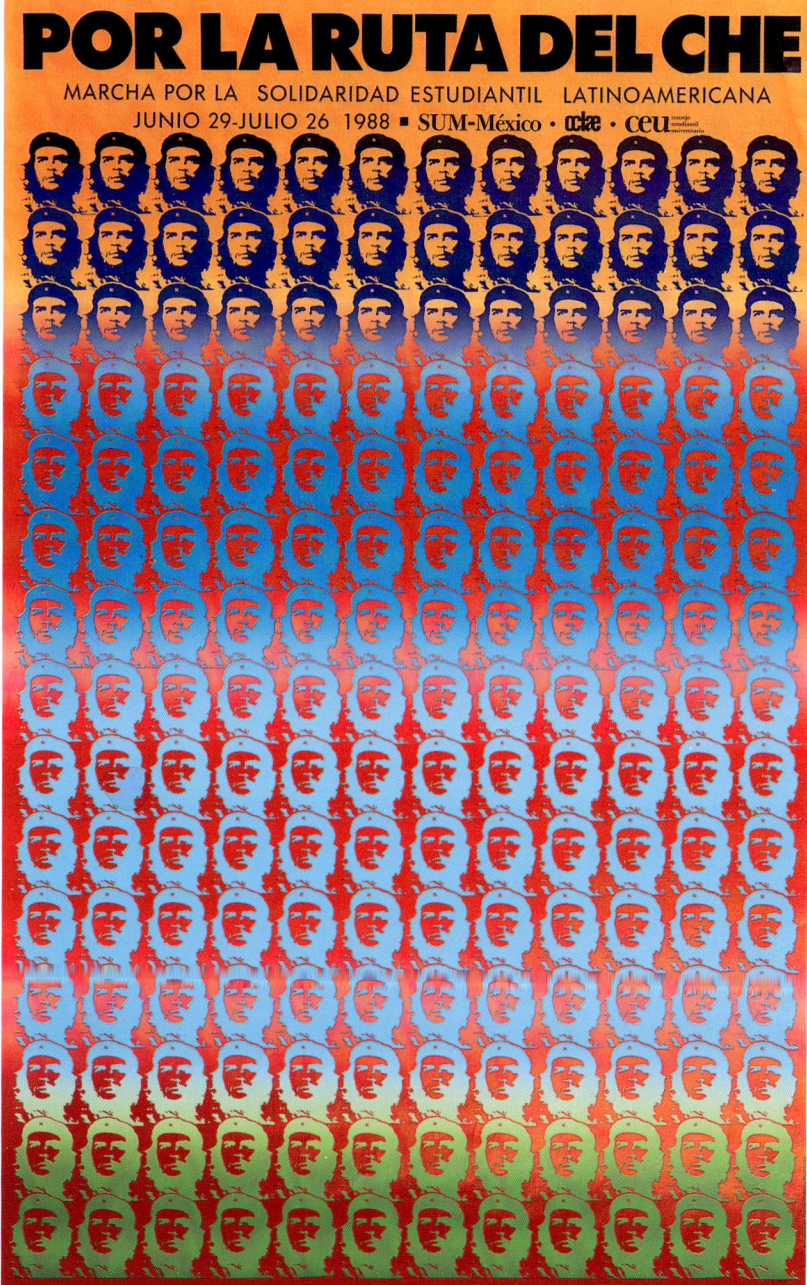

Figure G.1. Raphael López Castro/Gabriela Rodríguez (Mexico), *On the Path of Che, March for Latin American Student Solidarity 29 June–26 July 1988*, SUM-Mexico, OCLAE, CEU, 85 x 55 cm.

Figure G.2. Lázaro Abreu, *Day of the Heroic Guerrilla, 8 October*, OSPAAAL, 1970, 53 x 33 cm. Andean poncho woven with face of Che among traditional designs, supported on a rifle. The poncho looks real, even if Che failed to realize his hopes of integration into the Bolivian peasantry; the rifle seems (ideologically?) abstract. The willingness of the Bolivian miners to engage in armed struggle was undermined by the Communist Party; the peasantry were generally atomized, terrorized by the army, indifferent, and pacific.

Figure G.3. Victor Manuel Navarrete, *Ever Onward Unto Victory! Day of the Heroic Guerrilla, 8 October*, OSPAAAL, 1970, 99 x 75 cm. Lower left shows Che shaven, disguised for his Bolivian campaign.

Figure G.4. Rafael Enríquez, *Che Vive*, OSPAAAL, 1984, 60 x 41 cm.

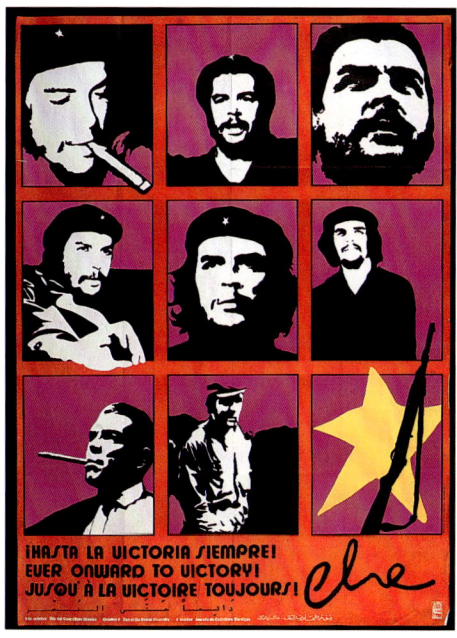

Chapter 6.
Mederos's Life of Che

In his series of twenty-five paintings, previously exhibited in Che's hometown of Rosario, Argentina, in 1992 for the twenty-fifth anniversary of his death, and scarcely seen since, René Mederos gives us in painted form the most extensively known version of the hero's life. It may be described as "mythic," but seen in the grandiloquent tradition of pictures recounting the lives of military heroes with which the history of art is replete, it is remarkable for its lack of conventional heroics, and two absences: that of visible enemy, and that of scenes of battle; indeed, there is no violence at all. This is the life of Che purified, and to a degree pacified, with the revolutionary leader cast as physical adventurer, explorer and dreamer of uncharted lands, leader of men, simple worker, chronicler in *El Diario* of his personal history now become world history (fig. 6.8).

The nearest Mederos comes to actual military events is a scene of Che watching Fidel tracing a strategy in the ground with a stick (this is also the only picture where Guevara is not the protagonist, with three others he shares equally with Fidel). Always armed with a rifle, Che is shown in combat position only once: at the end, just before capture in *Quebrada del Yuro* (fig. 6.14). The chief military-related scenes show him rather as a bold venturer into wild enchanted forests, braving adverse conditions but never the truly frightful ones of reality. Wading ashore from sea to swamp, in the disembarkation from the yacht Granma (*Birth of the Heroic Guerrilla*, first scene of the series, fig. 6.5), which brought about the initial disaster of the invasion of Cuba, November 1957; resting in camp (*Campamento Central*, presumably Ñancahuazú, Bolivia, actually posing for a well-known photograph); doing the watch beneath a fig tree, in a rocky but dreamy ravine (*La Espera*, fig. 6.6); crossing a dangerous river (*Río Grande*, fig. 6.11) which would in reality claim several lives; perched in a tree, observing, correcting a map perhaps or writing a poem? *(Punto de Observación*, fig. 6.12), also based on a photograph; finally, bowed down in a blizzardous asthma attack (fig. 6.13). These are all different emotional states rather than "episodes from revolutionary wars."

The scene of evacuating the wounded (fig. 6.2) is not particularly military in allure, nor is that of Che speaking to Camilo on the radio (based on a well-known—and posterized—photograph (fig. 6.7); Che helped create the first guerrilla radio station, Radio Rebelde). The only feature, apart from the rifles and uniforms hung with small impedimenta, which locates Che's wars in mid-twentieth century and as conducted against an enemy equipped with modern weapons, is to be found in *Santa Clara* (recalling Che's greatest military triumph, in December 1959), where he was wounded in the arm, and is shown by Mederos thus, backed by a large tank captured from the Batista army.

Demilitarized as it is, the series is dedicated entirely to Che's life as a guerrillero (omitting the African campaign, the diary for which was not published until 1995), with only two exceptions: the *Ministro Machetero* (fig. 6.1) hacking with a machete at sugarcane figured as a carnival of polychrome, swirling ribbons of vegetation more Mederos than real. Cutting sugarcane was the "classic" and most arduous form of voluntary labor, in which Che engaged systematically and exemplarily, as "relief" from sedentary marathons as Minister of Industries and President of the National Bank. To exclude, as Mederos does, Che's heavy labors as bureaucrat (albeit an anti-bureaucratic one), enhances one "mythic" element in the man's life: his essence as man of action. To show him as a common laborer, the archetypal Cuban proletarian working in the cane fields, which Mederos has idealized beyond all recognition of the monotonous reality, is both to heroize that labor (as revolutionary ideology and posters liked to do) and to proletarianize the hero.

There is just one other picture illustrating the years between military campaigns: it shows him as the ideological voice of the Cuban revolution, speaking at a microphone, in reference to his numerous speeches at the United Nations and elsewhere (fig. 6.8). The political elite of all nations heard him repeatedly denounce imperialism and social injustice, the gulf between North and South, between the rich, whom he portrays symbolically in a fancy blonde posed before a sexy car, and the poor, represented, Frémez-like, in a starving woman and child, and a crouching African

Figure 6.2. René Mederos, *The Wounded*, Che attending to casualties after the battle of Uvero. (Life of Che no. 2.)

Figure 6.1. René Mederos, *The Minister with the Machete*. (Life of Che no. 5.)

child resembling the one used by Frémez (fig. M.10, p. 113).

In one important respect, the methods of painter and his subject matter converge: both are idealists, constructing utopia in the (artistic) imagination. Che's imagined social utopia is physically realized in Mederos as a utopia of natural forms. The artist's tendency, already manifest in his two Viet Nam series (1969–1971), to see even (or especially) in war-torn countries not war but beauty of environment and people, is brought to a higher pitch in the Che series. It was not of course hard, given existing iconography, to preserve the distinctive physical beauty of Che's appearance, but another level of skill was required to both idealize and individualize the sixteen (male) guerrillas of the Bolivian campaign (fig. 6.10; Tanya la Guerrillera is oddly missing entirely from the series). With their differing physiognomic types, they all look morally alike, tough and determined.

Mederos's chief form of idealization throughout is however that of the natural environment, which was in reality even more hostile in southeastern Bolivia than in Cuba's Sierra Maestra. The plant erupting in the foreground of *Los Heridos* (The Wounded, fig. 6.2) is so alive with color and movement that one is inclined to see it as an instantly available herbal remedy for the wounded in the stretcher. In *Otras Tierras* (Other Lands, fig. 6.3), magical, luminous vegetation seems to grow into the very head of Che, and accompany his figure advancing into the distance. This is an allegory, I think, rather than a specific historical moment, of Che's yearning both for a more hospitable future and the beauty of new adventure (in Latin America). The luscious effect will remind North Americans of "Disney magic," but it is Mederos magic too, with roots actually deep in eighteenth- and nineteenth-century European romantic landscape painting.

The supernatural is more present in *Otras Tierras* than where one would expect it, a priori, from the title *Resurrection*, a relatively straight (and sweet-faced) bust of Che emerging from grasses, against a backdrop of sea. *Sus Manos* (His Hands, fig. 6.4), however, embodies perhaps the most directly a mythic aspect of the man, shown standing meditatively in a dream-coated, multicolored, fertile lake-and-mountain landscape. Those hands that would be severed after death and constitute the only known surviving physical remains, which are shown just touching at the fingertips and suffused with a "magical" pale blue glow beneath, seem to reflect onto the surrounding uniform, turning it from olive green to pale yellow. The painting, despite its reference to the Santa Clara victory of December 1958, where Che was injured in the arm (he is shown wearing a sling, as in a well-known photograph), makes a fitting mythical ending to the series.

Figure 6.3. René Mederos, *Otras Tierras (Other Lands)*, (Life of Che no. 8.) The "other lands" are those of the Latin American continent beckoning him, referred to in his farewell letter of 1965.

Figure 6.4. René Mederos, *His Hands*, (Life of Che no. 14.)

Chapter 6.

The Mederos Paintings (From a series of 25 acrylic paintings)

Fourteen of Mederos's *Life of Che* paintings, executed in 1992, acrylic on board, are reproduced in this book. All titles (italicized) are those of the artist and the paintings measure typically 60 x 90 cm. The secondary numbering is that of the artist.

Figure 6.5. *Nacimiento del Guerrillero Heroico* (Birth of the Heroic Guerrilla). Landing of Granma, 2 December 1956, at Alegría Del Pío. Che described the event as "not a landing, but a shipwreck." (Life of Che no. 1.)

Figure 6.6. *La Espera* (Waiting). (Life of Che no. 3.)

Figure 6.7. *Camilo, Camilo, Aquí está el Che* (Camilo, Camilo, Che here). Founding Radio Rebelde in Sierra Maestra. (Life of Che no. 4.)

Figure 6.8. At the UN in 1964. Che makes a speech denouncing social injustice. (Life of Che no. 9.)

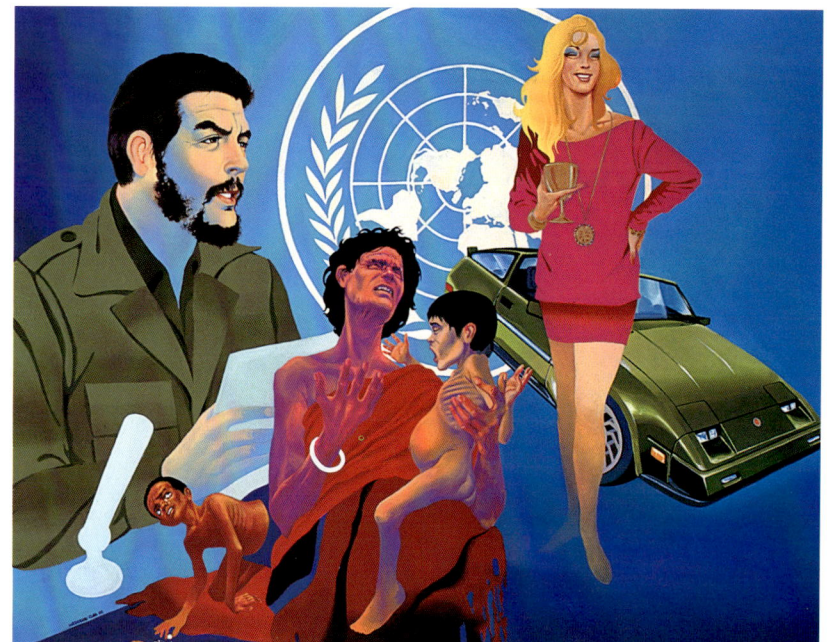

Figure 6.9. *Rocinante*. In a farewell letter of 1965, Che refers to his feeling the ribs of Rocinante, the steed of Don Quixote, under his legs. (Life of Che no. 6.)

Figure 6.10. *El Diario*. Che with portraits of sixteen of his principal comrades of the Bolivian campaign. He is writing in the diary which he kept rigorously throughout the eleven-month campaign, and which has become celebrated in its own right. Che also kept notes separately on the qualities of all his comrades. (Life of Che no. 12.)

67

Chapter 6.

Figure 6.11. *Río Grande*. Crossing the river could be perilous; two of Che's comrades drowned in it. (Life of Che no. 10.)

Figure 6.12. *Punto de Observación* (Point of Observation). Based on a photograph of Che. (Life of Che no. 11.)

Figure 6.13. *El Asma*. Throughout his life Che was assailed by asthma attacks. (Life of Che no. 25.)

Figure 6.14. *Quebrada del Yuro*. Che was finally caught in a ravine near La Higuera named after the Yuro stream. (Life of Che no. 18.)

Chapter 6.

Cuban Murals

Many murals with and of Che are scattered throughout Cuba, although some have disappeared or been altered over the years.

Figure H.1. José Delarra, monument to Che in Santa Clara, Cuba, site of a great victory by Che in December 1958. The statue is twice life size, the monument seven meters high. There is also a Guevara museum in the town. Another sculptural monument to Che is in the University of Marcos, Lima. The statue (c. 1973) in San Miguel, Chile was destroyed under Pinochet.

Figures H.2–H.3. The most visible and monumental Che of all is on the facade of the Ministry of the Interior building, facing Plaza Revolución where Fidel for many years gave his great quarterly public orations. The image, typically seven or eight stories high, was constantly changed, but has achieved permanence apparently in the steel silhouette by sculptor Enrique Avila González, now in place.

Figure H.4. José Venturelli (Chile), *Mural of Revolution*, Ministry of Health, Camilo Cienfuegos Hall, Havana, late 1960s. Detail of Che tending the wounded (figures are about life size).

Figure H.5. Orlando Suárez, *Dawn of Revolution*, provincial bus station. Havana. 1975. Detail of Che and Camilo Cienfuegos (figures are about life size).

Figure H.6. Raúl Martínez, Che with daughter Aleida, and Fidel. Detail from a mural in Palacio de los Pioneros, near Havana, 1982 (figures are about life size).

Figure H.7. Hyperrealist fiberglass figures of Camilo Cienfuegos and Che (full-length and life size) emerging from the jungle, in the Museo de la Revolución in Havana.

Figure H.8. *"Voluntary labor is the cornerstone of our communist education."* Based on a photograph of Che doing voluntary labor, sold also as a poster. Che's example of voluntary labor inspired countless brigades in Cuba and the Venceremos Brigade in the US, which in its twenty-eight years of existence has sent twenty-eight brigades to Cuba and brought over seven thousand people to the country. These brigades were pioneers in the breaking of the blockade.

Chapter 6.

Latin American Murals

Figure H.9. Argentinean artists: Paintings based on a photograph of Che, arms linked with comrades, in a May Day demonstration. On 21 November 1967 an exhibition—surely the first of its kind—opened in Buenos Aires, hosted by the Sociedad Argentina de Artes Plásticas and composed of pictures of Che by twenty-two Argentinean painters. The exhibition was ordered closed after only four hours, and it was reconstituted in Havana in October 1969, with versions by fifteen of the original artists. Subsequently, the artists donated their work to Cuba via the Casa de las Américas, where three of the paintings are still to be found as reproduced here. Another three paintings are with Aleida March, Che's widow. The artists were Alano, Capino, Ricardo Carpani, Castagnino, Clemen, Colombres, Erlich, Juan M. Sánchez, Martínez Howard, Obelar, Pereyra, Plank, Sahiseh, Sessano, and Ventura (see *Granma*, 24 October 1969).

Figure H.10. Bolivia: *"Our whole action is a war cry against imperialism—Rebeldía."* Painting on a wall of an external courtyard of the Universidad Mayor de San Andrés, La Paz, by pupils of Walter Solón Romero in 1987. The mural, approximately three meters high, is very visible from the main artery of the city, Avenida Mariscal Santa Cruz. Rebeldía is a political group; the word means defiance.

Figure H.11. Nicaragua: Mike Alewitz (US), "Che Commander you are the way, we the wayfarers," former Sandinista youth center, Estelí, 1988, 3 m high (Kunzle, *Murals*, p. 149, no. 153). The mural has been destroyed.

Figure H.12. Grenada: mural, 1981–1983, over 3 m high. Destroyed during US invasion in 1983. One of the pretexts for the invasion was the Cuban aid to that country.

Figure H.13. Venezuela: *"We must struggle every day so that this love for humanity becomes a reality."* Mural in Caracas, Habitación 22 Enero, with portrait of Simón Bolívar. The signature of Che creates a trail followed by guerrilleros, based on a Cuban cartoon. Photograph by Alan Barnett, 1983.

Chapter 7.

Che, Chicanos, and Cubans: The Struggle Over a Symbol
Shifra M. Goldman

> In the early 1970s, [a] good friend... introduced me to listening to short wave radio from Cuba. We used to hear the speeches of Fidel. One of those talks was dedicated to "El Día del Revolucionario Heroico," el Che Guevara, remembering the day he was killed, Oct. 8, 1967 [*sic*]. Since then we started celebrating Che's day by trying to do something significant. In 1977, highlighting the decade of his martyrdom, I designed and printed [an] offset poster of Che...I heard in my mind him telling La Raza, "You Are Not a Minority!"
> —Mario Acevedo Torero[1]

Che and Chicanos

Torero's original black-and-white offset poster established the iconography and composition that was later used for the mural painted at Estrada Courts Housing Project[2] in 1978 on a wall facing Olympic Boulevard in East Los Angeles. Known as "We Are Not a Minority!!," the mural features just the head of Ernesto "Che" Guevara wearing a brown beret (lacking the usual star) over his flowing hair that merges with his mustache and beard to form an irregular halo. His large foreshortened left hand, with a dramatically pointing index finger, is extended straight toward the viewer. The poster clustered the slogan "YOU Are Not a Minority!!" almost directly under the figure to accommodate to the verticality of the paper. The mural, however, is horizontal, its shape determined by the full wall of a house. The letters of the same slogan were fancifully spread across three lines beside the image in decorative type and color. "We Are" appeared in a curlicue script, followed by an orange-colored "NOT" in Bold Gothic outlined in yellow; an invented A in yellow follows, looking like a perforated pyramid; and finally the word "minority" appears in white lower-case letters with a deep three-dimensionality established in black. Framed with thin brown lines that open to allow the words "We Are" and the head of Che to protrude, the mural still maintains its essentially poster format. Che's face and hand were originally painted in a pinkish-yellow skin color in keeping with his European-Argentine origins. Strong black forms delineated his eyebrows and features, with a white spot left in each deep-set eye to increase the intensity. The hand was outlined in black surrounded by a thick white line where it crossed the dark beard to increase its impact through contrast. In fact, the high-contrast techniques of photographic screening, so popular in posters since the 1960s, were used throughout.

This mural joined the approximately sixty major murals, 20 x 30 ft. each, that were painted on the exterior walls of the housing units between 1973 and 1980. The subjects are as varied as the artists who produced them, including renderings of pre-Columbian carvings and paintings; tributes to the United Farm Workers Union; celebrations of life; the overlapping flags of Mexico, Japan, and an African liberation banner; a history of flight stretching from a child on an inner tube to an astronaut; a tribute to Northwest Coast Indians; images of Zapata, Christ, and the Virgin of Guadalupe; dedications to children of the world; a memorial to a "homeboy" of the local Varrio Nuevo Estrada youth; portraits of Abraham Lincoln and John F. Kennedy (both also assassinated), and a black-and-white mural commemorating the 1970 Anti-Viet Nam Moratorium during which *Los Angeles Times* reporter Rubén Salazar and two others were killed by Sheriff's Deputies. This last work (1973–1978) is displayed along the same series of building walls that include the image of Che Guevara. Both face Olympic Boulevard, a broad major thoroughfare that traverses the city. Torero's knowledge of the posters and great billboards in Havana containing images of Che and other Cuban heroes doubtless prompted his choice of a simplified poster format for his mural so it would impact both pedestrians on the two sidewalks fronting the roadway, and speeding cars. Many of the murals are only accessible from inside the complex.

In the upper left hand corner of the mural, to heighten the effect of the slogan "We Are Not a Minority" which presented a new idea in 1978—one that ran directly contrary to common usage[3]—Torero wrote "In memoriam to the guerrillero Heroico, el Doctor Che; Día del Rebelde Internacional (In memory of the heroic guerrilla, Doctor Che; Day of the International Rebel), XI Aniversario, Oct. 8, 1978." Below, the painters were identified in capital letters as "El Congreso de Artistas Cósmicos de Aztlán" or CACA, San Diego, Califaz.[4]

To understand this mural and its location, we need to briefly outline the conjunction of Los Angeles street murals with the politics of the fledgling Chicano movement in the late 1960s. Che Guevara did not arrive casually at the Estrada Courts Housing Project; his portrait and its maintenance were a direct consequence of the politicization and new militancy of Chicano youth and students. The 1968 "blowouts" from five East Los Angeles high schools for a nonracist education were followed in 1969 by the Fiesta de los Barrios, organized at Lincoln High School by the Educational Issues Coordinating Committee, that drew an unprecedented ten thousand persons to a three-day display of Chicano culture. Demonstrations in East Los Angeles against the war in Viet Nam (in which Chicano soldiers suffered casualties highly disproportionate to their numbers in the national population) began with about five thousand people in 1969, and culminated with twenty thousand to thirty thousand from throughout the Southwest in 1970. An attack by the police, who killed three participants, resonated throughout the Mexican community which had long suffered from police brutality.

By 1971, local government monies had been advanced for a series of murals in various locations of the city and county of Los Angeles whose stated purpose was to discourage the extensive graffiti on the walls of Latino neighborhoods—a purpose which failed almost immediately when a mural by "Magú" (Gilbert Sánchez Luján) was covered with graffiti several days after it was painted. Other Chicano muralists actively integrated graffiti into their paintings to celebrate its status as an original Chicano calligraphy. Nevertheless, the notion of graffiti obliteration motivated "mothers, fathers, and children of all ages [to come together] in May 1972 to paint out the graffiti which covered many of the exterior walls of their homes" in Estrada Courts.[5] In later years, the residents of the Courts undertook to protect the finished murals from graffiti on their surfaces—a protection that included the Che mural.

By 1973, Charles "Cat" Felix became the mural coordinator for Estrada Courts. Himself a muralist, he assigned walls to the artists (who generally worked with teams) and/or local residents who wished to paint a wall or create decorative motifs for the low cinder-block fences. It was he who approved the Che Guevara mural in 1978. The work was completed in one day.

Estrada Courts was far from being the only location of murals. In addition to the housing projects, murals sprouted all over East Los Angeles on buildings of every variety and use, including libraries, schools, playgrounds, and other public locations. A certain number were also commissioned by private businesses who, at first, supported the anti-graffiti campaign, but subsequently saw the murals as attractions for customers. The private clients, of course, were more worried about "controversial" thematic content. Estrada Courts artists, on the other hand, were free to use the theme of their choice if approved by Charles Felix. For example, Willie Herrón and Gronk (both from the group known as ASCO (meaning "nausea") painted a black-and-white mural centered on the 1970 Chicano Moratorium and the attack on it by police, as well as the struggle for education and against racism, not far from Torero's mural of Che. Neither would have been countenanced by private clients.

Torero's source for his Che poster and mural was a poster from World War I regarded as a classic and very well known today in the US and British versions; there is even a Cuban adaptation (fig. M.7). The US poster by James Montgomery Flagg shows a nineteenth-century Uncle Sam, a respectable, vigorous, but civilian elderly gentleman with the stars of the nation on his hat band, appealing to the passing young man with "I Want You for US Army; Nearest Recruiting Station." His expression is stern, almost accusing; he is a grandfather, a member of the family who addresses the passerby directly as "I" and "You." In the image of Torero the summoning finger is on the right, rather than the left hand; both of the others show a sleeve with a white cuff, while Uncle Sam, rendered in a highly painterly fashion, is depicted to the waistline which allows a blue coat, a white shirt, and a red bow tie to echo the US flag, along with the stars of his top hat. Che, on the other hand, is not shown in either a patriotic or a military garb—but the beard was *de rigueur* for the Cuban revolutionaries. Another variant is the beret. Che actually wore a black one, but the mural's original brown version was associated in the community with the regalia worn by a popular Chicano paramilitary group of the 1970s called the Brown Berets, well-known throughout East Los Angeles as defenders of Chicano rights. A final consideration is that of the slogan. From the "I - You" configuration of the military recruitment posters, Torero changed the pronoun into a social pronouncement: the collective "We."

For about five years the Che mural aroused no special concern among the residents or among the increasing number of visitors who toured the site. It had been chosen on 1 January 1976, on the occasion of the US Bicentennial, as one of the "Horizons on Display" communities in the nation, two years before the Che mural was painted. "Estrada Courts had been drafted into a local, state, and national cultural campaign in which the residents—through their work—would be showcased under governmental programs directed by 'outsiders.'"[6] Charles Felix attended the Washington, D.C., Horizons' events, and was given an exhibition of his work at the Smithsonian Institution. In either case, Estrada Courts became increasingly visible and attracted many tours locally and from out of town.

By 1981, the Che mural, among others in Los Angeles, was recognized and reproduced in *Newsweek*, *U.S. News and World Report*, the *Herald Examiner* and *Newsline* of Los Angeles, and in French filmmaker Agnes Varda's much-acclaimed documentary *Mur Murs* about Los Angeles murals.

Che and the Cuban exiles

Trouble began to brew with the advent of the Olympic Games, scheduled for Los Angeles in 1984. By September of 1983, Cuban exile Abel Pérez, editor and publisher of the anti-communist *20 de Mayo* Spanish-language newspaper of Santa Monica, raised objections to the Che mural before officials of the Housing Authority. He damned it as a "propaganda tool" for idolizing Guevara.[7] The manager of Estrada Courts asked Charles Felix to cover the mural within a week, but he refused. He also refused to remove the wording.[8] By October 1983, vandals had thrown black paint at the mural. In February 1984, the Cuban exile publisher attempted again to have the mural destroyed. The Housing Authority was once more contacted. This time they checked with the office of Councilman Arthur Snyder, who represented the district but who refused to take a position, and with the residents of Estrada Courts and their representative to the Housing Authority Advisory Committee (HARAC), both of whom wanted to keep the mural. The HARAC representative of Pico and Aliso Villages (some miles further west in East Los Angeles) submitted a letter in defense of the mural.

On 25 February 1984, the author wrote to the executive director of the Housing Authority deploring the censorship of *any* work of art opposed by an individual or a segment of a community, and comparing the insistent demand for destruction of the Che mural to the whitewashing some years after its completion of Mexican muralist David Alfaro Siqueiros' similarly controversial mural, *Tropical America*. This had been painted in Olvera Street in 1932, and its loss was that of an important cultural symbol.[9] My letter said that "it would be ironic if the City of Los Angeles, which is paying muralists to paint the freeways for the great influx of visitors to the Summer Olympics, would at the same time be considering the destruction or censorship of an existing mural. When Chicano and Latin American artists paint murals that represent their point of view...and choose symbols meaningful to them, whether they are Zapata, César Chávez, or Che Guevara, that is their right."

By 22 March 1984, the censorship battle was won. Both the Housing Authority and the Deputy Mayor advised the author that the mural would remain intact; any further complaints from the Cuban exiles (who, after all, did not even live in the community) would be taken up at a public meeting open to all interested parties. This was verified in an official letter dated 27 April 1984. However, in the face of this consensus, the Cuban group struck again. Sometime during the night of 3 May, plastic bags filled with gray and yellow paint were hurled at the mural, defacing seventy-five percent of the figure of Che Guevara. Charles Felix once again restored the mural, but was forced because of the black and gray paint used by the vandals during the two defacements to change Che's skin color to a much darker tone. He angrily warned the perpetrators in a press interview that they already owed $6,000 for the earlier restoration.[10] Finally, there arrived a letter addressed to the author as "Shifra Goldman 'Judío'" (Jew) postmarked 17 May, Santa Monica, and signed (with no address given) "Lopez." "What does a Jew like you know of the butcher 'Che?'" it asked in red ink. To date, there have been no further attacks on the mural.

Chapter 7.

US Murals

Che and the Cuban poster were powerful ideological and formal forces in the renascent US mural movement since the late 1960s. The selections here represent just a small sampling. Other uses of Che in murals include:

Marcos Raya, Peace Mural, Chicago

Joan X and other students, La Causa/Peace, Love and Perfection, 1969–1970, Merritt College, Oakland, California

Local residents, People's Wall, 1969, Berkeley, California

Chicano artists and residents, on Coronado bridge abutment, 1973, Chicano Park, San Diego, California

The last three are reproduced in Alan Barnett, *Community Murals: The People's Art* (Philadelphia and London: Associated University, 1984, pp. 61, 73, 160). For Che depicted in the work of Avado Mauricio Peña, Jr., see Goldman, p. 173.

Figure 7.1. Chicago: Mark Rogovin, National Headquarters, Young Lords Association (a militant Puerto Rican group), People's Church, Chicago, 1971 (destroyed). For Che as symbol of the Puerto Rican separatists, see Goldman, p. 435. Photograph © by James Prigoff.

Figure 7.2. Chicago: Aurelio Diaz. Che with Zapata at left. Photograph © by James Prigoff, 1978.

Figure 7.3. San Diego, California: Gonzalo Placencia Ochoa, Chicano Park, 1980. "*Let us say, at the risk of seeming ridiculous, that the true revolutionary is guided by great feelings of love. Déjeme...*"—Che. Photograph by Tim Drescher.

Figures 7.4–7.6. Los Angeles (Estrada Courts): Mario Torero, *We Are NOT a Minority!!*, approximately 3 m high, before vandalization (fig. 7.4), vandalized (fig. 7.5), and after second vandalization, when the face was painted darker (fig. 7.6). Photographs by Shifra Goldman.

Figure 7.7. Portugal: Mural with four different portraits of "Commandante Ernesto 'Che' Guevara," second and fourth portraits marked "negative" and "positive," respectively. Death and birth dates appear below. Photograph by Bob Jensen, 1977. Courtesy of James Prigoff.

Figure 7.8. Northern Ireland, Derry (Londonderry), Cable Street: Che with Northern Ireland martyr Bobby Sands, 1988. Below Che, against a Soviet flag, is the silhouette of Lenin making a speech. Photograph by Bill Rolston. Courtesy of James Prigoff.

Chapter 8.
Chesucristo: The Christification of Che

Christ as the armed revolutionary

From the perspective of historical probability, as opposed to millennial myth, there are more similarities between Ernesto Che Guevara and Jesus Christ, and between Latin America in the twentieth century and Galilee in the first century, than conventional (Christian) scholarship would allow. Historically it is most unlikely, indeed incredible, that Jesus, or any other popular charismatic Jewish leader of the age, was a pure pacifist, and even less likely that the movements they engendered were pacifist, nonpolitical and dedicated to an exclusively "spiritual" revolution. To suppose so is to divide unnaturally and unhistorically body from spirit, life in the world from the life of the mind, society from individual. A notorious (much banned) poster by the Cuban Rostgaard showing Jesus with a rifle is not mere rhetoric, but puts a finger on the probable truth (fig. 8.1).

Jesus was part, surely a leader, of a movement of dynamic messianism which threatened Roman rule and was cruelly and finally crushed in the war of 66–70 CE. During the previous generations, and especially after the time of the birth of Christ, there were frequent insurrections against oppressive Roman rule, led by Judah the Galilean and his like. These militants were called Kingdom of God activists, or Zealots, some of whom, as the Gospels tell us, became followers of Jesus. It is evident that even before Jesus' ministry, St. John the Baptist was organizing armed resistance, for which he was executed. Jesus himself paid tribute to the violence of St. John's suffering, and the need he represented to "take the Kingdom of God by force" (Matthew 11:12).

For political reasons Jesus was subsequently, when the Gospels came to be written, whitewashed to appear not a political agitator but as a purely spiritual revolutionary. One act of egregious violence did, however, survive the whitewash: the cleansing of the Temple. This must have been a major event, militarily comparable to Che Guevara's greatest military achievement, the taking of Santa Clara, for the temple was guarded by a Roman cohort of five hundred to six hundred men, and a special temple force of twenty thousand. To have brought off a coup of this magnitude, Jesus' followers must have been well armed, and it was this outrageous act against Roman authority that quickly led to the arrest of the perpetrators, and the crucifixion of Jesus between two fellow activists. And the arrest did not pass off unopposed, either, to judge by the remnant of forcible resistance surviving in the Gospels, the cutting off of the ear of the High Priest's servant (Mark 14:47). Jesus was explicitly executed as King of the Jews, as Che was executed as king of the Cuban-style Latin American revolution. "King of the Jews" is obviously a political title given to and taken by a leader of sedition. "Behind the skimpy, distorted, and obscure Gospel references to the events preceding this arrest, there was a real-life, stark event—an abortive insurrection."[1]

The friction between Jesus and the Romans, as opposed to the Jews, is suppressed in the gospels, and that "vast movement of religious and political disaffection that churned up the country in grinding oppression" is never referred to because at the time the gospels were written, Christianity saw its best chance of survival in peaceful integration into the Roman empire. As it does still largely today, living at peace with the "grinding oppression" of the imperial rule of transnational capitalism.

The Church recrucified: liberation theology

Jesus would have suffered worse if he had fallen into the hands of the Argentine torturers who boasted to Father Rice in 1976. "Now you'll find out that the Romans were very civilized towards the early Christians compared with what's going to happen to you." Penny Lernoux in her heartrending *Cry of the People* says that the persecution of Catholics in Latin America is greater than it was under Hitler or Stalin. In Latin America in the 1960s and 1970s, an estimated 850 priests, nuns, and bishops were arrested, tortured, and then murdered or expelled, and thousands of Catholic laity were killed and jailed. This repression followed the Vatican Council of 1962–1965, and the meeting at Medellín, Colombia, where in 1968 the "Magna Carta" was drawn up of the new persecuted, socially engaged church launching the "Theology of Liberation." Latin American priests

Figure 8.2. Rafael Enríquez, *Foreign Debt*, OSPAAAL, 1980s, 69 x 48.5 cm.

Poor Puerto Rico, now nailed with the nails of torment by your treacherous sons who hammer your bones on a cross of dollars.
—Pablo Neruda

"We'll have to hand over $40 billion each year for the next ten years in interest payments alone...[Latin America] is handing over $70 billion to the wealthy industrialized countries every year...while the investment and credit income is only around $10 billion.... We say that it is economically, politically, and morally impossible to pay it.... Our thesis...is that the rich and powerful creditor states...allocate 12 percent of their military spending—which now amounts to $1 trillion a year [to solve the debt problem, still leaving] $700 billion to spend on weapons.... We have suffered not only the torment of Calvary, but also that of Sisyphus...if we've had our Calvary, we should also have a resurrection" (Fidel Castro, cited in Betto, pp. 253, 256, 261).

Figure 8.1. Alfredo Rostgaard, Christ armed, OSPAAAL, c. 1969, 54 x 37 cm.

committed themselves to the poor, as Jesus had done and as the Church institutionally and historically did not.

To stop this threat to capitalist interests, the CIA trained armies, police, torturers, spies; their master plan, mature by 1975, to persecute church liberals was adopted in ten Latin American countries. In the years 1950–1973, sixty-four thousand Latin American soldiers and officers, including 170 heads of state, ministers, and generals were trained in the US Military School of the Americas, popularly known as the "School of Coups." The training worked, for to the great satisfaction of big business, real wages fell (in Brazil, by 64.5%).

Latin America became the "Galilee of our time," in the words of Cardinal Sebastiano Baggio, describing the scene of poverty, ignorance, sickness, and malnutrition maintained and exacerbated by the presence of an invading force rejected by the Galilean people. It was a time of massacres, of which only one survived the whitewash of the Gospels, probably synechdochically for all the others, the Massacre of the Innocents, a theme translated by Latin American artists into their own times. The Indian population of Brazil, estimated at two million around 1900, had shrunk to two hundred thousand in 1963 and half of that fifteen years later.[2]

Che and the Christian word

The Christian religion and texts, the tenets of liberation theology, were never strangers either to Che Guevara or Fidel Castro. Neither ever advertised their atheism, both showed respect to revolutionary Christians. There was room for professing Christians in the Cuban revolution, although not to the extent that Christian Nicaraguans helped make the Sandinista revolution of 1979 or Christian Brazilians helped make liberation theology.

In his first letter home to his parents from the Sierra Maestra, Che ends on the hope, both ironic and sincere, that "God is Argentine." The night before his execution, Che was questioned by a Bolivian soldier, who had been taught that he was fighting godless communists: "Is there religion in Cuba? Do Cubans believe in God?" "They believe in God," replied Che, "there are religions. Cubans are free to believe. But in Cuba there is no official religion." "You are not Catholic, right?" "No, I am not. But personally I support Christians."[3]

On their "training march" in Bolivia, arriving at last at the Rio Grande, wildly joyful, Che suddenly appealed to Inti Peredo: "Pacho, we have arrived at the (river) Jordan. Baptize me." The baptism would be, alas, as Che also noted, one of death, for the river drowned some of his best comrades.[4] Che baptized the brave young Communist Party youth leader Loyola Guzmán "Ignacia" after the famous sacrificial saint of the sixteenth century. He gave the name "Bread of God" to one of his guerrilleros who was always ready to carry the heaviest burdens and who called himself Christ bearing his machine-gun like the Cross.[5] If not explicitly as Christian, Che saw himself at the very least as "a little itinerant prophet announcing the advent of the Last Judgment in a stentorian voice." In the words of Jon Lee Anderson, Che's most recent biographer, "Writing of the peasantry's own gradual acceptance of the revolution, Che employed religious symbolism, rendering their travails as a kind of Pilgrim's Progress in which individuals found redemption through sacrifice, attaining final enlightenment by learning to live for the Common Good."[6]

Fidel

> "How on earth can you compare Fidel Castro to Jesus Christ?"
> "Because he has a beard like Jesus, he had twelve disciples like Jesus, he loved children and the poor, and wanted justice for all."
> "Then why in hell don't you crucify him?"
> —Cuban joke

It is commonplace to observe that Fidel (the name means faithful) inspires a kind of religious devotion in the Cuban people, and that he has a "charismatic" personality. Beneficiary (and victim) of a Jesuit high school education, Fidel was always fascinated by the "fabulous" content of the Bible, and was much impacted by the "whole process of death and crucifixion of Christ."[7] He was observed in the Sierra Maestra to wear around his neck a chain with a cross, a gift to him from a child, as a gesture toward her faith in him; he also wore

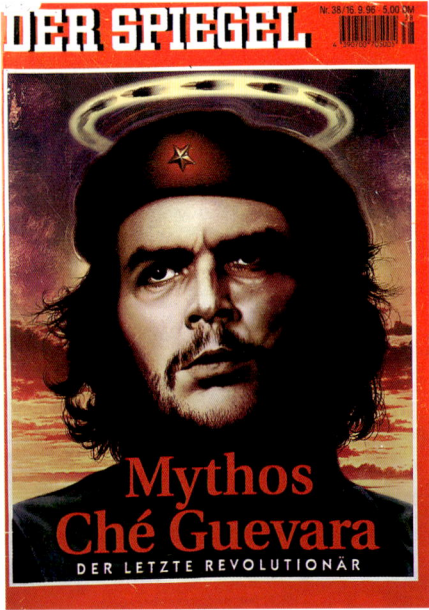

Figure 8.3. Braldt Bralds. "Che Guevara Myth. The Last Revolutionary." Cover of *Der Spiegel*, 16 September 1996. The article inside is titled, "The Leftist Pop Star."

Figure 8.4. Fernando Rodríquez: Fidel gives nuptial kiss in church to the Virgin of Charity, patron saint of Cuba, below a picture of the crucifixion. A picture of Che and Camilo, as witnesses, hangs lower left. Wood sculpture about 40 cm high.

such a cross at the triumphal entry into Havana. He was rendered by an artist in *Bohemia* magazine "with a Christlike countenance, complete with halo."[8] And he was happy to be godfather to countless children during the struggle. His recent meeting (1996) and concordat with the pope should have surprised no one. In the first years of the revolution he was saying "He who betrays the poor betrays Christ." In Chile in 1971, addressing Catholic clergy, he claimed, "There are 10,000 times more coincidences between Christianity and communism than between Christianity and capitalism...." In Jamaica 1977 and Nicaragua 1980, he said, "Christ was a great revolutionary." In 1985 he told the Dominican friar Frei Betto, "Upon the same pillars on which today reposes the sacrifice of a revolutionary, yesterday reposed the sacrifice of a martyr for his religious faith."[9] In an interview with Dan Rather for CBS in 1996, Castro compared the fate of fighters for socialism like himself with that of Jesus Christ, persecuted and crucified.

The idea of Fidel as "married" to Cuba or the Cuban people is not perhaps surprising, the idea of literalizing the marriage in specifically Christian terms more so. Yet this has been done in popular art. A series of fourteen folkloristic wood sculptures[10] by Fernando Rodríguez recounts what was supposedly vouchsafed to the artist by a blind man in a vision, Fidel marrying the Virgen de Caridad, the patron saint of Cuba. In one of the pieces, *Besándose en la Iglesia* (Giving the [Nuptial] Kiss in the Church), Fidel kisses the Virgin, with Che and Camilo as witnesses (fig. 8.4).

The cult of Che

It may be that some of the awe, reverence, and love surrounding the living Fidel has been diverted towards his martyred Cuban second, whose death facilitates a cult of personality. Che as Christ, or Christ substitute? Or at least as secular saint? The biographies seem to concur with the popular sentiment which makes him so. For Peter Weiss, who wants no saints or Christ-models, no depositions or resurrections, "Che galvanized the youth of the planet, perhaps because they had ceased to believe in Christ."[11] But in Catholic Latin America Che is not substitute for but an accretion of and tributary to Christ: the use of the term "Christlike" recurs again and again, not unaffected, of course, by the photographs, starting with Freddy Alborta himself, author of the best known photograph of Che dead, who has used the terms freely and insistently in interviews. In Vallegrande, where the body was laid out, witnesses say Che looked alive and "como Jesús," and parish priests testify that masses have always been said for Che, at the request of residents who used to write just the name "Ernesto" for safety; in recent years, they put openly "El Che." In Argentina, within days of Che's execution, a priest scandalized his compatriots with a homily dedicated to Che as a "Christian hero" inspired by thirst for justice, social redemption, and neighborly love.[12]

It has been frequently reported that in La Higuera, the village where he was shot to death, "Santo Che de la Higuera" is believed to work miracles: to cure a sick cow, to find a stray goat, to bring good weather. It is implied that he is even believed present in certain stones honored in the village with flowers and candles, like the murdered pre-Incan god Vilacocha, and awaiting resurrection.[13] These accounts may be taken with a pinch of salt, and Higuerans are now aware of visitors' desire to confirm and build the myth. At the very least, honoring Che, who has a small, amateurish monument in the village "plaza," is an act of atonement for having permitted foul murder in their midst. Locally the words "miracle" and "miraculous" are used loosely, as we discovered talking to a twelve-year-old boy who had created portraits of Che on the outside and inside walls of his house (see cover), and who averred that Che helped him "miraculously" (i.e., gave him wonderful encouragement) in his studies. Che was also a father substitute, since the lad had recently lost his real father in unfortunate circumstances. The juxtaposition of portraits of Christ and Che in popular art, in market stalls, and in private homes is so commonplace (figs. 8.5–8.7) that it is impossible for the one not to rub off on the other. A reporter for the *San Francisco Chronicle* claimed that Che now (in 1996) outnumbered statuettes of Jesus on taxicab dashboards.[14]

Figure 8.5. Necklaces on display in market stall, Cathedral Square, Santa Cruz, Bolivia, 1996.

Figure 8.6. Humberto Mayol, Havana, 1987, from *Aperture* 141 (Fall 1995), p. 9.

The local clergy in and around Vallegrande tend to look askance at the externals of homage to Che, insofar as they may distract from his message. "It's not by lighting candles to Che that you do him homage, but by understanding the political message of his struggle for liberation." This admonition from a local priest was reported in a Cuban source in 1971,[15] and confirmed for me by Alsace-born Francisco Bopp, parroquiano of Vallegrande in 1996.

Che and Christ in Bolivian literature

Bolivian literature is replete with the Che-Christ analogy and religious imagery applied to Che. The cover to a volume of Bolivian poetry inspired by Che carries a reproduction of a scrap metal relief sculpture of Christ in the "Ecce Homo" role. The first Bolivian art work inspired by Che, it was shown in August 1969 (when Che was still very much taboo in the country) in an exhibition of religious art. Christ's hands are (anachronistically) padlocked; even more curious, and incorrect for this pre-crucifixion moment of Christ's passion, is the wound over the heart: the spear-thrust of Longinus, or the bullet that killed Che? The artist said the piece derived from a photograph of Che dead.[16]

A verbal graphic in honor of Che and Néstor Paz Zamora, the Christian mystic and guerrillero of Bolivia, by Ignacio Siles del Valle and called *Nails as Bullets*[17] is thus configured:

CLAVOS COMO BALAS

néstor
clavados los ví en la guerrilla
ernesto
erchesto
ercresto
ercristo
el cristo

Says another Bolivian poet addressing Che: "So across time, I summon you to arise and be the gunshot Christ (*Cristo de metralla*), who redeems better than the ancient cross."[18] And Che shows up in unexpected places. A Bolivian lawyer who works in the Ministry of Defense describes the hero in a poem as having the "beard of an American Christ...your hands torn from your body to embrace the peoples, and the ashes of your asthmatic lungs sown in the earth."

More problematical is the mixing of the voices of Che and Judas Iscariot, and the diary of Inti Peredo with the gospels, in a strange novel by Bolivian Julio de la Vega, called *Matías El Apóstol Suplente* (La Paz: Amigos del Libro, 1978). Here Judas, whose legendary suicide by hanging from a fig tree evokes Che's being held captive by the fig tree (*higuera*) in the Quebrada del Yuro before being shot in the village called La Higuera, is seen as a victim, betrayed by Jesus who turned spiritualist and pacifist, after promising a real revolution to save the Jews.

Che's humanitarianism in combat

> "The true revolutionary is guided by feelings of great love."
> —Che (posters)

How far does Che's own life justify this famous assertion made in a famous essay "Socialism and Man in Cuba" (1965)? There is no armed revolutionary, no guerrilla fighter whose humanitarianism is better documented, not just theoretically, not just in the revolutionary social programs he espoused, but also in actual combat, where mercy is not always seen as a winning tactic. Che learned and taught the necessity of hating, but hating the idea of oppression, not the persons of its representatives. Love motivated him too: "It was precisely love for man which conceived Marxism, it was love for man, for humanity, the desire to combat misery, injustice and all exploitation."[19]

The principle was enunciated and observed from the start in Cuba's Sierra Maestra, to the finish in Bolivia, of sparing prisoners, tending enemy wounded with resources however scarce, and releasing them as soon as was safe. This principle was publicized early on and to good effect, in contrast to the army's practice of torturing and killing enemy prisoners and abandoning their own wounded. They also abused, raped, and stole from the peasants, while the guerrillas respected them, paid them for food, befriended them, taught them and rewarded them. The superior moral caliber of the rebels won hearts and minds to the

Figure 8.7 Alain César Ríos, *El "Che," Love Emblem, Christ*, drawings by a 13-year-old boy, displayed in the Casa de Cultura of Vallegrande, Bolivia, the town where Che's body was exhibited. Photograph, 1996.

cause among Cubans and people everywhere even (or especially) among Batista's soldiers, who were rendered more likely to surrender, less likely to fight to the bitter end, if guaranteed their lives and decent treatment when captured. The degree to which the guerrillas resisted the temptation to retaliate in kind, which is natural and is often seen as a deterrent ("if you treat us so badly, we will be forced to treat you the same"), may be unique in military history. The guerrillas did, however, execute spies and traitors, as they did notorious war criminals after their accession to power, and Che himself in his *Episodes from the Revolutionary War*[19] describes one lamentable incident of having to execute a hardened spy and would-be assassin of Fidel.

Che was certainly no natural killer. Enthusiastic for battle, he took no pleasure in the death of the enemy, only in the idea of victory. His concern to minimize deaths turned at times militarily to a disadvantage: in his *Bolivian Diary* (3 June 1967) he describes how on one occasion a truck carrying sleeping soldiers drove into view, but how he did not have the heart to shoot at them, letting them pass unscathed.

The humanity of Guevara extended to love for animals, evidenced already in his youth, as recounted in his *Motorcycle Diaries*, where he braved a fire to rescue a cat.[21] It is apparent too in his remarkable account, already considered a classic of Cuban literature and a masterpiece of a short story in poetic prose, called "The Murdered Hound" *(El Cachorro Asesinado)*, which was reprinted in an article called "Che and the Contemporary Way of Love."[22] The incident evokes the pain of having to execute a dog which had attached itself to them, but whose barking was threatening to reveal their positions in an ambush; the spirit of the dead animal came to haunt them, through the eyes of another dog which shortly thereafter approached—and reproached them. Dogs were a military liability, but Che's attraction to small pets was well known, and in a text coupled with the story, we read how two heroic women added to the essential supplies they were bringing to the guerrillas from Havana a small dog that he coveted; they were betrayed and murdered before they could fulfill their mission. Che included dogs in the tally of war casualties. He kept a dog in the Ministry of Industry that was notoriously spoiled, and he was known as the protector of street dogs in the area. There are anecdotes of Che's scarcely contained fury when confronted with Chinese culinary cruelty to monkeys. And he banned cockfighting in Cuba, substituting more civilized cultural activities. According to Jon Lee Anderson, Che's attachment to pets and mules was a sign that he craved tenderness and solace to ease the harsh life he had adopted.[23]

Che's humanitarian love expressed itself in the most immediate and practical way in his choice of medicine for a professional qualification, and in his specialization, which he put into practice even as a student, in leprology, a disease of the poor and outcast. He was always a doctor. He tells of a famous turning-point in his life, how soon after the disastrous landing of the Granma at Pinar del Río, under heavy aircraft and other fire, he had to abandon either a box of ammunition or his medicine chest, because he could not carry both. At this moment he left the latter, putting his role as soldier first, doctor second. But, in fact, he never stopped being a doctor, and when his comrades were able to rest after a battle, or secure their safety during one, Che was busy tending the wounded—on both sides, for he gave no preference to his own. As he put it, laconically, in his *Episodes of the Revolutionary War*, "I had to exchange my soldier's uniform for a physician's robe; actually, all I did was wash my hands."[24] This was true in the Sierra Maestra, as later in the Congo, where as "Doctor Tatu Muganda" he was considered a magical healer.

In Bolivia, at the moment of his capture, while immobilized by the many guns pointed at him, Che saw soldiers passing with his dead and wounded comrades, and asked, in vain, to be allowed to tend to them. An hour or so later, as he was being led, bound and limping from a leg wound, to La Higuera where he would be executed, the party encountered wounded soldiers of the Bolivian army, whom he asked to be allowed to help, an offer which was roughly refused by the commanding officer Gary Prado.[25] After being decorated for heroism and patriotism, the common soldier captors and executioners of Che

Figure 8.8. View in La Higuera, Bolivia, with Che graffito and Cross.

Figure 8.9. Primitivist carving in wood of Che (twice) and Jesus (twice). Private collection, Havana.

mutinied in anger at, among other mortifications, the army's failure to treat the wounded by getting them to hospitals.

Facing death in the schoolroom of La Higuera which served as his jail cell, Che found himself confronted by a peasant with a crumpled, gap-toothed face. "What a pity we didn't meet before," said Che, "you are missing two teeth. I would have given you new ones. You must look after your teeth to keep up your health." This was pity, rather than humor, for the peasant left full of tears, saying "Che's gaze melts your heart."[26]

His grief at losing his friends in battle flows clearly from his Cuban and Bolivian campaign chronicles. In the Sierra Maestra, Che gave himself the painful duty, which he always executed punctiliously, of himself writing the next-of-kin of the fallen. The need to rescue the bodies of those killed, and to help the wounded to safety, overrode considerations of military expedience, not to speak of his personal safety. His comrades with him when he was besieged in the Quebrada del Yuro testify that his concern for the sick impeded his movements at a critical moment of the encirclement by the enemy, leading directly to his own entrapment.[27] Loyalty, which is one of the highest forms of love, weighed heavier than military prudence, or he would never have allowed "El Chino" (Juan Pablo Chang), executed with him at La Higuera, to have joined his troop, for this brave fighter was partly deaf, lame from torture, virtually blind without his glasses; even wearing them he could scarcely see to walk at night. When El Chino lost them, causing Che to stop and help him look for them, it may have cost them both their lives.[28]

Family love

Che had strong family instincts. His was a happy childhood, and his attachment to his parents, especially his mother, lasted as long as their or his life. After leaving home, he saw them little but kept up a substantial correspondence with them. A long film called *Mi Hijo el Che*, consisting of interviews with his father, Ernesto Guevara Lynch, who lived into his eighties, and a book of the same title, are eloquent on his qualities as son and parent. Father of one child by his first marriage, and of four by his second, Che showed as much affection and attention to them as was possible for a man who kept impossible working hours (1 PM to 6 AM was typical, "come early, come at midnight"), and who spent so much time traveling. The biographical sketch published by his first wife Hilda Gadea is warm on the subject of his love for and time spent playing with their daughter, born in Mexico: "One of his traits that made me believe in him from the first was precisely his deep love of family."[29]

Che's Bolivian diary, kept in conditions in which some lapses of memory would be pardonable, always starts out noting any birthday of his children. His farewell letter from Bolivia to his elder daughter Hildita is a poignant mixture of paternal advice, simple affection, and regret at his absence. His last letter, written for all his five children and in the expectation of his death, has become famous for its modest self-satisfaction, and the way paternal love is enlarged to an all-embracing revolutionary love. It was published in the issue of *Tricontinental* dated to the month of his death.[30] A number of photographs, and a mural in the Palacio de los Pioneros (figs. H.6, p. 71; B.2, p. 17), testify to Che's close relation to children.

On a silkscreen poster,[31] framed within the unmistakable outline of the beret and beard of Che, bust-length, Christopher Logue placed this poem:

> O come all ye faithful
>   here is our cause,
> all dreams are one dream
>   all wars civil wars
>
> Lovers have never found
>   agony strange
> we who hate change survive
>   only through change
>
> Those who are sure of love
>   do not complain
> for sure of love is sure
>   love comes again!

Figure 8.10. Che with puppy in bed. Poster for book and videocassette by Roberto Massari (Rome: Erre Emme). Recent posters from Italy, where Che has always been more honored than in any other European country, confirm the tendency toward informality, softening, even sentimentalization of the Che image. Other Italian posters proclaim, "We must be hard without ever losing our tenderness" (Feltrinelli Publishers) and "For a lasting passion," a phrase also used on the Communist Youth membership card.

Figure 8.11. Alejandro Aguilera, detail of haloed Che from a group of life-size, scrapwood figures entitled "*En el Mar de América*" (In the Sea of America, whole group repr. in Camnitzer, p. 262), 1988. The other figures—all with haloes—are Jesus, Bolívar, José Martí, and Bartolomé de las Casas. From the cover of the exhibition catalog *Art in Cuba Now*.

Figure 8.12. Adolfo Pérez (Argentina), Capture of Christ, from *Viacrucis of Latin America*, published by Misereor, 1980, 69.5 x 50 cm. The graffiti and poster read: "No more repression," "Where are the children," "Liberty for political prisoners," "No to impunity," "Where are the disappeared," "Where is my son," "They took them away alive, we want them back alive."

Che as the Christian knight

"Guevara was no Christ."
—John Berger

I am no Christ, nor a philanthropist. I am the very opposite of Christ…. I will fight with all the arms within reach, instead of letting myself be nailed to a cross.
—letter from Che to his mother, from his Mexican jail, 1956[32]

It is possible, but unlikely given the difficulty two millennia later of destroying or concealing so much evidence to the contrary, that Che will be mythified some day as a pacifist and purely spiritual revolutionary. But I believe that the process is already well under way of seeing him less as the incarnation of armed struggle, than the proponent of something much larger, the New Human Being, imbued with what have been traditionally regarded as essentially Christian values: self-sacrifice, spirituality, and idealism, summed up in the Christian cardinal virtues of faith, hope, and charity.

The iconography shows that the process of fitting Che to the times has already undergone a detectable shift. In the posters of Che and on other themes in the late 1960s and early 1970s, Cubans did indeed emphasize the principle of armed struggle, climaxing perhaps in 1973 when the twentieth anniversary of the attack on the Moncada Barracks was celebrated. There were guns in posters everywhere, and the overthrow of Allende seemed to prove that there was no peaceful road to socialism. Outside Cuba, and particularly in the US, where the "romance" of armed struggle was short-lived and never much embedded except in a very small (if conspicuous) minority, the Che poster favored his famous quote, "The true revolutionary is guided by feelings of great love" (figs. M.49, M.50). That same quotation is now blazoned (since about 1990) by the Cubans, who have long since abandoned overt support for armed revolution elsewhere, at the entrance to the Comandancia del Che, a small museum located in the part of the Havana fortress where Che had his office and command post immediately following the triumph. And now the symbols associated with Che, even in Cuba, are the flowers and the dove of peace (figs. M.52, M.53). The latest poster from Italy, for Roberto Massari's video and book called *Man, Companion, Friend*, shows Che snuggled up in bed with a pet dog (fig. 8.10). Guevara may yet take his place with Gandhi, whom he so much admired and at whose tomb in India he laid a wreath, as an apostle of revolutionary peace.[33]

There was always from the start a tendency outside Cuba to hype up the image of Che with decorative, even psychedelic or Peter Max-ish effects; to turn him into an aesthetic object (fig. 5.6), and to intensify face and gaze in a way that is both more sensual and spiritual (fig. 5.4). Christian art has been doing that with Jesus for centuries. Outside Cuba, the aesthetic sanctification of Che set in early, maybe because he was less real, maybe because armed revolution was never a serious option (in the capitalist First World). But by 1988 the Cuban artist Alejandro Aguilera gave Che a halo, and set him in a life-size sculptural scrap wood series called *En el Mar de América*, grouped with Don Quixote, José Martí, and Bartolomé de las Casas, other Cuban secular saints (fig. 8.11). In a recent portrait, appearing on the cover of *Der Spiegel* (16 September 1996), Che is given a halo studded with what seem to be bullets, and the pained intensity of the inwardly suffering as he awaits his martyr immolation (fig. 8.3). In Richard Dindo's film on Che (*Ernesto Che Guevara, The Bolivian Diary*, 1995), a cross is held conspicuously in close-up for several seconds, burning in a fire at which Che is described—by a peasant who saw him thus—to have sat brooding over his defeats and losses of comrades, and perhaps over the prospect of passing through the fire of martyrdom.

The daily crucifixion of Latin America

Liberation theology encouraged Latin Americans to see themselves and their continent as suffering like Christ, even as it offered Christ's concern for the poor as the springboard of action to reduce that suffering. In 1932 David Alfaro Siqueiros scandalized the righteous by painting in Los Angeles *Tropical America*, a mural in which a peasant appeared bound to a double cross. The mural was quickly covered over. *The Crucifixion of Central America or The Triumph of Neo-Liberalism* is the name given to a crucified Christ by the Italo-

Figure 8.13. Sergio Michilini, *Che with the Yellow Christ*, oil on canvas, 1996, 60 x 70 cm. Based on Gauguin's *Self-Portrait with Yellow Christ* (c. 1890) in which the French artist rendered himself bust-length in front of his Yellow Christ painting of 1889. This is itself based on a Breton medieval sculpture. Gauguin added a mask behind him; Michilini has placed in his own painting a mask he made from a cannon shell. Michilini has turned Che in the other direction but in the same relation to the background. His beard is very sparse, as if in imitation of Gauguin's beardless (but mustached) face. Che is posed in front of a Michilini painting of the crucified Christ (Kunzle, *Murals*, p. 108, no. 37), in the Oscar Arnulfo Romero Spiritual Center near Managua, rendered more similar to Gauguin's Christ by being colored yellow. If we recognize the reference, Che is cast in the role of the self-portraying artist. At the same time, the Italian Michilini, a Nicaraguan resident since 1983 and a militant Sandinista muralist, identifies with Che—and with Gauguin.

Figure 8.14. Raúl Arellano (Nicaragua), Crucifixion with Che as Christ, National Guardsmen as Roman soldiers, and Nicaraguans in the role of the Holy Women, part of a *Via Crucis de Solentiname* series of paintings published as posters by Peter Hammer Verlag, 1980s.

Nicaraguan muralist Sergio Michilini in a spiritual retreat center near Managua named after Oscar Arnulfo Romero, the Salvadoran archbishop murdered by US-funded death squads while saying mass (see fig. 8.13).[34]

In the same spirit, the Argentine Ricardo Cinalli made a beautifully crafted crucified figure suspended over the maw of a monster, itself constituted of dismembered body parts.[35] Tomás Sánchez, hyperrealist landscape painter from Cuba, painted crude, papier-mâché-like people, including some circus performers, raising a crucified Christ in a circus arena; a large crowd enjoys the cheap spectacle. In another work, *Man Crucified in the Garbage Dump*, we see the crucifixion of the common man whose suffering is regarded as no better than rubbish, and/or destined for the rubbish pile of death squad victims.[36]

In Nicaragua especially, where Christians contributed so much to the Sandinista revolution of 1979, and where the blend of Christian and Sandinista revolutionary iconography expressed itself perfectly in Michilini's major cycle in the church of Santa María de los Angeles, the revolution was seen in biblical terms. A Via Crucis series by an Argentinean artist and Nobel laureate, massively distributed around the world by the progressive Catholic organization Misereor (I saw the series posted on the pillars of the little mountain church in Evolène, Valais, Switzerland), is clearly set in a desperately oppressed contemporary Latin America, complete with protest posters (fig. 8.12). With even greater geographic specificity, a comparable biblical series, originally paintings in a primitivist style which were then reproduced in Germany as posters, cast soldiers of the Nicaraguan dictator Anastasio Somoza as the torturers of Christ, and Nicaraguan peasant children as the Innocents massacred by Somocistas as by the soldiers of the biblical Herod. In the Nicaraguan series, hanging on the cross, Christ is almost as naked as when he was born (this makes him even more vulnerable, and more Nicaraguan). He is crowned by a beret and star and, lo and behold, he bears the features of Che Guevara (fig. 8.14). In another quite orthodox Christian context, a church community center in Batahola, Managua, Che is with other Nicaraguan heroes and folk, an astonished spectator at the birth of the New Man, Jesus (fig. 8.15).[37]

The most striking pictorial contribution to the Christification of Che must be a recent Bolivian one by the most distinguished muralist of that country, Walter Solón Romero, whose career stretches back to his assisting David Alfaro Siqueiros in Chile in the early 1940s. Solón's mural in the Faculty of Medicine at the Universidad Mayor de San Andrea, La Paz (pyroxyline on panel, 3 x 17 m), includes as its pivot Che Guevara (fig. 8.16). He is the only historical figure present in a multifigural triptych illustrating the passage from magical, traditional herb-based medicine, dating back to the pre-Columbian age, to the modern social and scientific practice, and ending on a vision of the twenty-first century.

Although Che was himself a medical doctor, he is characterized in Solón's mural more as a supernatural spirit emerging directly from the earth, and presiding over the future. An arboreal, Siqueiresque hand reaches from the soil, holding symbols of new humanity, justice, and time, while out of the same earth sprouts an anthropomorphic tree (higuera), within whose branches and green foliage Che appears, his arms interlaced with them, in a gesture of patronage and pity and sufficiently apart to suggest, obliquely, a crucifixion. Unarmed, empty-handed, he is entirely (face, hands, dress) transfigured in whitish and pale colors, which increases his transcendental aura. He is at once a force of nature and a divine spirit. He seems to be watching the surgical operation going on to the right. The whole is infused with the air of sacred ritual, with much specificity in the Incan and modern medical instruments.

The happy family below Che to the right is crowned by a child modeled on the artist's grandson José Carlos, named after a son "disappeared" by the military. His gesture imitates that of Che. Here, as everywhere in Solón's oeuvre, hands are expressive and powerful. When the artist was in prison, under torture, the Bolivian military (the same institution that killed Che) threatened to cut his hands off.

The injection of a Cuban into a mural for the major Bolivian medical school gains added relevance from the fact that the school has benefited much from Cuban technical assistance. And it is Cuba which, through the Félix Varela Center, set up and maintains the medical post on the very site

Figure 8.15. Boanerges Cerrato Brigade (Nicaragua): *The New Dawn*, Batahola Church Community Center, Managua, 1988. Figures half life size. Detail of Che with Nicaraguan revolutionary heroes Carlos Fonseca and Augusto César Sandino, and martyred Salvadoran Archbishop Oscar Arnulfo Romero, helping celebrate the birth of Jesus (off to the right) (Kunzle, *Murals*, p. 100, no. 18).

where Che was murdered in the village of La Higuera, where there were no services previously.

Jesus and Che

> He was like a Christ taken down from the cross...
> —Peter Weiss[38]

What external similarities and differences does the historical record show between the passions of Che and Christ? Both died young, in their thirties. Both were betrayed like so many martyrs by those who should have supported them (Jesus by his disciple Judas and the crowd at his Presentation, Che by the Bolivian peasants and Communist Party). Both were mocked and insulted by soldiers after capture, and suffered despoliation of their paltry belongings after death. Both were exhibited in public to be reviled, in a manipulated public response, with two other victims. Both were executed in the military manner appropriate to the age as seditionists. In some respects, however, Jesus was treated better than Che, which says a lot about our current level of civility: Jesus was at least given a trial with some legal trappings, even if not a fair one. Che was murdered, period, without the merest show of a trial, which would have risked garnering worldwide sympathy.

More difference in the Romans' favor: Jesus' body was not desecrated by being exhibited postmortem to public obloquy. Nor was it subject to mutilation by having parts cut off. And above all, Jesus' family was allowed to take the body down from the Cross, and bury it decently. Che's body was quickly "disappeared" in order to prevent mourning, reverence, the germination of myth. The attempt failed, dramatically, and as with the disappearance of Jesus' earthly remains (and as with that of another notable Argentinean, Evita Peron) it became a primary factor in the mythification. Jesus' death was followed by a resurrection, the belief that he was and is spiritually present among us. Che's death, too, was followed by a spiritual resurrection: *Che vive*.

Che like Jesus was a healer, a doctor with special gifts for, or interest in, leprosy, the disease of social outcasts. The attribution of miracle cures, with Jesus an essential part of his ministry as told by the gospels, is not lacking with Che, credited by grateful peasants with having saved the lives of their children. Che, like Jesus, was uncompromisingly egalitarian, as is evident from his manner of strictly sharing food during his guerrilla campaigns, and refusal to accept material privileges when in power. The severe discipline he imposed on himself, he enjoined also on his followers: "He was superstrict, like Jesus Christ."[39] The famous miracle recounted in the gospels of the multiplication of loaves and fishes illustrates the principle of equal sharing. As Fidel explained to Frei Betto, "Christ multiplied the fish and loaves to feed the people. That is precisely what we want to do with the revolution and socialism."[40]

The physical sufferings of Che and the guerrillas in the jungle may be compared to those legendary with the Christian martyrs. When captured, the rebels were routinely and terribly tortured, although Che himself was spared what was inflicted on his comrades (jailed in Mexico, he was threatened with the torture of his wife and baby). Much worse than the three light wounds he received in battle were the deprivation of food, drink, and sleep, as well as the heat, the rain, the insects, the lacerating stones and vegetation, and the diseases, which Che shared with others in the jungles of Africa and Latin America. In Bolivia, the rebels were reduced to drinking their own urine, and eating disgusting wild animals. But Che alone had to bear the cross of the disease which harried him all his life: his paralyzing attacks of asthma.

No, Che was no Christ. His most recent French biographer, Jean Cormier, explicitly distances himself from the term "Marxist Christ," but confesses that his 444-page book started with an epiphany, finding the effigy of the "Guerrillero Christ" on a wall in Paris, and talking about it to a homeless man who expressed himself in outright religious imagery: "He will return...." Then, ecstatically: "Even in the blackest nights, there is always a star up there, that of the true shepherd, the star of Che."[41]

> Our father, that art in heaven of tin and condor, protect us; hallowed be thy name, thy kingdom come, of peace, bread and justice; thy will be done, that of a living man, for we cannot believe you dead, no.[42]

Figure 8.16. Walter Solón Romero (Bolivia), *The Christ of La Higuera*, Faculty of Medecine, La Paz, 1994. Detail of mural shows Che (top left) presiding over modern medicine from within the *higuera* (fig) tree. La Higuera is the name of the village where Che was executed.

Figure 8.17. José Antonio Burciaga (US), *Last Supper of Chicano Heroes*, Stanford University, California, 8 x 15 m. The heroes in this mural in the Chicano-themed Casa Zapata dormitory at Stanford were selected through a poll the artist conducted among students, faculty, and staff. The Virgen de Guadelupe, patroness of the Americas and the spiritual heroine of Mexican and Chicano culture, did not place first but she was positioned above out of respect. Leading the poll was Che Guevara, shown here as Christ. Other heroes at the table include Benito Juárez, Dr. Martin Luther King, Emiliano Zapata, César Chávez, Dolores Huerta, Frida Kahlo, Joaquín Murieta, and Augusto Sandino. On the tablecloth is the additional dedication from one student's hero list: "...and to all those who died, scrubbed floors, wept and fought for us [so that I could be here at Stanford]." (*Los Angeles Times*, 3 May 1988; *San Jose Mercury News*, 2 June 1989).

Chapter 9.
Che Dead, Che Vive: The Alborta Photograph and the Belkin Variations

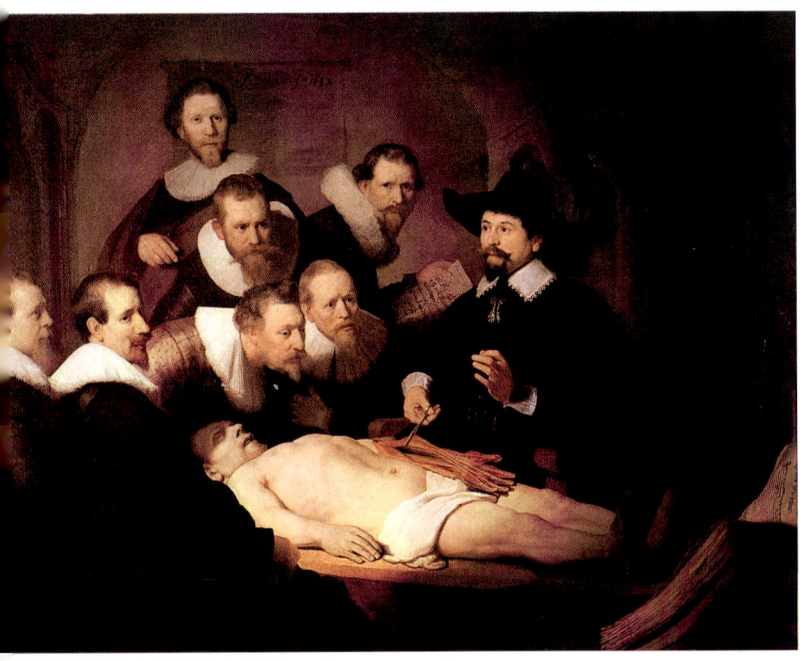

9.1

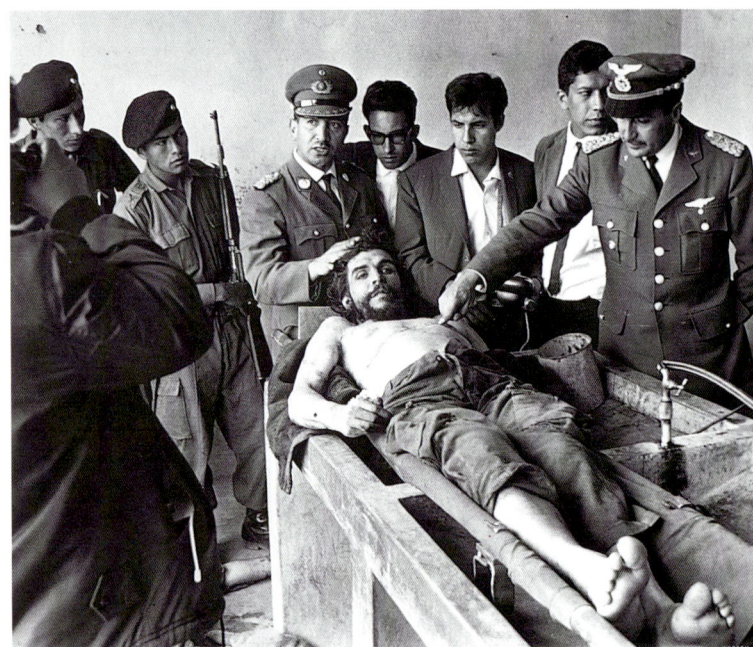

9.2

9.3

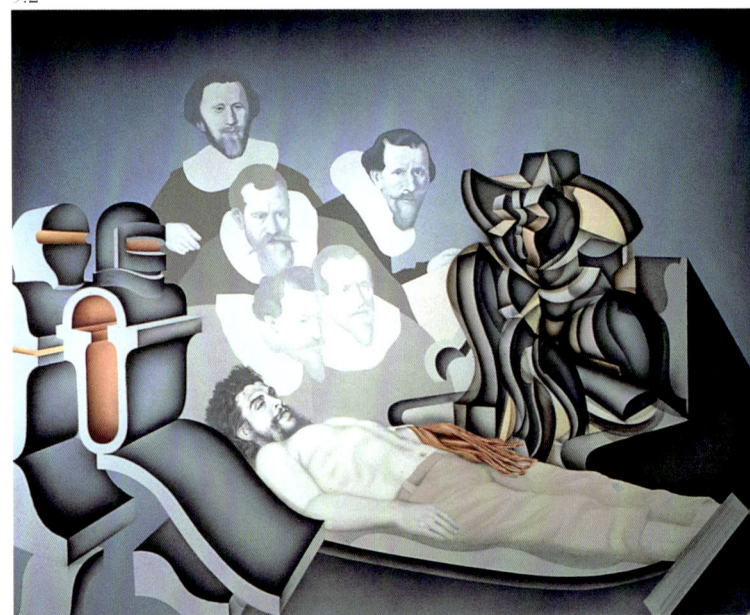

9.4

9.5

9.6

Belkin's variations on Rembrandt's *Anatomy Lesson of Dr. Tulp*

A remarkable group, these acrylic paintings, executed 1972–1975 by the well-known Canadian-born Mexican Arnold Belkin, were arranged by the artist in a sequence for a 1975 exhibition called *Historical Deaths*. They offer a strange narrative, jumbling historic moments and personalities, using the best-known photograph of the death of Che by the Bolivian photographer Freddy Alborta (fig. 9.2) to turn a classic of art history and a primary visual document of early modern medical science into a lesson in revolution, its defeat, and—perhaps—ultimate triumph.

The first version of Belkin's *Annual Anatomy Lesson*[1] (fig. 9.3) starts with much of the famous Rembrandt painting *The Anatomy Lesson of Dr. Tulp* (fig. 9.1) intact —the faces of the surgeons tense with concern, listening to the professor's words, watching how he exposes arm muscles of the corpse which the professor's hemostat clamp points to rather than grips. Belkin's corpse, however, is an inert, robotic assemblage of volumes, forms not evidently human in origin although ending in an ovoid shape which should represent the head, to the right (where Rembrandt has the corpse's head half in shadow to the left). In the Rembrandt painting, the corpse is that of a criminal, a bad man, hanged for theft and bodily violence and condemned to what may be regarded (and was regarded by many in the seventeenth century) as supernumerary and arbitrary punishment and degradation, that of being anatomized postmortem on behalf of medical science. The body of a good man could not in law or custom be used in such a way in Rembrandt's Europe as still today in many parts of the world, including Latin America. For Dr. Tulp, for the surgeons, for Rembrandt, the *Anatomy Lesson* is the judgment of divinely sanctioned science over human, individual evil. Now, for Belkin, the role of evil has become anonymous, inhuman, abstract—like the immeasurably ubiquitous evil of imperialism? The bodies of the surgeons to the lower left are left blank: is their judgment still in suspension?

Then in *The Anatomy Lesson II*, subtitled *Tableau Manifeste, Homenaje a Che Guevara, Pablo Neruda, Salvador Allende* (fig. 9.4), roles of good and evil are abruptly reversed. Rembrandt's learned, elegant professor of anatomy coagulates into the kind of robotic form he was previously shown dissecting, with a touch of sinister ingratiation in the forward flowing, slightly less than rigidly geometric arms, while two of Rembrandt's surgeons to the left have become helmeted, marching military robots, their mechanically polished shapes derived as it were out of the monumentalized letters of the words of the slogans to which they march. The other surgeons are still Rembrandt's; the lower ones are fading.

And the corpse is now the world-class "criminal" Che. Drawn carefully from the famous photograph of him laid out on the washtub, only with the fingers of the right hand stretched as in Rembrandt, perhaps he is to be understood as the human sacrifice to a modern, inhuman, (extra-)judicial apparatus which, having killed him, is now engaged in leaching out his blood, muscle, and fiber. In the seventeenth century, anatomical dissection was done by the book, some canonical medical text, seen propped up in the right lower corner of Rembrandt's painting. Today, political dissection is conducted by or filtered through the media. The Death of Che, the Death of the Revolution, is now dissected in public before the world press, in word and image. The book, retained by Belkin, may be read as part of that stream of righteous literature, judiciously, judicially anatomizing, through the example of Che, the failure and death of Revolution. The divided characterization of the surgeons as partly militaristic robots and partly sentient, sympathetic humans suggests that the jury—the verdict of history—is divided, or not yet in.

In *La Lección de Anatomía III* (fig. 9.5), robotization, mechanical acceptance of existing, market-mechanical world orders, has achieved absolute predominance. All—professor, surgeons, and victim—are robotized, in a pulsating, triumphant efflorescence of mechanical forms, leaving human only Che's face, his portrait-in-death, arms and legs truncated.[2] Is the hero to be imagined as part mythically resurrected? Less fancifully, formally he looks abbreviated like a sculptural monument. Che is painted to resemble white marble. In Rembrandt, the dissected arm (lacking in the Belkin) was cut off in advance, for convenience of demonstration; Che's hands were also cut off for purposes of demonstration, of identification. With a wonderful "rhetorical" explosion of his head the professor lays a robotic, curved panel of an arm on the torso, which is (by his touch, as it were) instantly eviscerated, internally robotized. Che, with his slightly elevated head, seems to watch the process of mechanical reduction of himself. The robotization has now transformed the witnesses, the surgeons as well; they are grandiose, architectural, science-fiction constructs, *sensuously* mechanical. Can they also be seen as transnational (towering, dictatorial) corporate entities?[3]

The fourth and last painting in the series, called *The Final Anatomy Lesson* (fig. 9.6), reverses roles again and puts Che in power. The corpse is now, fully, the dismembered robot, stretched out before us, "anatomized," into its complex mechanical parts. The wreck of imperialist oppression? Analysis of it, at the very least.[4] Che is in the role of Dr. Tulp, Che the teacher (as he always was in reality) with the *adlocutio* gesture addressing the audience. Five of his comrades (portraits, from a photograph of the Bolivian campaign), stand guard, combat ready, embodiments of audience to the leader's words that we, not they, need to hear, surgeons of the new order with automatic rifles for scalpels.

The interpretations made here are hypothetical, subjective, and politically loaded. But the association we make and imply of robotic with bad—military/imperialistic/dictator—which may be traced back to a tendency in Siqueiros, can be confirmed through other paintings by Belkin of political denunciation: the My Lai Massacre, where robotized US soldiers stand over well-humanized bodies of Vietnamese victims, based on a famous photograph; and the Tlatelolco Square massacre, where the Mexican army, backed by tanks and composed of "tankoid" mechanical bodies, attacks the civilian protesters whose bodies are stacked in a photographically realistic pile. Complication sets in when we realize that in the latter picture at least two of the figures we see on the civilian, victim side, in the foreground gesticulating wildly, are of a rubbery kind of robotic makeup.[5]

The tendency of Belkin in much of his work since the 1960s to robotize figures, and to do so sometimes (apart from the cases cited) without distinction of moral character, to cast them as neither good nor bad and also both, causes one to pause and reflect on the seductions of visual and philosophical ambiguities in what was evidently contrived as a pervasive and deliberate aesthetic signature. It was carried out necessarily with a sophisticated, "high-tech" airbrush technique. We must be aware that there are often within Belkin's robotic forms nuances of style, structure, and characterization

Figure 9.1. Rembrandt, *The Anatomy Lesson of Dr. Tulp*, 1632 (Mauritshuis, The Hague).

Figure 9.2. Freddy Alborta (Bolivia), photograph of Che laid out on the washtub in Vallegrande, 9 October 1967. Courtesy of Freddy Alborta.

Arnold Belkin (Mexico), *Four Variations on Rembrandt's Anatomy Lesson of Dr. Tulp*, acrylic on canvas, 1972–1975, all 163 x 218 cm. Private collections.

Figure 9.3. *Annual Anatomy Lesson* (first version).
Figure 9.4. *The Anatomy Lesson II, Tableau Manifeste, Homage to Che Guevara, Pablo Neruda, Salvador Allende*, 1972.

Figure 9.5. *The Anatomy Lesson III*, 1974.
Figure 9.6. *The Final Anatomy Lesson*, 1975.

evident also in the *Anatomy Lesson* group, which should warn us against facile, polarized moral identifications. Reality teaches that there are always nuances and indeed contradictions within ideologies, be they imperialist or liberatory. In Belkin, both photographic and robotic modes of rendering are subject to many gradations.

In a distinction made by Shifra Goldman, robotization, imbued a priori with the negative, can be stretched to the cybernetic, as well as to the purely decorative, and to scientific utopianism as we see it in Belkin's Managua murals, where it is combined with human anatomization (of Zapata and Sandino).[6] There are echoes in Belkin of the scientific utopianism of Rivera and Siquieros, whose stylizations are often not without a mechanical flavor. The *Anatomy Lesson* group is unique however in its permutation of roles, as can be gauged from a comparison with a directly preceding series, also of an art-historical victim: twelve images based on Jacques-Louis David's *Death of Marat*, in which an icon of art history is overwhelmed by the ways of seeing of a post-cubist-futurist-abstract-science-fiction-animated-cartoon era.[7] It is impossible to see the *Anatomy Lesson* group in this detached, formalist way, and not merely because the death of Marat is now two hundred years away, while Belkin took up the death of Che within a few years of the event. The Che group—permutating the roles of the victimizer/victim, living/dead, robot/human, and ending positively on the "guerrillero heroico" in command—enforces reflection on his legacy as a living and instructive force.

Belkin, raised in Canada and fluent in English, must have got the idea of combining the photograph of the dead Guevara and the Rembrandt painting from a short essay written by the English art critic and novelist John Berger two weeks after he first saw the photograph on 11 October, the day after it was first radiographed around the world. Berger compared it with two famous paintings: Rembrandt's *Anatomy Lesson of Dr. Tulp*, and Mantegna's *Dead Christ* in the Brera, Milan. The latter is an *ostentatio vulnerum* demonstrating the sacred wounds of Jesus, surrounded by mourning family; while Che is surrounded by the military, his executioners, mingling with journalists and photographers, in a demonstration of how a revolutionary gets killed. A Bolivian officer points to the wound on Che's chest. The purpose of an ostentatio vulnerum, and of Dr. Tulp's gesture, is similar: to reveal truth; the Bolivian officer's is to affirm a lie, to show the lethal wound supposedly received in combat, as the military high command first claimed. All the chest wounds were soon known to have been inflicted in an execution committed in cold blood. To Berger's remarkable repertory of resemblances between Che and Mantegna's Christ—the angle and height of viewpoint, the form and creasing of the drapery, the curve of the fingers, the expression of the head—we may add one more derived from another and similar photograph, taken at a moment when the Bolivian officer raised a handkerchief to his nose, like the mourners of Christ, only not of course in pain, but against the stench (this lesser known photograph was used in the Twentieth Century Fox film *Che!*, in a very devotional atmosphere, fig. 10.1).

There is another photograph showing a man holding up a book open at a photograph of Che, next to the head of the dead man, to demonstrate the identity: a photograph within a photograph, the one proving the authenticity of the other. And, inevitably, with so many photographers battening on the corpse, there is a photograph reflecting its own means of production, where the chief figure around Che is another photographer who engages in another kind of pointing, that of the camera lens itself, in an *ostentatio photographica*, a visual capturing of the captive. (Only) seeing is believing, as Jesus knew, showing himself as physically present after the resurrection to his disciples; likewise, only the photograph can make and preserve physical truth. Belkin, using photographs and painting "photographically" as the airbrush can, subverts this claim. He reminds one of the subjectivity inherent in viewpoint, proximity, opportunity, and intention by choosing oddly to include in his *Muertes Históricas* catalog, as if it were the source of his *Anatomy Lessons*, that other one referred to, showing another photographer at work, rather than the one he must have relied on in reality, the best known, Freddy Alborta's, as used by Berger and so many others.

In death, in his photographic death certificate, Che's eyes are open, as if he were still alive. His eyes were closed, soon after his execution in La Higuera, by the Swiss priest Roger Schaller, then later reopened at Vallegrande in order to increase the resemblance to Che when alive and the documentary value of the exhibition. This was surely the only motive; and the counterproductive effect which soon emerged, of having made Che appear to come alive again, post-mortem, thus facilitating his transcendence into myth, must have shocked the Bolivian authorities.

It is rare to see representations of the dead with eyes open; a hardy superstition dictates that the dead be shown at rest, asleep. Here again the tradition of Christian art allows us to experience this aspect of the photograph, which has seemed to so many to make Che come alive again, to make him immortal, mythic, "*jesucrístico*," as following a known type of Jesus represented after death, the "Man of Sorrows" type, where he sits on the tomb, after the crucifixion and before the resurrection, facing the spectator, challenging her. Jesus' eyes are open also in some versions of the Pietà or Lamentation, a type of which the Mantegna cited is an example, where the eyes are, as was customary, shut.

The open eyes, by which the dead accuse us still, are one of the many astonishing features of Holbein's *Christ in the Tomb* (1521, Basel), which has also been compared to the Che photograph, and which, together with some depositions by Rembrandt, is perhaps the most unheroic picture of Christ ever made. There, in addition to the open eyes, the mouth is open and the beard juts upwards, as if to denounce out loud the crime, even as it is forgiven. Like Che in the photograph, Holbein's Christ is extraordinarily emaciated and broken; he is decaying, his wounds and the whole of the visible right hand have turned a purply brown; one experiences here also what unnerved Berger looking at the Che photograph, "the smell of Formol, the untended wound on the unwashed body, flies, the shambling trousers: the small private details of the body rendered in dying as public and impersonal and broken as a razed city."[8]

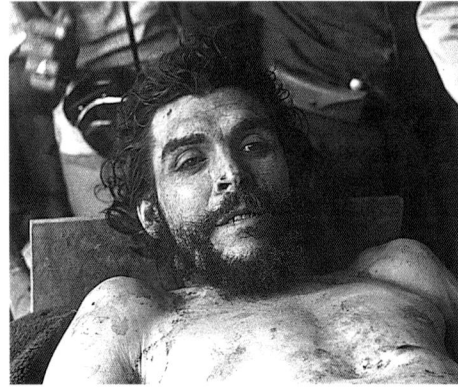

Figure 9.7. Freddy Alborta, photograph of head of Che dead, Vallegrande, 9 October 1967, 30 x 40.5 cm. Courtesy of Freddy Alborta.

The Dead Che in Art

The photographs of Che stretched out on the washtub, and those taken at the same time of the head in close-up, seen frontally, have inspired a number of artists. In two paintings by Barcelona-born Chilean artist Roser Bru, one called *Imagen Grabada* (Graven Image, 1979), shows Che as a picture within a picture, on the crossing point of a perspectival X and seen within a frame half rased by white lines—Che merging into/out of himself-as-image. In the other painting called *At the Dawn* (1976), the very face is being erased—by myth, by time?[9]

The young Costa Rican artist Adrián Arguedas Ruano did a *Descent* (from the Cross) series (1992) with the recumbent Che "mourned" by classical and art historical figures, and executioners, intended to be evocative of Mantegna.[10]

Another young Costa Rican, José Miguel Rojas, did a print entitled *Lección de Anatomía* (1994), consisting of a "straight" juxtaposition of the Rembrandt painting and the Alborta photograph, flanked by skulls. American Joe Tilson did a silkscreen and collage, called *Is This Che Guevara?* (1969), combining the head of the dead Che with cartographic material and a photograph of a young woman smiling on a rocky beach.[11]

It is only recently that photographs of Che dead are acceptable in the Cuban public domain. When a painting by Raúl Martínez with a reference to the Alborta photograph was included in a retrospective exhibition of his work in Havana in 1989, it caused quite a stir, despite the fact that the cadaver with the pointing officer constituted a minor lower part of the painting, which was dominated by the face of Che very much alive.

Weisberg's *Deposition*

In 1968–1969 the Los Angeles artist Ruth Weisberg did four aquatint etchings based on dead Che photographs. One, entitled simply *Che*, shows just the feet, seen against the background of the stretcher on which the corpse was brought from La Higuera to Vallegrande, and seen from above. Dark patches in the center of the shoes might evoke stigmata, and the shoes generally remind us how Che replaced his boots, destroyed by the lacerating rocks and thorns of the ravine where he was caught, with thongs of goat-hide, reminiscent of the sandals we imagine worn in Jesus' time. Another print, based on a close-up of the head, called *The Dead Che*, shows the curly hair stiff and somewhat barbed, like a crown of thorns; there is rust-colored blood in the right eye and eyebrow, and in the neck.

The blood at the neck comes not from a bullet wound, but from the incision made to insert the formaldehyde for preservation of the body—as may be inferred from another Weisberg etching. That work was based on a little known photograph of the head, taken from above, so that the eyelids appear closed (or, more probably, before they were reopened), with a clamp oddly (but coincidentally) similar to the hemostat held by Dr. Tulp.[12]

The largest and major work of the Weisberg quartet is called *Deposition*, and uses the standard (Alborta) shot with the pointing officer. Kept in focus (in the photograph they are blurred), the feet obtrude upon us further, the toes enlarged as it were by disease or inflammation, the washtub emphasized to make a tomblike monumental slab, into which Che is lowered. This "tomb" is surrounded by a dense black, from which emerge, behind and cut off at the waist, the military and journalists. The head and whole left side of Che, shadowed in the photographs, is banded in a shroud of light or else a kind of corporeal halo. Either way, the effect offers some solace of hallowed burial.

Weisberg's most incisive artistic intervention, however, is the dense perspectival network of mathematically calculated red lines, reminiscent of Renaissance architectural painting, injecting a fictive ceiling and floor flowing together and cutting across the figures, and interrupted at the most important parts—Che's body and the pointing officer. The place he points to, the wound in Che's side, collects a number of horizontal lines so closely placed as almost to form a pool—of blood? The perspective grid, which seems for a moment to classicize, historicize, distance the event, suddenly functions as red arrows of pain. Is it accidental that in the foreground, where the lines are much further spaced apart, they are so arranged that they point to the feet where Christ was wounded by the nails?

Here, too, is that "global stillness" seen by Berger in the photograph.

Figure J.1. Andrea Mantegna, *Dead Christ With Mourners*, c. 1500, 66 x 81 cm., Pinacoteca Brera, Milan.

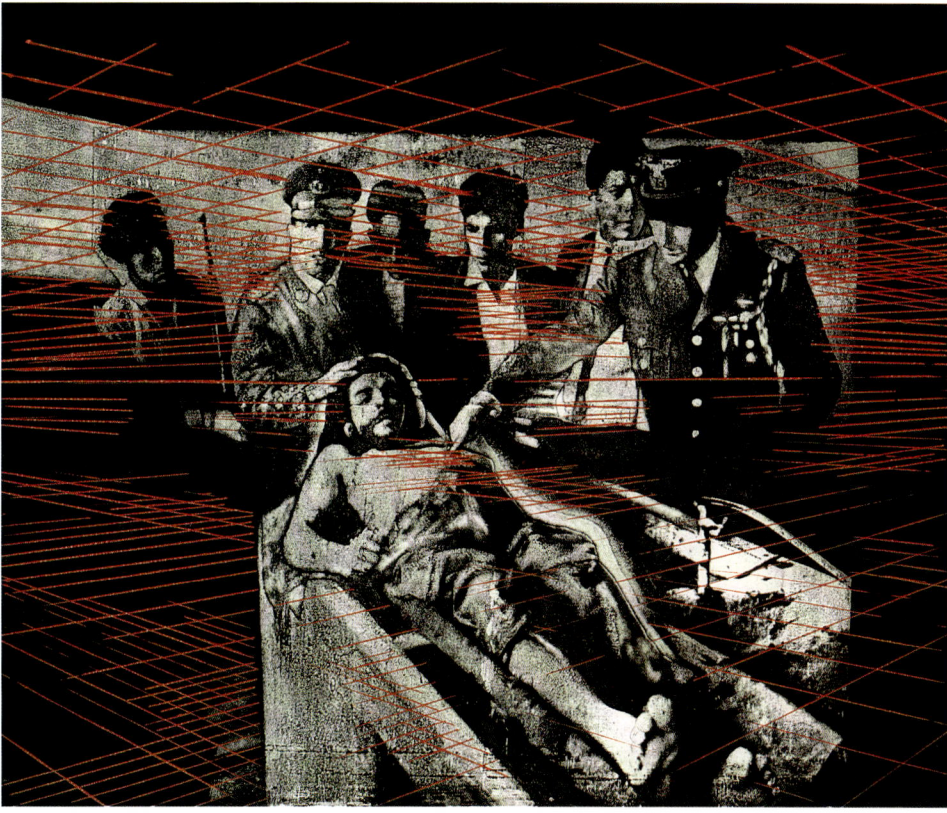

Figure J.2. Ruth Weisberg (US), *Deposition*, etching, 1968–1969, 50 x 64.5 cm. Courtesy of Jack Rutberg Fine Arts.

Chapter 9.

The Alborta Photograph in Film

The most striking filmic use of the Alborta photograph is in British Director Roger Spottiswoode's *Under Fire* (1983), a fiction film based closely on the Nicaraguan Sandinista insurrection, where the hero, an American photographer, is asked by the guerrillas, initially against his professional conscience, to fake a photograph of their leader. Called Rafael, he is evidently a composite of Che Guevara and Carlos Fonseca, the real-life Nicaraguan premier hero-martyr killed in combat during the Sandinista insurrection. Rafael has just been killed in combat by Somoza's army at a critical moment in the struggle when the setback must be concealed for the sake of revolutionary morale: a photograph of his corpse is staged, propped up, eyes open, staring somewhat unnaturally, like Che, but sufficiently lifelike to pass muster with the world press. The photographer of Rafael in the film fabricates a documentary lie in order to save the revolution. The photographer of Che in Vallegrande, in a photograph no less staged for propaganda purposes, represents a documentary truth designed to kill the revolution.

Christ-Che in Three Contemporary Works of Art *Christophe Blaser* [13]

The figure of Ernesto Che Guevara has recently inspired artists who have reconsidered the story of his death from a Christian viewpoint. The fusion of ancient Christian motifs with a modern revolutionary theme was already apparent soon after the disappearance of the famous guerrillero. Then it became popularized. But in recent years a new meaning has attached itself to the supposed resemblance between Che and the traditional figure of Christ forged over the past two millennia. This is because the iconography originating thirty years ago is no longer subject to the desire to change the world. Instead, it has to be adapted to a post-communist context.

There is a famous precedent in the depiction of a dead revolutionary hero in Christian guise. In Jean-Louis David's *Death of Marat* (1793, Brussels), the artist opted for a sober, austere dramatization, answering to the simple tastes of plebeian viewers. Marat's corpse, like that of Che, had been exhibited to the public in a former church of Paris, but in a state of advanced decay, bare-chested on a pedestal. Like Marat himself, David's homage is radically revolutionary and far removed from conventional Christianity, yet it abounds in references to Christian iconography of the Deposition: attitude, wound, knife, lighting, the very concept of macabre naturalism.

Paolo Gasparini's photomural *Body of Che*

The procedure of Paolo Gasparini, born 1934 in Gorizia near Trieste and now living in Caracas, is comparable to David's, choosing archival images most evocative of medieval and renaissance iconography. His polyptych, one of a trilogy called *The Sacrificed Passion*, consists of thirty-six photographs, those relating to daily life in Latin America taken in black and white, in the classic photographical tradition (fig. J.3). The others consist of pictures of Che, printed in red monochrome through a filter, which the Bolivian military used to prove to the world Che had been eliminated. Several of them are reframed and fragmented. Gasparini completed the ensemble with other photographs, printed in red and often also reframed, referring to the heroic history of political struggles in Latin America, notably the *Murdered Striker* (1934), a photograph by Manuel Alvarez Bravo, in the lower right corner.

The color red calls to mind the great struggles of history and their tragic outcomes. It is the color of violence and blood—the blood of sacrifice, and (since the French Revolution) of the people, of revolution, of hope...and the cause of Che. The red stands forth as a mark of a heroic past, against the monotonous futureless present ("derisory scraps of the contemporary social scene")[14] evoked by the black and white photographs. Is there also implied here a pessimistic meditation on the defeat of revolutionary ideas?

The multicompartmental form reminds us of medieval altarpieces with their array of incidents from the life of a saint, or Christ. But in its monumentality and its genre

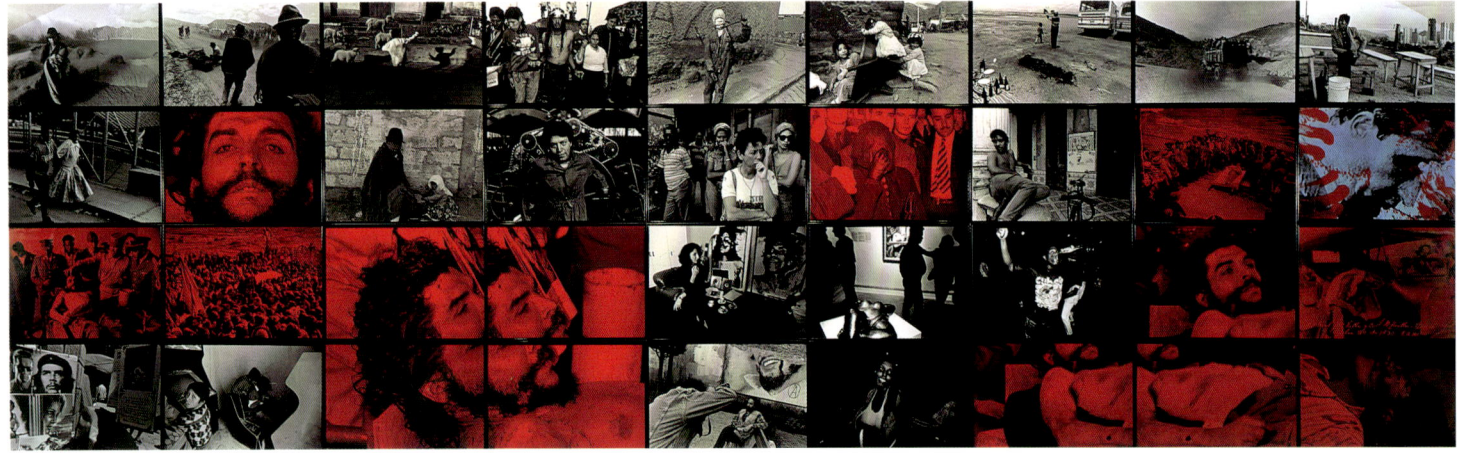

Figure J.3. Paolo Gasparini (Italian, living in Venezuela). *The Body of Che*, part of the trilogy *The Sacrificed Passion*, photographic mural, 1993, 164 x 549 cm. Artist's collection.

(history painting) Gasparini's photomural belongs rather to the great fresco mural tradition of the Italian and twentieth-century Mexican renaissance. At the same time, the multiplication of images is a tactic familiar in postwar and Pop Art (Warhol, etc.) that evokes the overbearing omnipresence and simultaneity of pictorial information in an electronic age. According to André Rouillé,

> There emerges a subjective, disillusioned reckoning, where violence and death, heroism and revolution, the impulse of Zapata, Villa..., Che, Tina Modotti, and even Trotsky, whose widow is represented..., seem to have been rendered useless, incapable of getting rid of poverty.... Together with the defeat of political ideals, this mural reveals other agonies, particularly that of photography confronting new media regimes. The single, unique image, which corresponded to a certain unity of social and historical project, is followed by the fragmented form which expresses explosion, atomization, loss of sense. The fragmentation is also manifested in the mixing of images from different sources (Gasparini's own photographs, archival shots, works of famous photographers, etc.), by reframing of the same image but also by the juxtaposition of several views on the same event, the assassination of Che....[15]

Dindo: Che's *Bolivian Diary*

In *Ernesto Che Guevara, The Bolivian Diary* (1995), the Swiss documentary filmmaker Richard Dindo reconstructs the last months of the life of Che, the encounters with peasants and the fighting with the Bolivian army. Dindo, too, sees a resemblance between Che and Christ, "his asthma...causing him to enter villages riding a donkey, like Christ...."[16] And although that resemblance is not the main subject matter of his film, it is present all the same—in the "march to death,"[17] the hunger, solitude, fatigue, and sickness which fatally overwhelm Guevara in the jungle, and finally the capture and execution reminiscent of the Passion and Calvary. The filmmaker is evidently anxious to add the human dimension—that of suffering—to the historical and political reality. The humanity of Che is thus affirmed, as was that of Jesus at various points in history, and as again quite recently in Martin Scorsese's film version of *The Last Temptation of Christ* (1988) of Nikos Kazantsakis. Do not the two films, moreover, play upon the same registers (human weaknesses, compassion)? Emotion and imagination are constant factors in Dindo's filmmaking. The dialectic conception of history having failed to transform society, he gives the impression of wishing to generate sympathy for the revolutionary project through an appeal to the emotions and sentiments of his viewers.

As a sympathetic witness of the events of May 1968 in Paris, Dindo belongs to a generation marked by the rise of revolutionary movements in the Third World and the great hopes bound up with them. For him and Gasparini, treating the death of Che is a means of mourning the demise of these great hopes. And so the cineast Christianizes the death of Che by suggesting that it was the destiny of Che to die for the poor.[18] But from the start, he conceives of death "as a metaphor for the defeat of revolutionary struggle, as a metaphor of the death of utopia." Like Gasparini, Dindo illustrates the defeat of ideals by the death of the hero.

"History written by the victors is not interesting," says Dindo. Certain victories (like the Russian revolution) are turned into defeats. It is the vanquished who deserve to be remembered. Furthermore, "After the pantheon of the left collapsed, leaving of the heroic figures of yesterday only banal bureaucrats and other tyrants, Che is perhaps the only one who merits being remembered...."[19] The vanquished are exalted for the beauty of the sacrifice which serves no purpose.

The aesthetic implications of such a vision are in accord with a certain philosophy of the absurd, and constitute a complete break with the militant ethics of Marxism, always preoccupied with efficacy. They reflect the state of mind of the generation of 1968, caught in the ebb of history. In a general way, the legend of Che reincarnated in Christian motifs poses the problem of the aestheticization of Marxism. One may ask whether Marxism is not engaged in a historical process akin to that adumbrated by Chateaubriand in the *Genius of Christianity* (1802), a process that marked the end of "pure" and self-sufficient religion, and the beginning of its afterlife in the form of art.

What memories does the vast historic mural of "applied Marxism" running from 1917 to 1990 offer to future generations? There is a real risk that only the most somber aspects, the black legend, will survive. In these conditions, the vanquished and the martyrs may offer the best alternative for transmitting a positive image of the Marxist legacy to posterity. It is this alternative that Dindo has represented in his film.

López Cuenca: *Corpus*

Rogelio López Cuenca, born 1959 in Nerja, near Málaga, has just completed (1996) his *Corpus*, a polyptych in the form of four photographs, framed, and two ceramic plates. Two of the photographs are historic: the head of Che, and the astronaut's boot treading the surface of the moon. The others represent the sole of a foot as if perforated in various places, and a torso scarred with deep gashes, taken from Richard Avedon's *Andy Warhol, Artist* (1969). Hands with the *fatma* (apotropaic eye) motif are inscribed on the lateral plates, which function as arms in a very schematic crucifix (fig. J.4).

Here Che is not just compared with Christ, but personifies him; ancient history tips into the late twentieth century, and at very different but chronologically close levels of American (US) triumph: the killing of Che, and the moon walk. *Corpus* consecrates—in connection with the approach of the third millennium?—the return of the protean "chameleon" Christ of the first centuries of our era.

Conclusion

The examples of Gasparini, Dindo, and López Cuenca show that some contemporary artists are more inclined toward the vanquished, dead, or condemned Che, than to the living and triumphant Che. Their work often harbors elegiac accents, inspired by the death of great utopias, deaths which tend to flow into religious molds. From this angle, the works with Che we have reviewed fit into the context of a contemporary art which has returned to the body as subject, to suffering, sickness, decrepitude, and death. Transcription into the macabre language of Christian art reinforces this artistic tendency.

Figure J.4. López Cuenca (Spain), *Corpus*, photographs and ceramic plates, 1996, 140 x 110 cm. Courtesy of Juana de Aizpuru Gallery, Madrid.

Alternative Views

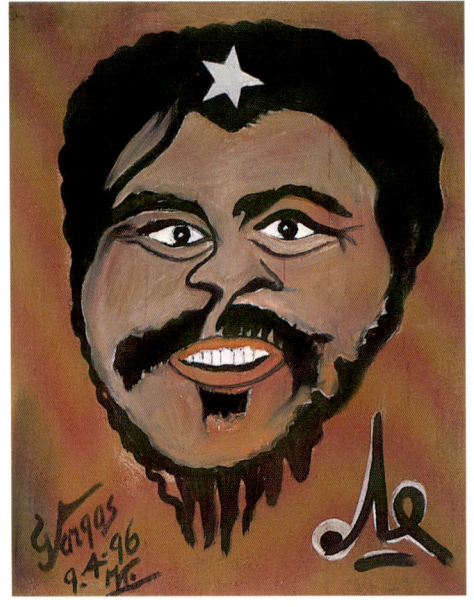

Figure K.1. Gilberto Vargas Cerveras, "Pintor Primitivo." Afro-Cuban Che, oil on canvas, 1996, 46 x 35.5 cm. Private collection.

Figure K.2. Gilberto Vargas Cerveras, Che with Santería and apotropaic (evil-deterring) symbols, oil on canvas, 1994, 75.5 x 55.5 cm. Private collection.

Figure K.3. Alexis Esquivel, Che on toilet, acrylic on paper, 1990, 70 x 50.5 cm. Artist's collection.

Figure K.4. Tomás Essón, *My Homage to Che*, 1987, 170 x 200 cm. Artist's collection. The eroticism, tending to the obscene, which marked Tomas Essón's work from the beginning, frequently led him into trouble with the authorities. In January 1988, he had a show in Havana which included My *Homage to Che*, a mural painting called *Strike*, and an installation involving a Cuban flag. The show was suspended the day of its opening, after much discussion, and moved to a less central gallery that the general public would less likely visit and thus not be offended. At this show, however, held four months later, Essón exhibited only juvenilia, in protest. The press in Cuba and abroad made much of the "scandal." Despite this and other censorious pressures, the artist remained a revolutionary and a patriot; it was only the quest for larger avenues for his career that led him to settle in New York. He thinks now he would no longer be censored in Cuba.

In late 1987, says the artist, Che had been forgotten. "Che is painted black for me, being black; Che was on the side of the poor, including blacks. In my picture Che is just watching the couple. Are they Cuban? I don't know. The painting is not overtly political, but in Cuba, everything gets politicized, and you have to explain too much," said Essón in an interview, 29 February 1995. More explicitly, the artist said the work was "about the hypocrisy of those people who applaud political speeches and then leave [Cuba]...[and the hypocrisy] of those bureaucrats...." (Camnitzer, p. 231; see also Tomás Essón, *Chá-Chá-Chá*, Monterrey, Mexico: Galería Ramis Barquet, 1993. Introduction and interview by Edward Sullivan describe censorship as a motive for Essón's leaving Cuba.)

Figure K.5. Liberating the Church, Photo Riehl, 83 x 59.5 cm. This poster was copublished (with the Dutch poster company Verkerke Reprodukties) by the German satirical magazine *Pardon*, which used the same photograph on the cover of its December 1969 issue. The glamorous pseudo-nun tears open her habit to reveal what is really on her heart, an image of Che tattooed on her chest. The photograph dramatized the theme of a serious report inside, "Rebellion in the Church," about monks, nuns, and clergy leaving the Catholic Church and flouting clerical rules and conventions to engage in social action. The report also discussed efforts toward ideological emancipation, democratization, and radicalization of the church. At the same time, the gesture of the "nun" is clearly one of sexual liberation; the image embodies a fusion characteristic at the time, especially in the US, of the political and the sexual.

Figure K.6. Chilean: "*Out of my fatherland, hypocritical assassins! My shadow will protect Chile*"—Manuel Rodríguez, 55 x 38.5 cm. Poster published c. 1972 by the US-funded Chilean fascistic organization Patria y Libertad, which helped overthrow President Allende in 1973. Such hostile caricatures of Che are extremely rare.

Figure K.7. Liliana Porter, *Untitled with Out-of-Focus Che*, vertical triptych, silver gelatin prints, 1991–1995, 8 x 11 in. each. Courtesy of the Monique Knowlton Gallery, New York. For the Argentinean-born, New-York based artist Liliana Porter, toys are metaphors. The bizarre juxtaposition here, which also appears in a larger work called *Simulacrum* (repr. in Liliana Porter, *Fragments of the Journey*, New York: Bronx Museum, 1992, p. 40), together with a photograph of a torn text from a book by Baudrillard (visible here below), reclassifies Che and Mickey Mouse, both popular heroes born in 1928, by combining them. The Mickey Mouse figure and the Che plate were found by the artist in Cuba, where Disney products have now officially reentered. Has Mickey Mouse, the imperialist cop, although "untitled" in the title, spiritually captured Guevara here, handed to him on a plate? (Regarding the "imperialist cop," see Ariel Dorman and Armand Mattelart, *How to Read Donald Duck*, New York: International General, 1984.)

Figure K.8. *Che Gay*, early 1970s, 76 x 51 cm. Collection of International Instituut voor Sociale Geschiedenis, Amsterdam. This contribution, surely by a gay artist, probably British, does not intend to suggest Che was gay, which would be bizarre, but rather to link an oppressed minority with a man who took up the cause of the oppressed everywhere. Che had nothing to say about gays or gay rights, but his cause has been linked to gays posthumously and indirectly by the Cuban Félix Varela Center. This German-supported foundation maintains the medical post established in honor of the martyr in La Higuera where he was killed, and also produced the video *Gay Cuba*, directed by the Sonja de Vries and shown at many film festivals, which documents the roots of homophobia. The Cuban film *Strawberry and Chocolate*, entirely sympathetic to the gay revolutionary, shows how far Cuba has traveled in terms of public acceptance of gays, in which Fidel himself has joined.

Alternative Views

Figure K.9. Gilberto Vargas, Che playing chess, acrylic on canvas, 57 x 70 cm. Private collection. A lifelong chess player who attained a high skill level, Che helped to promote the "game/science" when it had sunk in esteem since the days of the great Capablanca. His theoretical knowledge was good; he liked to play fast chess and to win. His tactics were audacity and readiness to sacrifice. He was capable of playing while blindfolded. A "very tense" game against international master and Cuban champion Eleazar Jiménez resulted in a draw, with only the kings and a pawn left (see Guevara Lynch, 283).

Figure K.11.

The Breccia-Osterheld comic book on Che

In 1968 the well-known Argentinean comic book artist Alberto Breccia, in collaboration with his son Enrique and the scenarist Héctor Oesterheld, published *Che*, a "mythic" homage to the hero in comic book form. It was, said the artist, an amazing success: "The day of its appearance, all the walls of Buenos Aires were covered with posters, and in no time some 60,000 copies were sold"—this despite a predictably hostile review in the pro-government *La Nación*. *Che* was to be the start of a series, continuing with the lives of Pancho Villa, Zapata, Sandino, and so on but it died with him. The military repression of 1973 completely changed the situation, as reading or possessing the book suddenly became dangerous. All the original plates and unsold copies were burned; the scenarist Oesterheld was disappeared and murdered. Reported Alberto Breccia, "My son and I were subject to very precise death threats, we had to go into hiding, the publisher died and people were so afraid that they themselves hastened to burn the copies they had bought. Scarcely three or four of the original edition are left, and given the apathetic public today [1992], a republication is improbable, at least in South America."[1]

Another edition was, however, published in Spain,[2] too luxurious and expensive for the taste of Breccia, who destined his book for poorer people. The original book was substantial, approximately 8 x 12 in., with ninety pages and 215 drawings. It constitutes, to my knowledge, the only attempt anywhere to render the whole life of Che as a sustained, primarily pictorial narrative. The book starts and ends on the theme of terminal sacrifice, works in a chronologically fractured (and thus modernist) way), so as to suggest a predestined life which may unfold in any order, seemingly written in advance as Jesus' life supposedly was.

Graphically, the style of the drawing is high contrast, "posterish." The rough, often brutal pen work and the refusal to admit any gray or intermediate tones, as well as the abrupt transitions from light to dark which are not so much naturalistic as determined by the need to convey emotional harshness, enhance the

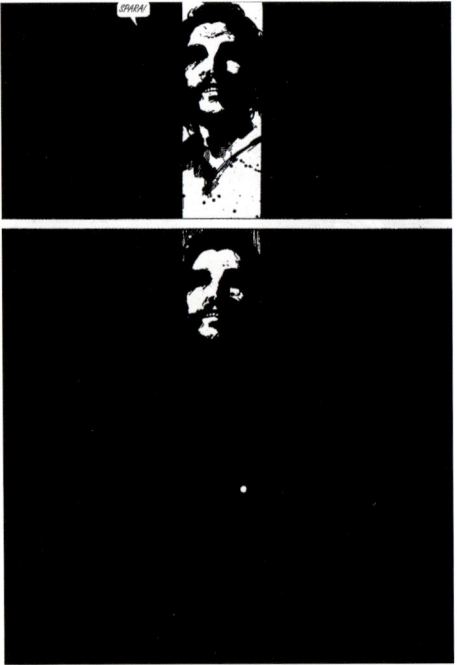

Figure K.10.

manichaeistic view of the world which is Che's and which is taken up by the authors. Day and night have no substance, only right and wrong. In its montage, the book is thoroughly modernist, indeed filmic, although the frequent intercalations of scenes of poverty which goad Che into action go beyond what I have seen in any film about Che. The parallel and "dissociative" cutting of filmic sequences and drawing composed like press photographs serves for scholar Jan Baetens an ideological function, that of transforming the failure of historic reality into a spiritual victory, a story of salvation. The deathly blackness of one of the last pages, in which Che tells his executioner to fire, is formatted to resemble a crucifixion (fig. K.10). This portrayal and a subsequent drawing evoking the Holy Shroud of Saint Veronica turn the comic book into a "casket closing on the direct, indicial imprint of Che, martyr and savior."[3]

Rius comic books: Che as Monk on a Mission

Rius (Eduardo del Río), Mexico's best known leftist cartoonist did two comic books on Che. One is included in the series *Los Agachados, Opus 91*, described as "a sort of comic book handmade by the Rius tribe for Posada Publishers, issue dedicated to Che" (1968, 32 pp.). The other, called *ABChe* (or *abCHE*, Mexico, DF: Grijalbo, 1978), declares on the cover that "most surely Che would have liked the book.... Why? First because Che was very fond of cartoons by this Rius, second, because in *ABChe* he is treated as a human being and not a saint...and third because it is done so as to be understood by everyone...." *ABChe* is longer (110 pp.; source of fig. K.11), and graphically much the superior of the two books.

Unlike Breccia's comic book, both of these are comic or comico-serious. Both use a unique mixture characteristic of Rius (who has in his long career become progressively more didactic), that is, funny drawings, designs borrowed from other artists in various styles—maps, photographs, and poster images—and above all, much more text (reproducing documents and testimonies) than is usually acceptable in the genre.

The jokes are simple: "Che was a doctor in allergies: allergies to dictatorships." Another (originating in Cuba) has become a classic that Fidel likes to tell: At a meeting to decide who should be president of the National Bank, Fidel calls for volunteers, someone who is an economist. Che raises his hand. Afterwards, Fidel, surprised, says, "I didn't know you were an economist, Che." "Economist!" replies Che, "I thought you said communist!" Adds Rius, "It was like putting Luther in charge of the [Catholic] Church."

Figure K.12. Alicia Leal, "From this murdered man are born all the men of tomorrow"—Félix Pita Rodríguez. 1997, oil on canvas, 165 x 133 cm. Artist's collection.

Chapter 10.
Demythification: The Twentieth Century Fox *Che!* *Christine Petra Sellin*

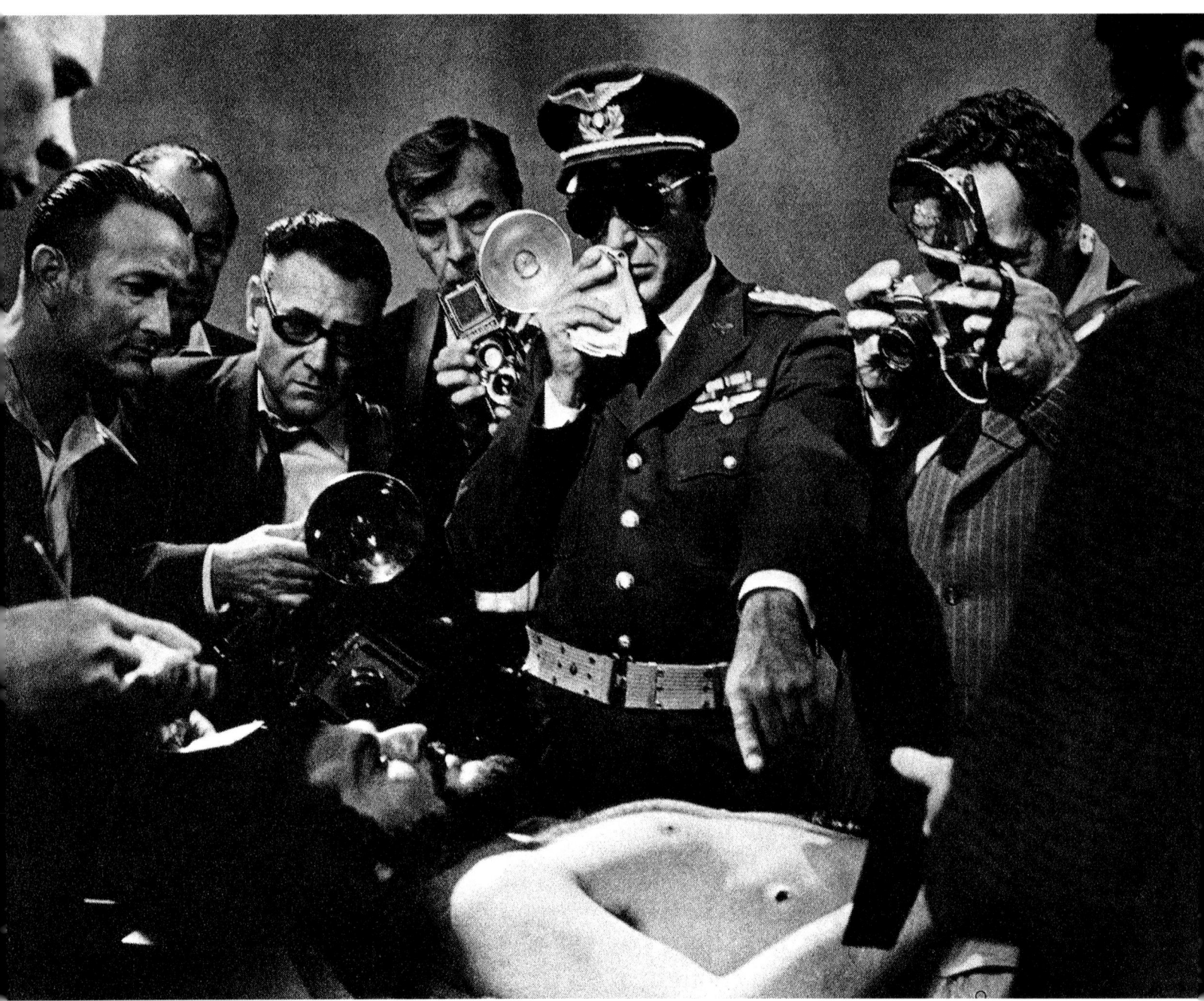

Figure 10.1. Still from Twentieth Century Fox film *Che!*, 1969. Bolivian officer points to bullet holes on Che's corpse.

In May 1969 Twentieth Century Fox released the major motion picture *Che!*, starring Omar Sharif as Ernesto Che Guevara, and Jack Palance as Fidel Castro, that promised to tell the "true story"[1] about the *guerrillero*. The studio attempted to portray one of the most controversial political figures in modern history—and to profit from one of the few icons powerful enough to generate a truly international cult following. But, as shall be shown, the Guevara character was politically contorted in mid-production, and became historically abused. The movie earned an avalanche of hostile reviews, gained an entry in a book called *The Fifty Worst Films Ever Made*,[2] and was withdrawn from theaters shortly after its release, a critical and financial disaster. It was buried by its producers: no video is available.

Why, after nearly thirty years, should one revisit a flop that few of us have seen and no critics have bothered with since? Perhaps because in the very failure of this film lies a historical lesson: the story of its making, here told for the first time, is a study in how a major studio, a group of notable filmic myth makers harnessing big stars, aimed at what they claimed as "objectivity"; but in giving cinematic life to their vision of Guevara, they found themselves fighting an ideological war on a battlefield of pixels. To countenance a film about a revolutionary hero at all, the studio appeared to be riding a wave of progressive films, such as *Battle of Algiers* (1965), *Easy Rider* (1969), *Medium Cool* (1969), *Z* (1969), and *Zabriskie Point* (1970). But was it possible at the height of national anxiety over the ever-worsening Viet Nam war to deal "fairly" with the man who wanted to create "two, three, many Viet Nams" all over the world and destroy US imperialism forever?

The film concept was first proposed by the studio's executive director Daryl Zanuck, who, following a trip to Europe, was impressed by the dead revolutionary's popularity among young people, and envied the commercial success of the poster makers. The project was accelerated by a race with several European filmmakers, British and Italian, bent on the same theme. To produce the film and oversee the preliminary script, Zanuck selected Sy Bartlett, a personal friend and a retired air force colonel and combat officer with close ties to the Pentagon and "international intelligence agencies."[3] Bartlett avowed his script would benefit from documentation gained from governmental and military sources in the US and Latin America. A promising beginning for "objectivity." According to the studio's press release, Bartlett was worried "that a picture based on Che's life could turn into a favorable propaganda platform for the Communists and Communism...[but] ultimately the Zanucks convinced him that [Che's] heroic exploits and his resultant failure [to spread 'revolution and violence' through Latin America] were of dramatic significance...."[4]

Bartlett's preliminary script was a cartoon, lacking in all political context: Che was depicted as cunning, ruthless, increasingly violent, eventually almost insane.[5] The script fabricated events and dialogue with little respect for the historical record: Guevara is depicted as the single mastermind behind the entire Cuban revolution, and his vision includes the risk of mass nuclear destruction. Bartlett's Che insults Fidel Castro as a "pig-brained clown!" and insists that "we better finish this war [Cuban revolution], before Fidel loses it for us." He tells an astonished Castro that he, Che, would have triggered off the Soviet missiles at the US and "set the world on fire...without a minute's hesitation." He spits in the face of a Soviet official, then announces he has been promised support from Mao Tse-Tung. Although Bartlett's preliminary script would later be shelved, some of the ideas that surfaced here would nevertheless make their way back into the final film version.

In Bolivia, his comrades want to desert him, preferring to go home to their wives. When Che threatens them with execution, they challenge him, "Then shoot us!" His philosophy is that "pain is the answer to a better world." He has only contempt for the people. "The masses are brutes—they understand [only] terror." The killing of Che comes as a relief, the proper ending to a narrative intent on obliterating sympathy for a man who at the end is virtually insane. He embodies no decent ideals at all, only violence, hatred, and strife. This wasn't creative license, this was creative licentiousness.

"I think Sy was certifiably insane," recalled the film's director Richard Fleischer (*Fantastic Voyage; 20,000 Leagues Beneath the Sea*), in a recent interview in his Los Angeles home. "Sy was probably the worst choice Zanuck could have made."

Under contract to the studio at the time, and unaware of the problem Bartlett would later become, Fleischer admits his general knowledge about the Cuban revolution and Guevara's life was very limited. Fleischer disliked and distrusted Bartlett's script, which Zanuck apparently found acceptable. Fleischer's suspicions were hardened following an odd visit to the studio from one of Bartlett's Pentagon contacts, who finally admitted to the lack of veracity in one of the more "ugly" scenes, as Fleischer called it. At that point, he agreed to direct only if "the complete and honest story about Che Guevara" could be pursued. Fleischer insisted on a total rewrite of the script, and requested that Michael Wilson, one of the

Chapter 10.

most successful screenwriters in Hollywood history, be hired.

Wilson was one of the "Hollywood Ten." A self-described Marxist and former Communist party member, Wilson had been jailed for his beliefs and blacklisted for years. "It was kind of a test for me," Fleischer explained, "to see if [the studio] would accept Michael Wilson or not. I felt that if anyone could write an honest story, it would be him...." So, Wilson came on board. From Bartlett on the right, past the moderate or neutral Fleischer, the pendulum of the project swung to Michael Wilson on the left, a microcosm of the larger shift in public opinion which had become newly attuned to issues of social justice through the civil rights movement and the Viet Nam war.

Wilson was also worried. "I undertook this project with grave misgivings, because I was not a naive kid anymore," he noted in an interview shortly before his death in 1978.[6] "I should have known better [than to suppose] that one could do an honest picture about Guevara in a stronghold like Twentieth Century Fox. But I was persuaded by close friends...and times were changing."

Wilson made these notes to himself about Bartlett's preliminary script:

> This screenplay...is a cop-out. It lacks balance and historical perspective on an evolving revolutionary era. It is a propaganda film.... The subject seen through a jaundiced and hostile eye.... The protagonist, already a legend before his death, is a revolutionary.... Any author worth his salt will portray him with an understanding, balance, depth perception, and will judge him in the social contexts of his time. But there's the [rub]—if he succeeds, the author may create empathy and understanding in the audience.... To avoid the charge of glorifying violent revolution and the movie being soft on Communism, this author reduces the stature of Che.... In an attempt to give this shrunken hero a slight superiority over the other principal figure, he reduces Fidel to the level of a clown.... Revolutions are made by conditions, not by men.

How did the director Richard Fleischer imagine Che Guevara? Twenty-seven years later, he recalled that he wished to portray Guevara as an idealist and a complex character, who wanted to eliminate oppressive rule in his adoptive country; but after the Fidelistas came to power, Guevara eventually left Cuba, perhaps discontented with bureaucracy and certainly with an inflated sense of power, heading for Bolivia. "But the surprise was, when he got to Bolivia, he made every mistake in the book...there was something wrong with him," for he acted against the very principles he had prescribed in his book on guerrilla warfare, alienating the peasants.[7]

A reasonable approach perhaps. Of Wilson's first draft, Fleischer remembered, "he wrote a wonderful script, beautifully done, very poetic." Wilson's screenplay created a multivalent portrait that allowed for a much needed ambivalence;[8] the Guevara character was reconstructed by eyewitness characters who appeared in two guises, as Wilson explained: "...in the past, during Guevara's life, as participants in the story, and in the present as witnesses, both those who loved him and those who hated him. So the structure of my screenplay was a constant debate about what kind of man he was, with witnesses appearing to say he was a saint, a Marxist saint...and others saying he was a monster.... Without forcing the studio or the director or anyone to take a position on the man, it revealed through those who loved him or those who hated him a great deal more...."[9]

Wilson's first draft screenplay presents a Cuban exile who calls Guevara a murderer; a Cuban schoolteacher who insists that Che is immortal, a living presence in every Cuban town; an American professor who calls him an incorrigible romantic, a Galahad questing for the Holy Grail; a Cuban army officer and former rebel who remembers him as an incompetent doctor; a woman, for whom, by contrast, Guevara was a true healer who introduced the first women's clinic in Cuba; another former comrade calling Guevara no better than an executioner; a survivor of the Bolivian campaign, from behind bars, recalling Guevara's increasing irrationality; another asking, what else could he have done, given the desperate circumstances? So the debates continued throughout, the witnesses themselves corroborating or discrediting one another, Guevara's portrait unfolding in a kind of cubistic mythography.

In the opening sequence, Wilson also included romantic, lyrical notions of Che, introducing Che as savior, as he sails to Cuba on the Granma, wind blowing through his hair, to a voice-over poem:

> We heard you calling Cuba
> Pearl of the Antilles
> Firstborn of the new America
> Eye of the Hurricane
> Island of Anguish
> Vale of Tears
> Island of Infamy
> Bastion of Butchers
> We heard you calling for deliverance...
> We heard your prayers and curses...
> We heard you calling Cuba—
> and we came.

But winds could not always be favorable and Wilson's script included chroniclers with darker tales, most of them post-1959. One anti-Guevara witness recalls a scene of the revolutionary dispassionately signing death warrants for executions of "traitors" in the immediate aftermath of the revolution, for which the historical evidence is mixed. (In reality, he was on occasion president of the board of appeals, responsible for approving death sentences.) Still, Wilson managed to slip in Guevara's explanation, which is important, and has always been reiterated by the Castro regime: that these executions were necessary in order to avoid far greater blood baths among the masses carrying out "popular justice" against members of the Batista regime found guilty of atrocities. This much survives in the final film version, which at the same time manages to show Che summarily and rudely rejecting a plea for mercy from a group of human rights advocates, whereas in Wilson's script, the pleas came from a tainted source: the brother of a proven criminal.

In Bolivia, by contrast, Wilson depicts Guevara as clearly disturbed and irrational, succumbing to desperation in a manner not supported by the historical record: he shoots the crucifix off the top of a tombstone in a moment of frustration (in Wilson, accidentally; in the final film version, deliberately); he angrily slaps the face of a Bolivian comrade for questioning his authority, provoking a physical struggle; both frustrated and incensed by the lack of peasant support, Guevara harangues the villagers, and refers to them as "stupid animals." (In his *Diary*, he does actually call them at one point "*animalitos*"—poor little creatures).

Wilson registered his "considerable pride" in a script which presented a kaleidoscopic Guevara for the viewer to judge.[10] Wilson began and ended the first draft with the public presentation of the martyr's corpse, surrounded by votive candles in the dark, obviously inspired by the internationally disseminated Alborta photos. Wilson's script also allowed Guevara to speak for himself, excerpting from his writings, underscoring aspects of his intellectualism, integrity, and vision. We hear his eerily whispering voice over the image of corpse and candles, reciting a passage from the end of his celebrated *Message to the Tricontinental* (and much posterized, e.g., figs. M.19, M.26, pp. 112-113): "Whenever death may surprise us, it will be welcome, provided that this, our battle cry, reach some receptive ear...." Wilson's scene of popular reverence, the locals filing past the corpse, is cut back significantly in the final film version: the religious questions posed by a reporter are eliminated, and we are left with a Bolivian official nervously dismissing the fascination of the dead Che as akin to the morbid curiosity raised by the spectacle of a slain gangster. In Wilson's end scene, we see a Bolivian officer about to extinguish the candles that surround the corpse. The writer leaves the question open: can the spirit of revolution be extinguished? In sharp contrast, the final film version closes the doors on this possibility, extinguishing all the candles, and literally closing the doors of the laundry room where the corpse is exhibited. The myth is shut away.

This image of the dead Che beginning and ending the film marks the crossroads, the place where all the witnesses' narratives meet and converge. Regardless of whether we consider the guerrilla fighter a failure or inspiration, a bandit or martyr, the story of Che's physical life ends here and a new chapter begins. His corpse serves as a bridge to past and future: the tousled hair, wounds, and emaciated limbs of the corpse evoke the struggles of the past; Guevara's eyes remain open and fixed beyond the viewer, on the future.

On the day that principal photography began, Wilson was astonished to receive notice of his termination—according to Fleischer, simply because his role as screenwriter was over. In any event, the moment shooting of the Cuban scenes began on location in Puerto Rico, politically motivated script revisions suddenly emerged.

"I started getting alarming phone calls from the studio," recalled Fleischer. Oddly enough, no one else had really read the script before filming began, not even Zanuck, who had walked away once the project got started. The story department told Fleischer that "complaints [were coming in] from the board of directors that the picture is too anti-American, and they insist we make some changes and tone down the anti-American or pro-Cuban scenes...."

These script changes continued almost daily, according to Fleischer. "I got very upset, very angry and threatened to walk off the picture.... I said, 'This isn't the picture we started out to make, we're making an anti-Che Guevara picture...and that's not our agreement!'" When Fleischer threatened to quit, he was faced with breach of contract. "I have never walked off a picture in my life...I decided to grit my teeth and get the damn thing over with," Fleischer said. "By that time I had become completely disillusioned.... I knew I was lost.... We were highly criticized—and I was personally highly criticized—for our interpretation of Che and I took the rap."

Principal actors Omar Sharif (Guevara) and Jack Palance (Castro) must have also been ill at ease under these circumstances. It was rumored that Palance asked for script changes during the shoot to reduce the "buffoonery" of the Fidel character.[11] The tension on the set must have been extreme—Sharif and Palance were anyway not on speaking terms. For a while, Sharif would not speak with Fleischer either. One film critic would later notice, "The performances are restrained to the point of disbelief, as if none of the principals wished to be nailed with pro or anti sympathies as a result of his impersonation."[12] Sharif told *Newsweek*, "Having this facial resemblance, I'm trying not to do too much more: I'm taking all the craft from the acting, just leaving the bare bones."[13] The director, retrospectively, liked the actors' performances overall, especially Sharif's Che, "wonderful all the way through, a brooding character." But to one critic Sharif was at his most convincing as the dead Che: "[The corpse] constitutes the best acting in Sharif's performance."[14]

"Sharif's own publicity people are at present trying to sell him as the Great Lover of our time, and they are succeeding," the *New York Times Magazine* pointed out, "...grafting that image onto the image of a revolutionary saint makes an imaginative sandwich only the mindless can munch...."[15] For another critic, "The idea of casting the actor who played Dr. Zhivago to be Che Guevara suggests, if not actual malice... [then] a devious attempt to make Guevara absurd."[16] Yet another objected, "Omar Sharif can no more interpret the fiery revolutionary than Elvis Presley could portray Lenin."[17]

Bigger trouble lay ahead. During the filming of the sequence of Guevara's execution, Fleischer discovered Bartlett had been tampering seriously with the script. "Michael Wilson was sending pages while we were shooting [via] Sy Bartlett. Sy would rewrite them before I saw them. So I wasn't seeing Michael Wilson's script, I was getting a Sy Bartlett rewrite!" Bartlett, secret saboteur of Wilson's script, had a taste for deceit and tactics worthy of the US intelligence agency sources he tapped for the film.

Wilson's end scene has Che noting that his death will be of no consequence, that "the dream can never be killed." To his captor's questions about whether he was hoping for a trial where he could "spout doctrines," he answers, no, history itself would absolve him. Che is depicted standing before a window, looking out at a schoolteacher and a goatherd; shots ring out, we hear a body fall. A villager crosses himself. In the final Bartlett (and film) version, the Bolivian military guard cuts Guevara's eloquence off, and mocks him: "In your brief contact with my people, you have contributed nothing but your arrogance and brutality...spare me your political theories, I've read your book." He is, however, reluctant to execute Che, "I take no pleasure in the orders I receive." Worst of all, the goatherd, posited as a representative of the Bolivian people, has become Guevara's judge and jury, saying to him, "Since you came, my goats don't give milk. You frighten them. You stink of death. I want to be free from you, and you." He turns to the Bolivian army officer. "Why you not go away [sic] and let us live in peace?" Then Guevara offers himself up, accepting his defeat and his fate, moving wordlessly into the other room to face execution mandated by the people as well as the military.

Fleischer was outraged at the tampering with the script and confronted Bartlett. "We almost got into a fight, it was very close...we had a screaming match...and I ordered him off the set." Richard Zanuck, Daryl's son, substituting for his father in his absence, called a meeting to straighten things out: "You two guys [have] got to work together and talk to each other, because you can't make a movie this way." Suddenly, Colonel Bartlett revealed other avenues of persuasion. "Bartlett walked in," Fleischer said, "and dropped a gun on the floor [which] he had in his belt—and that was the end of the meeting. I said, 'I don't have meetings with producers who carry guns!'" Zanuck tried to defend Bartlett's behavior, but thenceforth he was banned from the set and from the viewing of daily footage. Still, the wily producer managed to influence action on the set by planting a spy—a certain Nene (Inocente) Móntez, introduced by Bartlett as a former rebel under the direct command of Castro and Guevara during the Cuban revolution, to be a technical advisor to the director. "It all turned out to be absolute nonsense," said Fleischer. Móntez was an impostor.[18]

It must have been around the time the first editorial roughcut was viewed that Michael Wilson requested his screen credit be removed from the picture. He wrote the studio "Revisions of the script...have so drastically altered my screenplay, both thematically and stylistically, that I withdraw my name...." What an irony—after years of having been denied screen credit because of his blacklisted status—now he was demanding removal of his name as screenwriter, on the basis of "violation of principles and mutilation of material."[19]

The studio tried to appease him, realizing no doubt what dropping his name might cost them in terms of publicity. Wilson was shown a newly edited version of the film that eliminated or re-cut scenes to which he had objected. In a second letter to the studio, he rescinded his demand to withdraw his name. Michael's daughter, Becca Wilson, claims that the producers double-crossed her father, putting all the objectionable material back into the picture later, while legally retaining the right to use his name. "My name was back on something for which I am completely ashamed and humiliated," Wilson said later.[20] Despite his recognition that "eighty percent of the picture is mine" (in the credits, he is listed equally with Bartlett), he was bitter, and "anguished" at "revisions [which] *altered the political posture of the film* [stress original].... The producer's attempt to distort and bowdlerize my work was partially, but not completely thwarted and I winced, seeing and hearing his revisions in a projection room."[21]

The final film version is indeed a travesty of Wilson's intentions. Gone are many of the multiple voices—predictably, the sympathetic ones, among them the American professor and college student, and the Cuban female witness—together with newsreel footage of American protests (including Wilson's use of a 'Viva Che!' sign carried in a student anti-Viet Nam war demonstration through a small American town) linking the Latin American revolution to accelerating political youth movements in the US.

The vitality of Wilson's story is compromised in every way. Batista's tyranny, the motivating factor behind the Cuban revolution, is never properly established as such in the final film version, nor is any sense of the enormous odds that the rebels in Cuba or Bolivia faced, nor their courage, commitment, and sacrifice. We are not introduced to the terms of Guevara's philosophy or moral codes; we do not see him tending wounded Batista soldiers; helping Cuban peasants and teaching them to read; collaborating harmoniously with Fidel and their mutual admiration. We are left with Guevara the executioner, the Machiavellian schemer behind Castro, the ruthless and monkish disciplinarian, the abuser of peasants and comrades, the demented leader working out his own demons. There is, above all, no attempt to explain why the revolutionary after his death would generate such mystique among the American youth.

The most glaring historical fabrication is that which makes Guevara personally furious with Castro's acceptance of the Soviets' withdrawal of the missiles on Cuban soil, and willing to risk nuclear war rather than tolerate the humiliation. The reason for the placing of the missiles in the first place, the ongoing threat of US invasion, following the failed one at the Bay of Pigs, is not even mentioned, nor are any of the continuous US acts of sabotage or provocations against Cuba.

The director of the film touted as "the true story" admitted that Che's role in the missile crisis was "pure conjecture.... [The trouble was] 'my friend' [Bartlett] was feeding me falsehoods right down the line...and I thought [these] were Michael Wilson's scenes and it turned out [they weren't]."

Preliminary test screenings of *Che!* elicited some toxic responses. "Junk it!" sums them up. At the debut of *Che!*, leading critics indulged in some fancy flights of invective. "Stinkeroo.... All this movie inspires toward the Cuban Revolution is excruciating boredom, accompanied with nausea." "The old Hollywood Dream Factory still has the constitution of a goat. It can consume almost everything—including a subject as complex and abrasive as the late Cuban revolutionary—and reduce it to the consistency of strained spinach." "[A] galumphing attempt to substitute monkey glands for ideology...the result is objective, all right, objectively awful." "[The film] goes at the pace of a drugged ox...." "*Che!* is that rarest of birds. It is a no thing to no people." Few critics directly addressed the ahistoricity and political bias of the film: it was chiefly viewed cinematically, and as junk. Offended as they may have been with this bias, the critics preferred to express their revulsion in aesthetic or cinematic terms.²²

The hostility was not merely verbal. The film opened in New York in May 1969, with as many as 150 "Spanish-speaking people" (Cuban exiles?) demonstrating against it.²³ In front of one theater in Los Angeles, picketers reportedly carried signs with slogans such as "Movies are redder than ever!" in response to which UCLA's student newspaper opined that since the film was blatant right-wing propaganda, the demonstration was in fact antithetical.²⁴ A hand grenade was tossed into the lobby of one of the two New York theaters in which it premiered.²⁵ Police dismantled a bomb in a theater in West Palm Beach, Florida. In Los Angeles, seven Molotov cocktails were thrown over the wall of the Twentieth Century Fox lot.²⁶ Even Lalo Schifrin's musical score for *Che!* came under attack; released on Tetragrammaton Records, production of the soundtrack had to be shifted to another site after Cuban refugees staffing the company's eastern plant refused to package the album.²⁷ The film achieved some international distribution, but Mexico banned it in order to avoid endangering the country's relations with Cuba.²⁸ In Uruguay, the revolutionary Tupamaros destroyed a copy.

Che! is much more the portrait of a dilemma in cultural politics, than the portrait of a revolutionary. The making of *Che!*, or rather his unmaking, his demythification, offers a study of how Hollywood and national politics combined to come up with an aesthetic and political disaster. It also proves that Hollywood is not always market-driven: had the film been better, had its politics been attuned more to Guevara himself and to his numerous admirers (surely the film's natural, core audience) in line with the intention of Wilson's script, then it might have succeeded at the box office and with the critics. But the counterrevolutionary politics of Hollywood intervened against its own economic interests. Unfortunately, the example of Hollywood's bomb of a Che Guevara movie deterred others. A British film to be directed by Tony Richardson, for which a complete screenplay by Alan Sillitoe survives, was nipped in the bud. No feature length film reconstructing the life of Guevara was attempted for another twenty-six years until Richard Dindo's 1995 film, basically a documentary that focuses on the Bolivian campaign (see Chapter 9, p. 93).

Figure 10.2. Still from Twentieth Century Fox film *Che!*, 1969. Omar Sharif as Guevara and Jack Palance as Fidel Castro.

Mis*ch*ellanea

"Yo también tengo fotos de ustedes (Che)" (I, too, have photos of you), graffito in La Paz.

"Labor of Love" was the heading to the lead story in the Life and Style section of *Los Angeles Times* (18 February 1996) that also carried a photograph of Yanira Merino before a huge portrait of Che. Tortured by death squads linked to those trained by the US and operating in El Salvador, Merino organizes workers and immigrants in Los Angeles.

Rage Against the Machine, a rock group formed in 1991 in Los Angeles, hailed for its "raw, unfiltered extremism" and which has sold three million copies (US and abroad) of their eponymous debut album, used a Korda-derived Che as a logo and on their promotional T-shirts and album covers (including one called *Evil Empire*). In a poll taken in the streets of Los Angeles, respondents were asked to identify a Korda portrait of Che: several replied, "Isn't he the lead singer of Rage Against the Machine?"

A Che Tattoo Fails. At the 1996 Olympic Games a Swedish boxer, Kwameno Turkson, bearing a conspicuous tattoo of Che's face on his left arm, fought Cuban heavyweight champion Félix Savón. Despite the Che tattoo, he lost, floored in two minutes, twenty-nine seconds. "My Che was not for publicity, but for what was in my heart." (Reuters, 25 July 1996).

Papal Indulgence. On 25 May 1964, a very Catholic aunt of Che's requested from the Pope, and was granted, a plenary indulgence for him.

The total wealth of the 358 richest billionaires is almost equal to that of half the world's population of 2.3 billion.

Hang a Revolutionary in Your Living Room! "Tired of those Hollywood heroes? Get a bigger than life-size (22 x 28 inches) picture of Che Guevara. Worship him, throw darts at him.... Special offer: both the portrait of Che and a subscription to *The Movement* for only $3.00." Ad in *The Movement*, monthly of The Student Non-Violent Coordinating Committee (SNCC), October 1966. This is the earliest record I have come across of a Che poster sold in the US before his death.

"Yesterday, all of us who had not done it before swore an oath before a picture of Che Guevara. It will be a day of double memories for me—a double pledge of love for you and for the revolution. Deep down they are the same thing." (Nestor Paz, *My Life for My Friends: The Guerrilla Journal of NP, A Christian*, New York: Orbis, 1975, p. 39.) Paz died of starvation during the Teoponte, Bolivia, guerrilla campaign of 1970. The diary is addressed to his wife.

"In 1984, in a pure coincidence, Fidel Castro and I acquired Mercedes Benz automobiles. The are the same color: gray. They are the same model: 500 SEL. There is one difference. Mine has a license that reads simply: CHE." (Lyle Stuart, in M*emories of Che*, Guillermo Cabrera Alvarez, ed., Secaucus, NJ: Lyle Stuart, p. 29.)

Bosses of the top three hundred US companies earn 212 times as much as their average worker.

"Volveré y no seré poster" (I will return and not be a poster), headline in *Brecha*, 28 June 1996, p. 19), and graffito seen in Spain.

"Che is now totally dissociated from the meaning of action and the political discourse of social change...he is nostalgia." Jorge Castañeda (cited in *Brecha*, 28 June 1996, p. 20).

The Uruguayan football team Peñarol uses Che as their symbol (*Brecha*).

Letter to Los Angeles Times, 2 January 1996, from a military man: "About the left's respect and worship of Che Guevara...Che was respected by the right as much, if not more. His books were required reading at the JFK Special Warfare Center, Fort Bragg...Che's philosophy and work were to liberate the oppressed. The same philosophy is shared by the US Army anti-guerrilla branch whose members led the operation resulting in Che's execution."

"Religious In Their Own Right" "Famed Dissenters: Ernesto Guevara, Martin Luther King, and Mohandas K. Gandhi," two headlines of Religion column, *Los Angeles Times*, 2 December 1972.

"The last quarter-century of US foreign policy towards Latin America has consisted essentially of defeating the threat, the legacy, the legend of Che Guevara" (Brian Loveman and Thomas M. Davies, Jr., cited in *LA Weekly*, 8–14 March 1996, p. 14).

In the office of Mayor William Paparian of Pasadena, California, a line of photographs of his predecessors in office culminates in one of Che Guevara.

A Che Beer in England. In March 1996 the London *Sunday Times* and Reuters brewed up a small stir over the case of Joe Grahame, an enterprising young Englishman who financed the launching of a "Che Beer" in the UK out of his earnings as an employee in an American-owned investment bank. Since it contained Cuban fruit, the promotion for the beer was able to truthfully claim on both the poster and the label, which carried very soft versions of the Korda matrix, "Banned in the US. So it must be good." Grahame sold the beer by going from bar to bar with a backpack, in a tiny operation which can hardly have made much of a dent in the business, among the three hundred varieties of real ale sold in Britain. But it had media appeal: Fidel Castro was reported to have "hit the roof" at the "sacrilege" and elsewhere journalists claimed that the Cuban government had hired lawyers and secret agents to put an end to the beer, which had supposedly found its way into "trendy" London bars. Grahame, a friend of Cuba, quietly yielded. According to London's *Sunday Times* (3 March 1996) which gave the matter a five-inch headline, twenty-one inches of text, and three photographs, the reaction was part of a recently launched Cuban government crackdown on the commercialization of Guevara.

"Che's revolutionary tourist trail" is the headline over a report that "The Bolivian government is attempting to open up 'Che's Route,' a 500-mile long trail following the path taken by Guevara and his armed guerrillas in 1967."

Figure L.1. Bead hanging, bought in Havana, 1996, 15 3/4 x 22 in.

Mischellanea

The Swatch Watch Marks the Time

In the 68-page Swatch watch color catalog for spring/summer 1995, a watch with the face of Che derived from a René Burri photograph (Korda refused permission to use his), and with the Cuban flag and the word "Revolución" on the strap, was advertised with this exhortation and caveat: "The true revolutionary is the one who never stops—even after success has been reached, and who continues wanting to change the world, beginning with himself. With the 'Che Guevara' Swatch doesn't pay homage to a man or to an ideology but to the courage and freedom of thought that make true revolutions." The Che watch is the only political theme in the 86-strong collection featured in the catalog. Swatch launched an advertising campaign alleging, "Cuba orders 10,000!" There were complaints when the watch went out of production.

Che Watch Nemesis
Colonel Andres Selich, in command of the Rangers regiment which captured Che, and a former Bolivian interior minister who died supposedly "after falling down stairs in an Interior Ministry building while handcuffed, always wore the elaborate and distinctive watch (stolen from Guevara) on his wrist." (*Los Angeles Times*, 16 May 1973). The watch was then stolen from Selich; it was not among his personal effects handed over to his family.

Che Marks Time
> This [Che's] heart unified the time of America
> And this heart sounded all the hours of the new
>   America
> This heart was a great central station!...
> With twenty luminous-faced clocks...
> The new time belt of America
>
> What is the time and the weather? Che is out, is shining in the hills. It is Ernesto o'clock in our veins. Che is the new clock of history, against whose movements all events from now are measured. His death is the line of life tracing a destiny in the hands of all of us.

—René Depestre, Haitian poet (*Cantata de Octubre a la Vida y al Muerte del Comandante Ernesto Che Guevara*. Havana: Instituto del Libro, 1968, bilingual ed., French/Spanish).

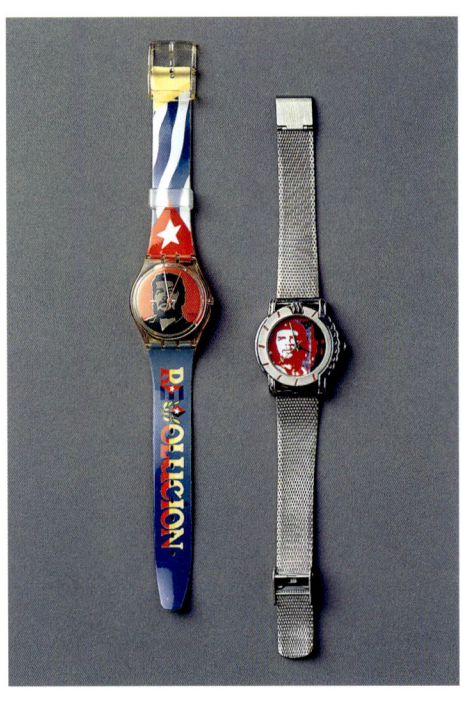

Figure L.2. Che on watches (Swatch, left).

Chicanos for Health Education
Chicanos of the University of California, San Francisco Medical School chose this name because it formed the acronym CHE.

"Don't Stick It Up in your dining room or your study, don't keep it in your bedside table. Don't misplace it. Don't collect it, don't archive it, don't keep it in your library. Don't give it away. Post it on the walls of the city."—Venezuelan Che poster

"Pope Meets With Castro," but not with Che. "Plain clothes Vatican security guards intervened when sympathizers attempted to display a banner picturing the Cuban revolutionary martyr Che Guevara" (*Los Angeles Times*, 20 November 1996, p. A4).

The Dutch poster firm Verkerke Reprodukties (Bennekom, Holland) in their catalog *On Wings of Color* (introduction by Simon Vinkenoog, c. 1972?) carried four different Che posters, more than for any other single figure. The *Pardon* poster (fig. K.4, p. 94) was placed in the erotica section.

In Gary Yanker's *Prop Art* (1972), Che appears fourteen times (nos. 109, 184, 561–72) He is topped by Nixon (fifteen times) appearing, of course, as a villain, but far ahead of Lenin (six), and Martin Luther King (five).

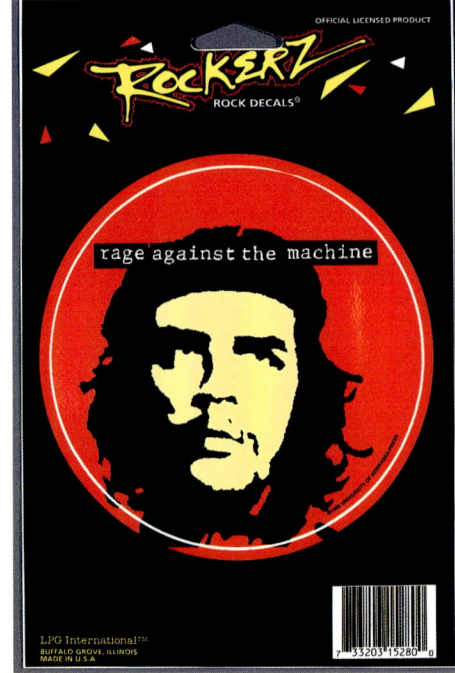

Figure L.3. Rage Against the Machine decal by Rockerz Decals, LPB International and (image) University of Nebraska Press.

Culture Clash Che
A skit by the Los Angeles-based satirical comedy group Culture Clash, written by Herbert Siguenza and others, uses the Korda Che in red and black as the continuous backdrop, covering the entire wall. The skit is a bitter mockery of Chicano political culture and its hypocrisies.

The protagonist Chewy calls upon Che to inspire revolutionary action, but immediately relapses into his visceral need for TV football and pizza. A friend returning from Cuba gives him a voodoo doll, which brings Che back to life, and with him the hope of reigniting the fires of revolution. Instead of the expected pizza delivery man, Che enters, and asks for an update on the history of the world since he left. Allende got killed, the Vietnamese won the war, but moved to Orange County. Communism is down, capitalism is up. Internationalism is dead; Marx, Lenin are out.

Che is in despair. "So I died in vain?" he cries, spreading his arms in a crucifixlike position. Chewy (in exaggerated Mexican accent): "Oooooy co-man-daaante, that's no reason to overreact and spit on the fascist subscribers in the front row!" Not to despair: Che, after all, inspired a whole generation of Yuppies, and "besides you made a handsome silkscreen poster." Enter the pizza man, who takes Che for a hippie. Chewy clobbers Che for treading on the pizza as a symbol of the oppressor, but Che and the delivery man go off to overthrow Domino's Pizza. Chewy turns on his TV for sports, which is interrupted by a news report that Che has been killed while holding up Domino's Pizza, while the pizza delivery boy-turned-guerrilla escapes.

According the US Department of Commerce, two percent of the US population controls ninety percent of the wealth in this country.

Che in Iran
A bibliography compiled by UCLA student Giselle Fahimian for my Che seminar contained a dozen items by Che or closely related to him and his writings. As the Tudeh (pro-Soviet) party lost appeal, Che gained. The Feda'iyan -e Khalq explicitly emulated him. Under a law from the Shah's era maintained under Khomeini, advocacy of socialism or collectivism was forbidden. Books were banned and destroyed. An ode to Che was written by the popular poet Siovosh Kasrai. There was much demand for Che posters in Iran, according to Massoud Valipour, now a Los Angeles resident, who helped distribute them; two of his friends were sentenced to ten years in jail for making them. To many in the exile community in Los Angeles, Che has a "godlike" status. In a children's book about Che, he is mythified as one "who could survive for weeks eating only grass and tree bark.... Anywhere he set foot, he started the fire of revolution."

In October 1987 in Westwood, the community surrounding the UCLA campus, the Iranian protester Neusha Farahi immolated himself by fire, watched by his brother Parham, who was wearing a Che T-shirt.

A René Burri photograph of Che showing him thoughtfully lighting up a cigar was used in a Nikon (Switzerland) ad with the words "a portrait that made such a noise in the world cost the camera a soft click."

In a recognition survey—conducted by UCLA students in May 1996—of Los Angeles residents who were shown a Korda matrix picture, Che was misidentified as a Black Panther, César Chávez, a Zapatista, and Manuel Noriega, among others. Comments included the following:

"Crops up often in my crossword puzzles."
"All I know is his face makes a great T-shirt."
"A Jesus look-alike with a beret."
"My name's Guevara. Maybe he's my uncle if I'm lucky."
"A Mexican Robin Hood."
"He unifies people just with his face."
"I've seen him in Bogota on the mud flaps of buses and trucks" (where US truckers put a sex symbol).
"With that beret he must be a revolutionary."
"Wasn't he killed by Fidel?"

As expected, recognition was much higher among Latinos over forty-five years old and those who were better educated. The musical *Evita* and the rock group Rage Against the Machine were primary vehicles of recognition.

The State of California is now spending more on the construction of prisons than on education.

Figure L.4. Wooden tourist artifacts.

Chapter 11.
The Passion of Che: Capture, Death, and Disappearance

[Major Andrés Selich screams:]
Hide him.
They hastily hide the body.
They will find him here.
They drag the body out again.
Do you want a Golgotha, and attract pilgrims.
Burn him.
They set fire to the body.
Christ the agitator
Slaughtered, and his well mourned death
Conquers the mightiest of empires, Rome.
Shall he be here resurrected. Let him disappear.
They bury the body in feverish haste.[1]

The tragedy of [Che's] death completes and exemplifies
the meaning of his whole life.
—John Berger

The story of the last days of Che is the stuff of myth. "It arises out of the mists, it has been told so often in accounts too readily believed. There were those who lied to steal a little corner in it, and smuggle their way in to the enormous photo of the story; those who lied to start a fable with ulterior motives; those who turned a half memory into a whole one, and ended up believing it themselves; finally there were those who fearfully and in the course of twenty-five years offered one element here, another there. Curiously, it was the smallest details which obscured the final text...."[2]

For months several thousand Bolivian "Green Berets," specially equipped and trained by the CIA, have been hunting the seventeen surviving guerrillas. By the beginning of October 1967 they are surrounded, cut off from the outside world, with no apparent escape route.

At the Huerta de Aguilar, near the hamlet Abra de Picacho, Che's M-1 carbine is smashed by a bullet, and he is wounded in the right calf. Che tries to stop the blood with a handkerchief, so intently that he does not hear the soldiers approaching, and, with Chino (Juan Pablo Chang), is picked up "like two fruits of the fig tree."[3] "What is your name?" Che asks the chief captor. "Cabo N. Balboa Huayllas." "What a lovely name for a guerrilla chief," he is supposed to have responded, before distributing his Astoria cigarettes. Summoned by Captain Gary Prado to identify himself, Che says, "I am Che Guevara." Taking out the Bustos drawings, Prado compares the features and asks Che to hold out his left hand to reveal the identifying scar.

With his two fellow captive guerrilleros, Chino and Willy (Simón Cuba), Che limps back painfully the several miles, most of it steeply uphill, to La Higuera, where the cortege, composed of nearly one hundred soldiers carrying their own wounded and several dead guerrilleros, arrives about 7:30 PM. They are greeted by the villagers with a mixture of respect and fear (fear that the village will become a battleground); the cries of "Kill him now, kill him" will remind Bolivian poet Juan Ignacio Siles of the crowd shouting to crucify Christ at his Presentation by Pilate.

The only medical attention given to the wounded man, who was himself always so punctilious in attending enemy wounded, is an aspirin and, later, the washing of his leg with disinfectant. He is put in a tiny, crude, two-room adobe shack of a schoolhouse. Interrogated, insulted, Che remains silent. CIA agent and Cuban exile Félix Rodríguez is prevented from torturing him. Colonel Andrés Selich suggests he be "shaved," and tries or threatens to pull out tufts of his beard. Che reacts angrily.

A gentler exchange takes place with the 19-year-old schoolteacher Julia Cortéz, who is initially hostile, but soon won over. In the latest version of her many interviews:[4] "You are a doctor, you are good-looking, you have children, who makes you go unkempt chasing after the misery of other people?" "You are pretty," replies Che, "you are young, you are clever, why do you teach in a tiny, muggy schoolroom at the end of the world?" And then he looked at her so charmingly, says Julia Cortéz, that the memory of it still brings tears to her eyes.

That night the soldiers celebrated their great victory in drunken revels. Che's left calf was bleeding, his hair was matted. He stank pungently of ancient sweat; it was in awe that the schoolteacher shrank before his beauty. He began to praise the drawings of her children hanging on the wall of the narrow schoolroom, and pitied them for having to learn in such a dark place. "In Cuba this would be a prison. How can one learn here? This is antipedagogic. In Cuba since the Revolution only large, well-lit schools have been built."[5]

Why are you not with your children, she asks. Because, he says, he has to make the revolution in the Andes, because he wants to build beautiful schools for all children, hospitals for the sick, and roads for the peasants, because he wants to bring freedom for all the oppressed and food for all the poor. He praises her legs and her eyes, which

Figure 11.1. Monument to Che at La Higuera, Bolivia, where Che was killed, the third monument on this site. The first (repr. in Diego Martínez Estévez, *Ñancahuazú*, p. 297) of c. 1987 was removed by the military, and replaced with a sign commemorating the "valiant soldiers who fought against communism." Another monument was put up, and also soon removed. Both were by students of the Bolivian University Confederation. The third monument, pictured here, dates from c. 1994. The paving stones on the ground make the shape of a star.

Chapter 11.

remind him of the beauty of Spanish women, and he promises tractors for the peasants. He speaks of the ideals for which one must fight and which are more important than one's own children. A teacher to the end, Che corrects a spelling mistake he sees on the blackboard. He says all this seated before the corpses of two friends placed in his prison, two of the forty-three guerrilleros who had died. "A man of integrity," she will say repeatedly of him, "of a fine nobility of spirit." She would be furious at his killing.[6]

In the morning of the ninth, Ninfa Arteaga, the wife of the village telegrapher (there are no telephones) offers to bring the prisoners food. The military refuse this mercy. "If you don't let me give him food, I won't give food to anyone." Her daughter Elida is allowed to bring Che a bowl of peanut soup (*maní*).[7] Most attempts by the military to engage Che in conversation fail. A soldier, seeing him lost in thought, asks mockingly, "Are you thinking about the immortality of the donkey?" "No, lieutenant, I am thinking about the immortality of the revolution."

At 6:30 AM Bolivian President Barrientos receives a phone call from his foreign minister, in Washington for a meeting of the Organization of American States, recommending Che be kept alive for a time and then disappeared as quietly as possible. But already the night before at 11:30 PM, Douglas Henderson, US ambassador in La Paz, has told Barrientos that Che should be presented as killed in combat—it was a mistake not to have murdered Régis Debray to avoid the bad publicity of a trial and the intervention of Charles de Gaulle.

CIA agent Félix Rodríguez arrives by helicopter in La Higuera with Colonel Zenteno. He photographs Che's diaries and claims to have spent an amicable ninety minutes with the comandante, which is universally viewed to be a lie (he was with Che for fifteen angry minutes at the most). There is competition for photographs: Rodríguez has himself photographed with Che, taken out of the schoolroom for the purpose; Che refuses to smile as bidden, or to look at the camera (fig. 11.3). In his biography, *Shadow Warrior*, Rodríguez will boast of having manipulated the camera of Air Force major Niño de Guzmán to prevent his photograph from succeeding, so that the CIA and Rodríguez would be the only ones to have the last photograph of Che alive. It is said that many other photographs were taken of Che captive; they have never been published.

The army announces that Che has been killed in combat. The order arrives in La Higuera to execute him. Mario Terán, whose birthday it is, tipsy, offers to do the job. He finds Che "serenely" waiting. "His eyes shone intensely. He fascinated me. I saw him as great, immense."[8] Given a drink to bolster his courage, Terán is still paralyzed. "Don't worry, " says Che, "you've come to kill me." The executioner turns away momentarily from the room, while Chino and Willy are shot next door. Again Che encourages him to fire. "Shoot, coward, you are going to kill a man." Then, says Terán, "I made one step backwards, towards the door, closed my eyes and shot a burst of fire. Che fell to the ground, legs broken, he convulsed, and began bleeding profusely. I plucked up my nerve, and fired another burst, hitting him in the arm, shoulder, and heart." It is 1:10 PM. The schoolteacher screams "murderers."

More photographs are taken of the corpse on the stretcher. The parish priest of neighboring Pucara, the Swiss Jesuit Roger Schaller, who arrives by horseback hoping to bring spiritual comfort to the condemned man, is too late. At a loss what to do, he begins to clean the blood from the schoolroom floor, "hoping to wash away part of the terrible sin of killing a man in a school." He keeps a handkerchief dipped in blood.[9] Schaller says a prayer over the body, which is already attached to helicopter skids, and with the help of Ninfa Arteaga wraps it in a blanket, and closes his eyes, "brown eyes suddenly turned blue, as if they were leaving the autumn of his life to enter the eternity of heaven."[10]

The body is carried aloft and away into the skies, which appeared supernatural, resurrectionary to some Higuerans. It arrives in Vallegrande, some thirty-five kilometers away, at 5 PM. Strangers, CIA agents, are there to greet it. When asked where they come from (Cuba? Puerto Rico?), one replies in English, "From nowhere," and Félix Rodríguez shouts to his companion in English, "Let's get the hell out of here."[11] Che is taken to the Señor de Malta hospital, where he is laid out on the hospital laundry washtub, and exhibited triumphantly to journalists and photographers whose pictures will next day astonish the world. The armed forces have announced that Che was killed in combat, one lie amid a mass of lies and inaccuracies; the nature of the wounds renders this unlikely and the autopsy

Figure 11.2. View of wall inside the medical post, which was built precisely over the site of the schoolroom in La Higuera, Bolivia, where Che was shot, and which was immediately destroyed. The theme of the large picture, showing Dr. Guevara with a little peasant girl and a sick infant, does not appear in posters. Photograph, 1996.

undertaken soon afterward proves it impossible. Vallegrandinos file past, some with candles and much reverence. Many remark on the vitality of his gaze (the eyes have been opened again to facilitate identification) and his Christlike look. The nuns who wash his body also find him Christlike.

General Ovando, commander-in-chief of the army, wants head and hands cut off for identification purposes; only the hands are severed, to be embalmed, and in a bizarre story worthy of a detective novel, eventually smuggled out to Cuba. The face has been destroyed in the course of making a wax face mask. Che's brother Roberto, arriving hastily from Argentina to claim the body, is told it has been buried, and then dug up and burned and the ashes scattered (cremation is contrary to Bolivian canonical law, and was technically impossible in Vallegrande). The body disappears; in fact it is probably buried near the landing strip of the airport. Extensive excavations undertaken in Spring 1996 uncover many guerrillero bodies but none that is demonstrably Che's. Another attempt is being made, by Cuban experts, currently (January 1997).

The old political fear that Che's remains might become a pilgrimage site has now dissipated. Vallegrande business people see an interest here, and hope that any remains found will become part of a Che museum to be built near the washhouse, a tourist attraction. At the moment the washhouse is unmarked, unused, visibly special only by the interior walls which are completely covered in reverent, hopeful, and inspired graffiti written by pilgrims from all over the world, all dating from the last decade.

The curse of Che

The following list has been drawn up by a Bolivian journalist[12] of what happened to the almost entire military hierarchy involved in the murder of Che. The list could be made longer, for it omits many minor actors. Ironically, only Mario Terán, the man who fired the deadly shots, has survived intact—if that is the word for one described by his latest interviewer, Jon Lee Anderson, as inwardly raging and who attempted suicide by leaping from a fourth-story window.

In descending rank:
1. President and Airforce General René Barrientos, killed in a helicopter accident, 1969.
2. Commander-in-chief Alfredo Ovando, future president, life marked by frustration and tragedy.
3. Chief of Staff and future president General Juan José Torres, overthrown in a coup and assassinated in Buenos Aires, 1976.
4. General Joaquín Zenteno, commander of Rangers division which captured Che, assassinated in a Paris street, 1967.
5. Chief of Intelligence Toto (Roberto) Quintanilla, assassinated in Hamburg, 1970, by the Bolivian guerrillera Mónica Ertl.
6. Major Andrés Selich, commander of Rangers regiment which captured Che, assassinated in La Paz, 1973.
7. Captain Gary Prado, commander of patrol which captured Che, wounded by a bullet in 1981 and left paralyzed.

Self-Portrait, Dark *Che Guevara*

From a young nation with roots of grass
(roots which deny America's rage)
I come to you, brothers of the North.

Laden with cries of dejection and faith
I come to you, brothers of the North,
I come from where we homo sapiens came,
I devoured kilometers in nomadic rituals;
with my asthmatic baggage which I carry like a cross
and in the gut of unconnected metaphor.

The trail was long and very great the burden,
the smell of vagabond steps still clings to me
and even in the shipwreck of my subterranean being
—despite the promise of the rescuing shore—
I swim fretfully against the undertow
keeping intact the state of the shipwrecked.

I stand alone facing the inexorable night...

Autoretrato Oscuro

*De una joven nación de raíces de hierba
(raíces que niegan la rabia de America)
vengo a ustedes, hermanos norteños.*

*Cargado de gritos de desaliento y de fe
vengo a ustedes, hermanos norteños
vengo de donde venimos los "homo sapiens,"
devoré kilómetros en ritos trashumantes;
con mi materia asmática que cargo como una cruz
y en la entraña de metáfora inconexa.*

*La ruta fue larga y muy grande la carga,
persiste en mí el aroma de pasos vagabundos
y aún en el naufragio de mi ser subterráneo
—a pesar de que se anuncian orillas salvadoras—
nado displicente contra la resaca,
conservando intacta la condición de náufrago.*

Estoy solo frente a la noche inexorable...[13]

Figure 11.3. Last photograph of Che alive, taken by CIA agent Félix Rodríguez, 9 October 1967. From Arnaldo Saucedo, *No Disparen, soy el Che*.

Gallery

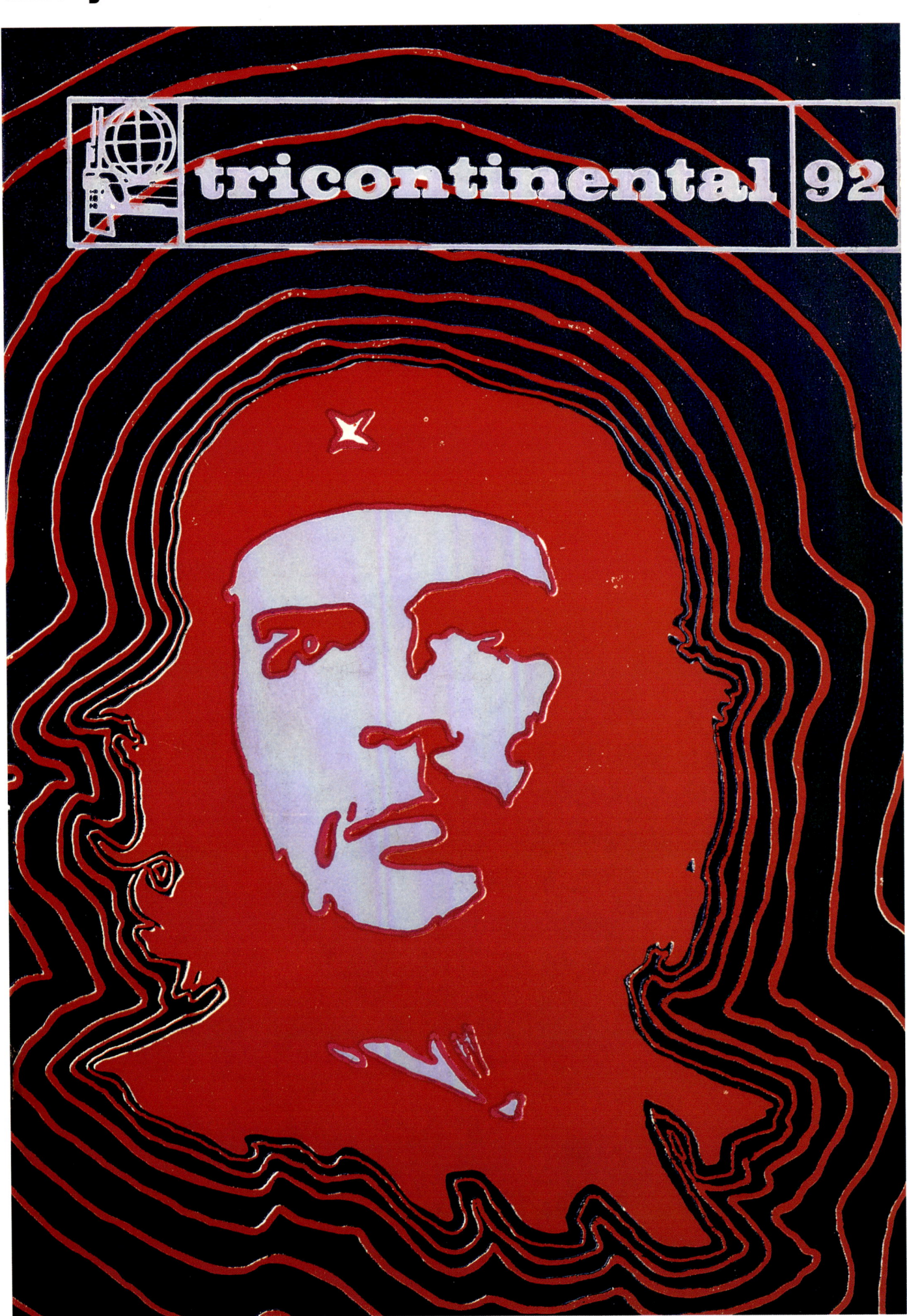

Figure M.2. Olivio Martínez, *Solidarity* (with Viet Nam), OSPAAAL, 1972, 54 x 33 cm.

Figure M.3. Rafael Morante, *Solidarity Congo*, 1973, 53 x 33 cm.

Figure M.4. Tony Evora, *World Day of Solidarity with the People of South Africa, 26 June*, OSPAAAL, pre-1973, 51 x 32 cm.

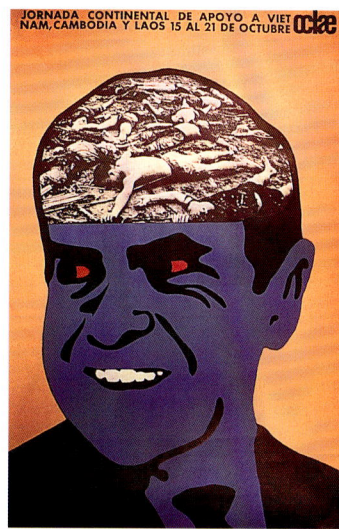

Figure M.5. *Continental Days of Support for Viet Nam, Cambodia, and Laos, 15–21 October*, OCLAE, c. 1972.

Figure M.6. Faustino Pérez, *Day of Solidarity with the People of Palestine, 15 May*, OSPAAAL, 54 x 33 cm.

Figure M.7. Victor Manuel Navarrete, *World Solidarity with the Cuban Revolution*, OSPAAAL, 1969, 75 x 51 cm.

Figure M.8. Frémez, lithograph, c. 1970, 46 x 61.5 cm.

Figure M.9. Frémez, lithograph, c. 1970, 58 x 44 cm.

Figure M.10. Frémez, lithograph, c. 1970, 61.5 x 46 cm.

Figure M.1. Cover of *Tricontinental* (29), 1974, 21.5 x 15.5 cm.

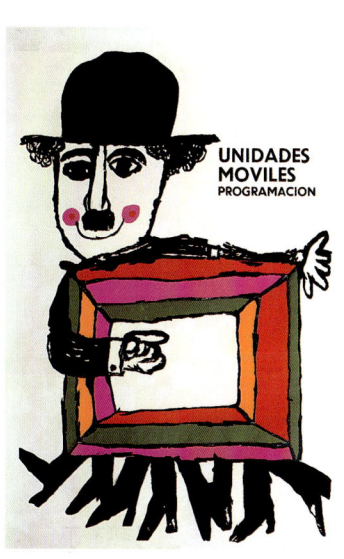

Figure M.11. Eduardo Muñoz Bachs, *Mobile Units Program* (with caricature of Charlie Chaplin), ICAIC, silkscreen, 1972, 76.5 x 50.5 cm.

Figure M.12. *8 March...International Woman's Day*, Commission for Revolutionary Orientation of the Central Committee of the Cuban Communist Party, 76 x 36 cm.

Figure M.13. Alfredo Rostgaard, OSPAAAL, 1971, 53 x 33 cm.

Gallery

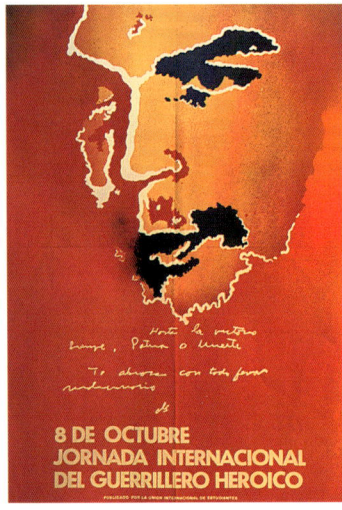

Figure M.14. *8 October, International Day of the Heroic Guerrilla*, "Ever unto Victory, Homeland or Death... I embrace you with all revolutionary fervor"—Che. Published by the International Student Union. Courtesy of Casa de las Américas, Havana.

Figure M.15. Enrique Agramonte.

Figure M.16. Lázaro Hondares, *Camilo Che, Ideological Days from 8 to 28 October, Ministry of Culture*. Courtesy of Casa de las Américas, Havana.

Figure M.17. Alberto Blanco, 1972.

Figure M.18. *Che Comandante, Amigo*, steel sculpture in patio of Palace of Pioneers, Lenin Park (see fig. 4.8).

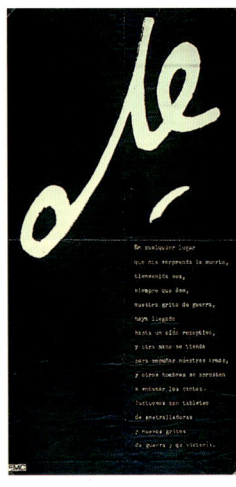

Figure M.19. *Che: Wherever death may surprise us, let it be welcome as long as this, our war cry, reaches a receptive ear, and other hands reach out to take up our arms, and other men be ready to intone the mournful songs with the rattle of machine guns and new cries of war and victory* (from the Message to Tricontinental, 1967). 98.5 x 52 cm.

Figure M.20. *Che, Debate "Crisis and Revolutionary Alternative in the Americas,"* 15 June 1987, Vanguardia Press (Managua, Nicaragua). 61 x 42 cm.

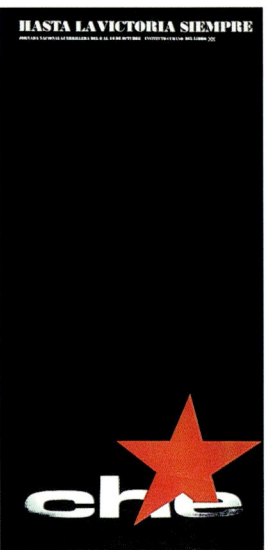

Figure M.21. *Che, Ever Onward Unto Victory, National Day of the Guerrilla, 8–28 October*, Cuban Book Institute. 21 x 34.5 cm.

Figure M.22. René Azcuy, *Che Heroic Guerrilla*.

Figure M.23. Jesús Forján, *Day of the Heroic Guerrilla Fighter—8 October*, OSPAAAL, 1973. 50 x 35 cm.

Figure M.24. Mario Gallardo, *Che*. Courtesy of the Center for Cuban Studies Art Space.

Figure M.25. Che signature over Palace of Pioneers, Lenin Park.

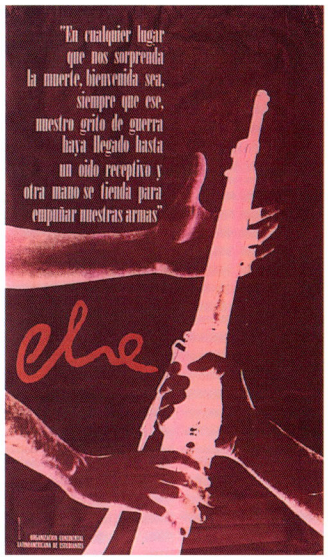

Figure M.26. *Che.* "Wherever death may surprise us, let it be welcome as long as this, our war cry, reaches a receptive ear, and other hands reach out to take up our arms." OCLAE, pre-1973.

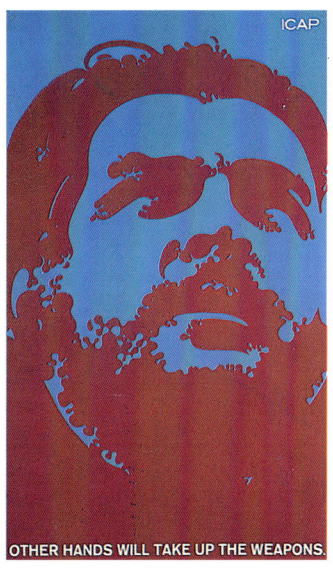

Figure M.27. Félix Beltrán, *Other Hands Will Take Up the Weapons*, Cuban Institute for Friendship with Other Peoples (ICAP), silkscreen, pre-1973, 53 x 33 cm.

Figure M.28. Félix Beltrán, 1970, 53 x 40 cm.

Figure M.29. Antonio Riverón, silkscreen, 1978, 64.5 x 49.5 cm.

Figure M.30. Netherlands, *Rather die on one's feet than live on one's knees—Che*, early 1970s, 61 x 43 cm.

Figure M.31. Jorge Hernández, *Che de América*, 65.5 x 43 cm.

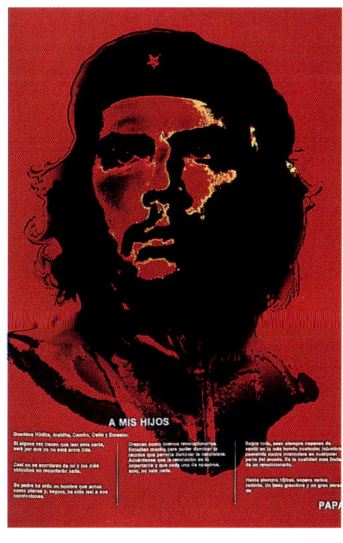

Figure M.32. "To my children...Papa" (extracts from Che's last letter to his children), 84.5 x 55.5 cm.

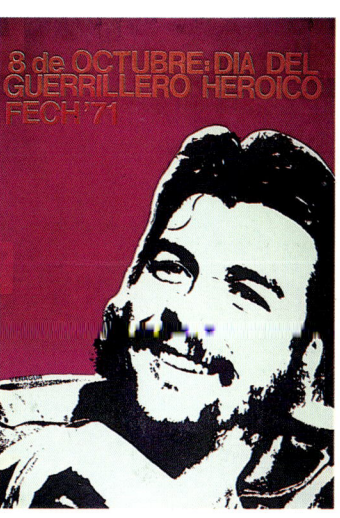

Figure M.33. Veragua (Chile), *8 October: Day of the Heroic Guerrilla*, FECH (Chilean student federation), 1971, 75.5 x 55 cm.

Figure M.34. *Day of the Heroic Guerrilla*, OCLAE, 68 x 45.5 cm.

Figure M.35. *Tardeada*, Salsa de Berkeley, Venceremos Brigade Benefit, silkscreen, 1977, 57.5 x 36 cm. Courtesy of Michael Rossman/The AOUON Archive.

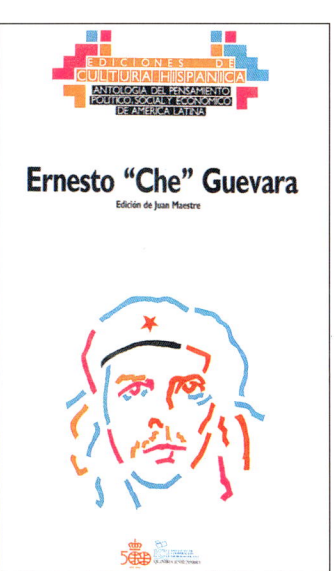

Figure M.36. Alberto Cerazon. Cover of *Ernesto "Che" Guevara*, edited by Juan Maestre. Madrid, 1988.

Figure M.37. Jorge Fornes, painting, 1970s.

Gallery

Figure M.38. Daisy García, ink drawing, 27 x 22 cm.

Figure M.39. Shuher and Yushiaki (Japan), electronic image (from "Che y los Ojos del Mundo," *Cuba Internacional*, April 1971).

Figure M.40. Sports stadium, Havana, photograph, 1973.

Figure M.41. Nicaragua: Detail of mural on former military barracks, Santa Ana, Managua, 1979, by the Felicia Santizo Brigade of Panama. Shows portraits of Marx, Lenin, and Che. The letters FSLN, added later to Che's beret, stand for the Sandinista National Liberation Front. The mural's theme is the insurrection (see Kunzle, *Murals*, p. 137, no. 109).

Figure M.42. Nicaragua: "*Che knows no frontiers,*" mural. The figure at the left is based on a famous photograph (1979) by Susan Meiselas of an insurrectionist preparing to throw a Molotov cocktail, a crucifix swinging from his neck.

Figure M.43. Haiti: *La Djé (Che). Ever Onward unto Victory. Lwi-Sidné*, mural. Louis Sidney is a local hero. Photograph by Donna Simchovitz, 1996.

Figure M.44. New York, Pathfinder Press: "*The truth must not only be the truth...It must also be told.*" Six-story high mural by 80 artists from 20 countries, 1989, now destroyed. Portrait of Fidel (bottom) by Aldo Soler; Che (left) by Ricardo Carpani of Argentina (see fig. E.6, p. 27).

Figure M.45. El Paso, Texas: Arturo Avalos. Photograph by Tim Drescher, 1994.

Figure M.46. Chicago: *Che–1928–1967*, 16th Street "Gallery." Photograph© by James Prigoff, 1973.

Figure M.47. Belfast: *We will meet force with force. Irish Republican Army. They may kill the revolutionary, but never the revolution. Che Guevara 1928–1967*. IRA mural. Photograph© by James Prigoff, 1994.

Figure M.48. Strabane, Northern Ireland: *Che Guevara*. Photograph by K. Denny, 1985. Courtesy of James Prigoff.

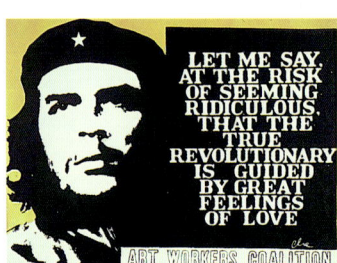

Figure M.49. "*...the true revolutionary is guided by great feelings of love.*" *Che*, Art Workers Coalition, 1970–1972. 39 x 54 cm. The quotation is from Che's famous essay, "Man and Socialism in Cuba."

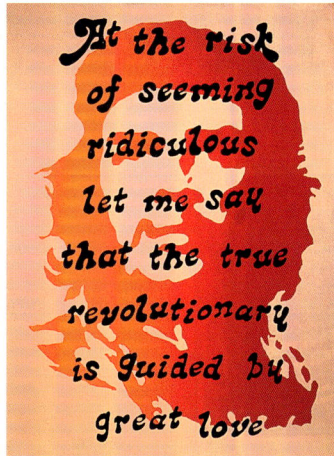

Figure M.50. "...*the true revolutionary is guided by great love.*" Courtesy of Michael Rossman/ The AUOUN Archive.

Figure M.51. "*How hard it is to die without seeing the triumph! I think Christ and Camilo [Cienfuegos] and Che Guevara felt the same way.*" Gaspar García Laviana, *priest, guerrilla, martyr, comandante.* Photograph by Conrad Contzen. Publ. Ministry of Culture Nicaragua, Peter Hammer Verlag, Wuppertal, and TVD Verlag Düsseldorf. Laviana was a Spanish priest who died in the revolutionary struggle of Nicaragua.

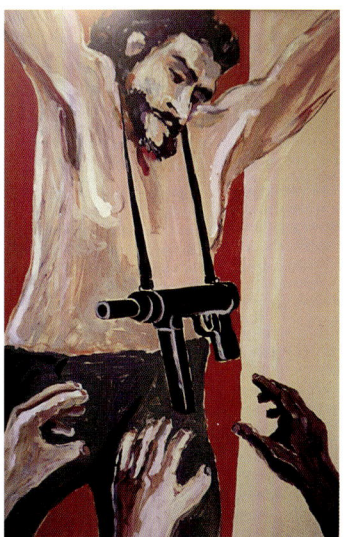

Figure M.52. Håkan Nyberg (Sweden).

Figure M.53. Laminario (plastic sign), one of several such signs in Havana streets, 1996, approximately 1.5 m high.

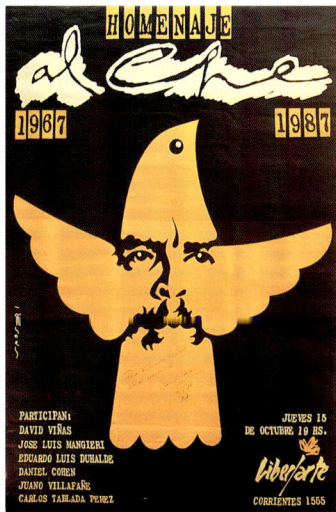

Figure M.54. Sposar, H*omage to Che Guevara*, 1967–1987, Liberarte.

Figure M.55. Caricature of Che, 1958, made while he was in the Sierra Maestra. (From *Signos 18, Gráfica de Cuba, 1976.*) This may be the first published drawing of Che.

Figure M.56. "The True Statue of Liberty," published by *Assayad* (a Beirut newspaper), 1967, José Veigas archive.

Figure M.57. Cigarette lighter holders, sold in the central market of Santa Cruz, Bolivia, as Christ (left) and "Indio del Oriente" (right). The latter, with a star in the headgear, was however identified for me by Santa Cruceños as Che.

Figure M.58. Betty Kano (US), *My Heart Belongs to Cuba*, mixed media with velvet, 1993, 44 x 27 cm. Collection of the artist. The piece incorporates a Cuban velvet hanging of the type sold to tourists around 1989.

Figure M.59. Betty Kano (US), *Make Trade (not War) with Cuba*, silkscreen, 1993, 77 x 57.5 cm. Collection of the artist.

Figure M.60. Italian T-shirt package: "*In a year as a banker I can say I have learned nothing about banking,*" Ernesto Che Guevara. From Cotton Words, producers of a series of famous quotations on T-shirts.

Figure M.61. Tran Huu Chat (Viet Nam), gouache, 1996, 54 x 78 cm. "There was a time when Vietnamese children liked to wear T-shirts with the image of Che."

Notes

Impressions
1. Goldberg, p. 156.
2. Alexandre, p. 90.
3. Berger, p. 44.
4. Richard Bourne, *Political Leaders in Latin America* (Harmondsworth, Middlesex: Penguin, 1969), p. 97.
5. Cormier, p. 430.
6. Alejo Carpentier in *Casa de las Américas*, 1970, p .151.
7. "Prologue," in Breccia et al., p. 6.
8. I.F. Stone in *New Statesman*, 20 Oct. 1967, p. 501.
9. Taibo, p. 100.
10. See note 6.
11. Cormier, p. 349.
12. From the introduction by Felipe, *Poemas al Che*, p. 5.
13. "Necessary Introduction" to the *Bolivian Diary*.
14. Alexandre, p. 69.
15. Ibid., p. 78.
16. Ibid., p. 71.
17. Ibid., p. 98.
18. Ibid., pp. 53–54.

Introduction
1. *Der Spiegel*, 16 Sept. 1996, p. 125.
2. Poem by Enrique Cisneros, on a poster titled *Chiapas, Zapata y "El Che,"* published by CEVA-CLETA, Mexico, DF.
3. "Hustling the tourist in Cuba," *Poliester*, Fall 1994, pp. 8–17. Cuba had eight hundred thousand tourists in 1995, up from a few thousand in 1985. Tourism has replaced sugar as the principal hard currency earner and could easily double in the next five years (*Cuba Update*, Sept. 1996, p. 14).
4. The Cubans have established a rule by which no living Cuban heroes are formally commemorated by having roads, schools, and so forth named after them. The image of Fidel, when it is used, is usually locked into some particular historical situation or reference (such as the famous attack on the Moncada barracks and the subsequent speech by Fidel, "La Historia Me Absolverá").
5. *Casa de las Américas*, Nov. 1968–Feb. 1969, p. 228.
6. "El Che y los Ojos del Mundo," *Cuba Internacional*, April 1971, pp. 14–23.
7. *The Art of Revolution: Castro's Cuba, 1959–1970*, texts by Dugald Stermer and Susan Sontag.
8. Anderson, pp. 584–85.
9. W. Mitchell, *The Reconfigured Eye* (Cambridge, MA: Massachusetts Institute of Technology, 1994), p. 95.
10. Cape/Lorrimer edition, 1968, p. 9.

Chapter 1. Che's Ideals in the Cuban Poster: OSPAAAL, Frémez, ICAIC
1. By 1980 Fidel Castro declared Cuba was prepared to suspend all expressions of solidarity (except symbolic ones) for revolutionary movements in the region, and follow the principle of nonintervention. See Martin Weinstein, ed., *Revolutionary Cuba in the World Arena* (Philadelphia: Institute for the Study of Human Issues, c. 1979), p. 83.
2. The total number of artists represented (with signatures) in the Cuba Poster Project list (see note 9) is about forty-one. Thirty are listed in the brochure for the OSPAAAL thirtieth anniversary show. The only non-Cuban name appears to be US artist Jane Norling.
3. See Susan Sontag and Dugald Stermer, *The Art of Revolution: Castro's Cuba 1959–1970* (McGraw Hill: New York, St. Louis, San Francisco, Düsseldorf, London, Mexico, Panama, Toronto), published in American, Dutch, English, French, German, Serbo-Croatian, Spanish, Latin American, and Swedish editions. This international capitalist enterprise carries excellent facsimiles, including some early OSPAAAL posters, and much useful text. Despite its earlier date, this remains unsurpassed. For a shorter essay, see David Kunzle, "Public Graphics in Cuba: A Very Cuban Form of Internationalist Art," *Latin American Perspectives* 7, 1975 suppl., vol. 2, no. 4, pp. 89–110.
4. See Camnitzer.
5. Chanan, p. 134.
6. Alexandre, pp. 92, 99.
7. *Cuba Internacional*, July 1971, p. 23.
8. Bonachea and Valdes, pp. 172–73.
9. I published the figure of twenty-four in an article for *Kunst und Krieg 1939–1989* (Berlin: Gesellschaft für Bildende Kunst, 1990, p. 74), in a country-by-country statistical breakdown. The figure of twenty-two (sixteen pre-1975) derives from the Cuban Poster Project OSPAAAL poster inventory, which is generally more complete than my list. The inventory is in the process of compilation by Lincoln Cushing and Michael Rossman, to whom I am indebted, in collaboration with OSPAAAL in Havana. Henceforth, all figures derive from this list. I owe a special word of thanks to Alfredo Rostgaard, who was so very generous with posters on my 1973 visit to Cuba, as were on later visits other OSPAAAL compañeros, notably Alberto Blanco and Gladys Acosta.
10. See Kunzle, "Killingly Funny: US Posters of the Vietnam Era," *Vietnam Images, War and Representation*, Jeffrey Walsh and James Aulich, eds. (London: Macmillan, 1989), pp. 112–22, and Kunzle, "From the Poster of Protest to the Poster of Liberation," *Graphic Design in America: A Visual Language History* (Walker Art Center and New York: Harry Abrams, 1989), pp. 177–91.
11. Now in the Southern California Library for Social Studies and Research in Los Angeles; see Kunzle, "A Cuban Donation...Mural by Mederos," *Third Text* 25, Winter 1993–94, pp. 33–42.
12. Marjorie Bray and Donald Bray, "Cuba, the Soviet Union and Third World Struggle," in *Cuba: Twenty-Five Years of Revolution 1959–1984*, Sandor Halebsky and John Kirk, eds. (New York: Praeger, 1985), p. 352.
13. This is the title of a compilation, *El Año que Estuvimos en Ninguna Parte*, Paco Ignacio Taibo II, Froilán Escobar, and Félix Guerra, eds. (Mexico City: Mortiz, Planeta, 1994). The best synthetic contextual accounts are Richard Gott, "Che Guevara and the Congo," *New Left Review*, no. 220, Nov./Dec. 1996, pp. 3–35, and Paco Ignacio Taibo's *Ernesto Guevara*, chs. 35–45.
14. Carlos Moore, *Castro, the Blacks and Africa* (Los Angeles: Center for Afro-American Studies, UCLA, 1988), p. 263.
15. Susan Eckstein, "Cuban Internationalism," in *Cuba*, Halebsky and Kirk, eds., op. cit. (see note 12), pp. 372–87, and Bray and Bray, op. cit., p. 353.
16. Repr. in Kunzle, *Posters of Protest* exhibition catalog (Santa Barbara: University of California, Santa Barbara, 1971), p. 91, no. 78.
17. Chanan, p. 187.
18. Ibid., p. 195.
19. Camnitzer, p. 350, no. 52, citing *Granma Weekly Review*, 22 Oct. 1989, and *Cuba Update*, Sept. 1996, p. 19–20.

Chapter 2. Che as Landscape
1. Marked on photograph of a billboard transformed by Arturo Cuenca (1987–1988), repr. in Camnitzer, p. 206.
2. "Ramón" by Enrique Gamarra, in Barrenechea Zambrana, p. 51–52. "Ramón" was a pseudonym of Che in Boliva.
3. Anderson, pp. 88–89.
4. Max Gallo, *The Poster in History* (London: Hamlyn, 1974). Significantly, the design was dropped in later editions.
5. María López Vigil, "Twenty Issues For a Green Agenda," *Envío*, 15 Nov. 1996, p. 24, ellipsis original.
6. Ibid., p. 34–35.
7. Arnaldo Saucedo Parada, *No Disparen, Soy El Che* (Santa Cruz, Bolivia: Oriente, n.d.), p. 31.
8. On this topic in general, see Hobsbawm, *Social Bandits* (Glencoe, IL: Free Press, 1960). These four paragraphs are based on the research of UCLA student Deanne Shey.
9. R. Schwartz, *Lawless Liberators* (Durham, NC: Duke University, 1989), p. 3.
10. Louis Pérez, *Lords of the Mountain* (Pittsburgh, PA: University of Pittsburgh, 1989), p. 192; cf. Hugh Thomas, *Cuba* (New York: Harper and Row, 1971), p. 1108.
11. Che Guevara, *Guerrilla Warfare*, ch. 1.
12. G.C. Infante, *Seven Voices*, 1973, p. 365.
13. Cormier, p. 147, says, "Their legend began to be hawked around like popular songs."
14. G.A. Geyer, *Guerrilla Prince* (Boston: Little, Brown, 1991), p. 174.

Chapter 3. Che-Man <—> Che-Project: A Collective Poetic Articulation
1. Lao, p. 136.
2. Nelson Osorio (Colombia), "El Gigante" (song), in Lao, p. 124.
3. Thomas Merton (USA), "Letters to the Che: Canto Bilingüe" (poem), ibid., p. 374.
4. Translation published in *Granma*, 29 Oct. 1967. See Keith Ellis, *Cuba's Nicolás Guillén*, Toronto: University of Toronto, c. 1983), p. 183.
5. Efraín Huerta (Mexico), "Cantata para el Che Guevara", in Lao., p. 270.
6. Eduardo Escobar (Colombia), "Oficios Peligrosos" (poem), ibid., p. 120.
7. Félix Pita Rodríguez (Cuba), "Cantata del Guerrillero Heroico" (cantata), ibid., p. 168.
8. Marcelo Arduz Ruíz (Bolivia), "De una Vez por Todas, Che" (poem), in Barrenechea Zambrana, p. 63.
9. Enid Vian (Cuba), "El Río" (poem), in Gónzalez López.
10. Matilde Bianqui (Uruguay), *Cantar del Che* (poem).
11. Alberto Guerra Gutiérrez (Bolivia), "En el Vado del Yeso" (poem), in Barrenechea Zambrana, p. 41.
12. Ruíz, op. cit.
13. Ibid.
14. Hector Miranda y Lucio Saavedra (Argentina), "Hombre Voluntad" (song), in Lao, p. 48.
15. Laurette Sejourné (France), "Oración" (poem), ibid., p. 222.
16. Carlos Puebla (Cuban), "Hasta Siempre" (song), ibid., p. 172.
17. Jaime Valdivieso (Chile), "Presencia del Che Guevara" (poem), ibid., p. 110.
18. Julio Cortázar (Argentina), "Yo Tuve un Hermano" (poem), ibid., p. 20; Merton, op. cit.; Bianqui, op. cit.; Victor Jara (Chile), "El Aparecido" (song), from *Canciones al Che* (audiocassette), Havana; David Viñas (Argentina), "El Hermano Mayor" (song), in Lao, p. 52; Nicolás Guillén (Cuba), "Che Comandante, Amigo" (poem), ibid., p. 152; Atahualpa Yupanqui (Argentina), "Tuve un Amigo Querido" (song), in *El Che*, Rosa Nassif, ed. (Buenos Aires: Editorial Agora, 1988), p. 86.

19. Merton, op cit.; Claudia Beck (USA), "Hola Che" (poem), in Lao, p. 368.
20. Pablo Armando Fernández (Cuba), "Che, Todos los Homenajes..." (poem), ibid., p. 150.
21. Guillén, op. cit., see note 18.
22. Pablo Milanés (Cuba), "Si el Poeta eres Tu" (song), in Lao, p. 164.
23. Manuel María (Spain), "Mensaje a Ernesto Che Guevara" (poem), in Fornet and Orrillo, eds., p. 50.
24. Antonio Conte (Cuba), "Che, el Poeta Saluda al Sufrimiento Armado" (poem), ibid., p. 226.
25. Andrés Machín Barrios (Cuba), "Sonoro Canto de Acero" (poem), in Gónzalez López.
26. Francisco Fernández-Santos (Spain), "El Che es Más que el Che" (poem), in Lao, p. 342.
27. Idea Vilariño (Uruguay), "Digo que no Murió" (poem), in Lao, p. 422.
28. Eduardo Escobar (Colombia), "Oficios Peligrosos" (poem), in Lao, p. 120.
29. Sejourné, op. cit., see note 15.
30. David Fernández (Cuba), "Epitafio para Llevar al hombre" (poem), in Lao, p. 148.
31. Bianqui, op. cit.
32. Valdivieso, op. cit.
33. Peggy Seeger (England), "Che Guevara" (poem), in Lao, p. 236.
34. Ernesto Aguero (Cuba), "Che" (poem), in Gónzalez López.
35. Fernández-Santos, in Lao, p. 344.
36. Coco Manto (Bolivia), "Che para Siempre" (poem), in Barrenechea Zambrana, p. 11.
37. Carlos Puebla (Cuba), "Que pare el Son" (song), in Lao, p. 172.
38. Claribel Alegría (El Salvador), "Quizá por Eso" (poem), in Fornet, p. 165.
39. Félix Pita Rodríguez (Cuba) in Gónzalez López.
40. Matilde Casazola (Bolivia), "Poemas del Amigo" (poem), in Barrenechea Zambrana, p. 105.
41. Julio Cortázar (Argentina), "Yo Tuve un Hermano" (poem), in Lao, p. 20.
42. Rafael Alberti (Spain), "Te Conocí de Niño" (poem), in Lao, p. 330.
43. Coco Manto (Bolivia), "Che" (poem), in Barrenechea Zambrana, p. 9.
44. Ruíz, op. cit.
45. Eduardo Ibarra (Peru), "Canto al Comandante Ernesto Guevara" (poem), in Fornet and Orrillo, p. 115.
46. Jorge Salerno (Uruguay), "La Senda está Trazada" (song), in Lao, p. 412.
47. Jaime Nisttahuz (Bolivia), "Sócrates de Fuego" (poem), in Barrenechea Zambrana.
48. Jara, op. cit. (see note 18).
49. Andrew Salkey (Jamaica), "Our Che" (poem), in Lao, p. 228.
50. Mario Benedetti (Uruguay), "Consternados, Rabiosos" (poem), in Lao, p. 394.
51. Alfredo De Robertis (Argentina), "Ay, Che Camino" (song), in Lao, p. 24.
52. Efraín Huerta (Mexico), "Cantata para el Che Guevara" (cantata), in Lao, p. 272.
53. Leoncio Bueno (Peru), "Este Gran Capitán" (poem), in Fornet and Orrillo, p. 91.
54. Daniel Viglietti (Uruguay), "Canción del Hombre Nuevo" (song), in Lao, p. 418.
55. Jaime Valdivieso (Chile), "Presencia del Che Guevara" (poem), in Lao, p. 110.
56. Félix Pita Rodríguez (Cuba), "Cantata del Guerrillero Heroico" (poem), in Lao, p. 170.
57. José Angel Valente (Spain), "Tiempo de Héroe" (poem), in Fornet, p. 46.

Chapter 4. Symbols: Hair and Beard, Cigar, Uniform, Beret, Star, the Name

1. From a poem by Enrique Cisneros on a Mexican poster "Chiapas, Zapata y 'El Che.'"
2. Ernesto Guevara, "América desde el Balcón Afro-Asiático", *Humanismo* 8, Sept.–Oct. 1959, no. 57, p. 48.
3. From Vicente Aleixandre, "Funeral por Ernesto Guevara," *Poemas al Che*, 1976, p. 9.
4. Carlos Franqui, *Family Portrait with Fidel* (New York: Random House, 1984), pp. 13–15.
5. The exploding cigar plot was satirized by a *Mad* magazine cover, Oct. 1963.
6. Edmundo Desnoes, "Castro's Beard," in Marshall Blonsky, ed., *On Signs* (Baltimore, MD: Johns Hopkins University, 1985), pp. 14–15.
7. Taibo, p. 478.
8. Ibid., p. 631.
9. Cormier, p. 357.
10. Taibo, p. 390.
11. This paragraph is based on the research of UCLA student Mary Wolfgram. See G. Cabrera Infante, *Holy Smoke* (New York: Harper and Row, 1985).
12. Anderson, p. 229.
13. Taibo, p. 352.
14. Rodríguez, p. 15.
15. Szulc, p. 44.
16. Anderson, pp. 566, 570.
17. Interview with Fidel Castro in Cuba by *Madrid Weekly* on 5 June 1991.
18. C. Soria Galvarro, "Tras las huellas del Che en Bolivia," *La Razón* (La Paz), 9 Oct. 1996.
19. From "Mensaje a Ernesto Che Guevara," by Catalan poet Manuel María in *Poemas al Che* (Barcelona edition), p. 51 (lineation not observed).
20. Guevara, *Episodes of the Revolutionary War*, p. 87.
21. Cover, endpapers, and inside *Atlas Histórico, Biográfico y Militar Ernesto Che Guevara I* (Havana: Pueblo y Educación, 1990).
22. Che quoted by Guillermo Cabrera Alvarez, ed., *Memories of Che* (Secaucus, NJ: Lyle Stuart, c. 1987), p. 127.
23. The well attested story of Che correcting the Higuera schoolteacher's spelling is made to involve Che's own nickname and virtually Che's last words in Hugo Gambini's *El Che Guevara* (Buenos Aires: Mundo Moderno, 1968, p. 13), where Che is made to say "Tell your colonel that Che is written without an accent, what he wrote on this blackboard is wrong.... Wait a minute. The wound in my leg hurts, but I want to stand upright. Now you'll see how a real man (macho) dies. Shoot now, dammit!"
24. Cormier, p. 76, was the first, I think, to suggest an Italian derivation—"Que cosa c'é"—which is too long.
25. "El Che y los Ojos del Mundo," *Cuba Internacional*, April 1971, p. 19.
26. Repr. in *Cubaansche Affiches* (Amsterdam: Stedelijk Museum, 1970).
27. Roberto Echazú Navaja, in Barrenechea Zambrana, p. 4.

Chapter 5. The Korda Matrix

1. Adys Cupull and Froilán González, *Ernesto Viro y Presente. Iconografía Testimoniada de la Infancia y la Jurentud de Ernesto Che Guevara, 1928–53* (Havana: Editora Política, 1989).
2. Taibo, p. 84.
3. Ibid., p. 669.
4. Ibid., p. 534.
5. An exhibition of Che's own photographs was held at the Galería Latino-Americana in Havana in November 1990.
6. They may be found reproduced in the fold-out series in the Italian *Album Fotografico: Che*, 1990. Interviews with Noval, Corrales, and Salas, September 1996; telephone conversation with Lockwood, January 1997.
7. Taibo, pp. 84, 481, where the "Cantinflas" photo heads Chapter 33.
8. See photo album in the three-part *Barbudos* series (Havana: Visual América, 1996).
9. Szulc, p. 514.
10. "Che: Historia de una Foto (Tal Vez la Más Reproducida del Mundo)," *Opina*, September 1980.
11. Giuliana Scimé, "Il negativo originale di Che Guevara," *Progresso Fotografico* (Milan), June 1983, p. 14.
12. According to Korda, interviewed September 1996, "in October or November."
13. See interview with Korda by Homero Kampa, *Proceso*, 6 Oct. 1996, p. 51.
14. Vicki Goldberg, *The Power of Photography* (New York: Abbeville, 1991), p. 156, with a Susan Meiselas photograph of the twentieth-anniversary version, and an excellent account of the dissemination of Korda's image, pp. 159–61. See also Taibo, p. 384, with a bibliography of the image (mainly Cuban), p. 797.
15. Interview with the artist, Sept. 1986. Cf. Sonia Sánchez, "Dimensión Plástica de la Imagen del Che," *Trabajadores*, 7 October 1982, p. 2. The article contains a list of six painters who have used Che as a theme.
16. Photographs by Lee Lockwood published in *Look*, 12 December 1967, in which Fidel seems visually to be saluting Che in the Plaza, and to be thrown back inspirationally before Che's gigantic gaze in the OLAS conference room. I have been unable otherwise to document the public agitational use of Che's image prior to his death. Hans Koningsberger, in *The Spirit of Che Guevara* (New York: Doubleday, 1971, p. 69) says that after Che met the President of Brazil in 1963, there were to be seen in the streets "thousands of Cuban flags and even pictures of Che on parade."
17. See *Album Fotografico: CHE, foto di Raul Corrales e Alberto Korda*, introduction by Jorge Amado (Milan: A & A Editori, 1990); there are also French and German editions.
18. Scimé (see note 11), with first-ever publication of the strip of four contact prints. The lithograph paired with the one making the Che-Mona Lisa comparison, shows the original Korda image larger, framed by the film edge, marked for cropping and complete with a figure in profile (left) and a palm tree (right); it also carries text from an article on the photograph by the Cuban Aldo Menéndez González from *Revolución y Cultura*, June 1974.
19. Taibo, p. 394.
20. Inés Morales García, *Ernesto (Che) Guevara en la Numismática Cubana*, typed pamphlet, 12 pp., n.d., in the National Library, and Gilda Pareja Lodosa, "El nuevo billete....," *Trabajadores* 6, 8 Oct. 1983.

Chapter 7. Che, Chicanos, and Cubans: The Struggle Over a Symbol

1. Letter to the author, 9 Feb. 1996. Though Mario Acevedo Torero was born in Peru, his long residence in San Diego, California, and his association with the large Chicano arts and activist community has caused him, since the late 1960s, not only to work with Chicanos, but to assume an honorary identity with the largest Latino group in the United States.
2. It is known that Los Angeles was home from 1907–1915 to the Flores Magón brothers, early leaders of the Mexican Revolution, where they had the support of many in the Mexican community. For those who remembered or revered the Mexican Revolution and its heroes of 1910–1920, the Cuban Revolution would probably have been understood and not necessarily rejected, though the pressures of the Cold War and the boycott of Cuba from the 1960s onward did leave their mark.
3. The use of the term "minority" gave rise to an impassioned essay printed in 1979 in a local Chicano publication. "Each time we hear ourselves referred to as minorities we are being conditioned to believe that we must take a secondary position among others. Then we come to use the word ourselves, without recognizing the harmful realities that go along with its acceptance." When minority programs were begun in the 1960s, they were accompanied with money. Since then, "we have begun to understand...that calling ourselves minorities" was a compromise. "For our own human rights [we] must begin to awaken the rest of the people of La Raza by telling them...you are not a minority." The writer referred not only to Torero's poster, but to the three murals he painted on this theme: the first (in 1977) was accompanied by the head and hand of a Chicana multiplied in-depth in Op-Art fashion and accompanied by the slogan "You Are Not a Minority!!" "Torero chose Che for his poster...because Che is an international figure, a hero of the struggles of all Latin-American people who have been oppressed by class poverty and racism. His image shows the extent of how the word America has been limited from a continent to a nation. In the poster and the [mural], Che dramatized the true meaning of the word minority." Rita Sánchez, "You Are Not a Minority," *Somos*, (July/Aug. 1979), p. 18 passim.
4. The group's identification translates as the Congress of Cosmic Artists of Aztlán (formerly the Congress of Chicano Artists of Aztlán). The name change occurred when non-Chicanos were admitted to the Congress. The term "cosmic" derived from Mexican philosopher José Vasconcelos who in 1925 wrote a book concerning the "cosmic race" which, he argued, was composed in the Americas of the mingling of the four "races" of the world: black, white, yellow and red. "Aztlán" is the mythical northern homeland of the Aztecs, and was the name chosen by Chicanos for the Southwest. The scatology of the term "caca" or excrement, functions playfully against the solemn titular identification. The term "Califas" has been regularly used by Chicanos to refer to California by employing the Arabic word "Califa" and thus acknowledging the Moorish contributions to the language of Spain. Torero spelled the word as Califaz—then crossed the Z with a reverse symbol of the swastika which, in this form, say Chicanos, refers to an ancient sun symbol of all Native American peoples. Finally, the artists are identified by their very "hip" nicknames: Zopilote, Rocky, Lion, Zade, and "el gran" (the great) Torero. Torero dated the poster which appeared at the tenth anniversary on 8 October 1977, signed it, and added c/s (Con Safos), a defiant expression (roughly, "the same to you") used by graffiti artists in the streets and adopted by many Chicano artists of the Southwest.
5. For a history and analysis of the Estrada Court murals, see Marcos Sánchez-Tranquilino, "Mi Casa No Es Su Casa: Chicano Murals and Barrio Calligraphy as Systems of Signification at Estrada Courts, 1972–1978," Master's thesis, University of California, Los Angeles, 1991.
6. Sánchez-Tranquilino, ibid., pp. 80–82.
7. Virginia Escalante, "Defaced Again: A Second Uproar Over the Che Guevara Mural," *Los Angeles Times*, 16 May 1984, Part IV, p. 5.
8. The conflicting versions derive from 1) a phone interview with Charles Felix by the author, 14 March 1984, and 2) an inter-office memo from the Housing Authority dated 24 April 1984, sent to the author.
9. See "Siqueiros and Three Early Murals in Los Angeles," in Shifra M. Goldman, *Dimensions of the Americas: Art and Social Change in Latin America and the United States* (Chicago: University of Chicago Press, 1994), pp. 87–100.
10. Escalante, "Defaced Again," p. 5.

Chapter 8. Chesucristo: The Christification of Che

1. Joel Carmichael, *The Birth of Christianity, Reality and Myth* (New York: Hippocrene, 1989), p. 189. I rely largely on Carmichael's interpretation in this segment.
2. Penny Lernoux, *Cry of the People* (New York: Viking-Penguin, 1982), pp. 4, 13, 59, 181, 265, 425.
3. Soria Galvarro, vol. 2, p. 49.
4. Taibo, pp. 649, 653.
5. J.I. Siles in Soria Galvarro, vol. 3, p. 366, 368.
6. Anderson, p. 299.
7. Szulc, pp. 47, 124.
8. Anderson, p. 379.
9. Betto, pp. 4, 13–15, 137, 233, and Szulc, p. 24.
10. The series was exhibited at the Whitechapel Gallery, London; I photographed the piece reproduced here in the house of Christina Vives and José Figueroa, where it is on loan.
11. Cormier, p. 434.
12. Siles in Soria Galvarro, vol. 3, p. 365.
13. Liliana Bucellini, *L'amore, la politica, la rivolta* (Milano: Zelig, 1995), p. 139.
14. John Otis, "Che's Ghost," *San Francisco Chronicle*, 12 March 1996, reporting from Vallegrande.
15. González Bermejo, "Che, su Paso por la Tierra," *Cuba Internacional*, Oct. 1971, p. 29. The conjunction of Che and Jesus goes back, according to Tad Szulc, to 1961 when "Guevara's portrait began to appear on the walls of homes of many parish priests...across Latin American, next to the image of Jesus Christ" (review of Anderson, *Los Angeles Times Book Review*, 4 May 1997, p. 3).
16. Barrenechea Zambrana, p. *i*.
17. Juan Ignacio Siles del Valle, *Medulamor* (La Paz: Letras, 1993). The crossbar translates literally: "I saw them nailed in the guerrilla."
18. José Arce Paravicini, a doctor who died in the Teoponte massacre in 1970 (Barrenechea Zambrana, p. 14).
19. Che quoting Fidel (Bonachea and Valdes, p. 110).
20. Guevara, *Episodes*, ch. 6.
21. See *The Motorcycle Diaries, A Journey around South America*, (New York: Verso, 1995), p. 46, where his friend Alberto Granado is credited with the exploit; Granado credits Che elsewhere.
22. By Nils Castro, *Casa de Las Américas*, Jan.-Feb.1970, p. 124.
23. Anderson, pp. 341, 385.
24. New York, 1968, p. 67.
25. Soria Galvarro, vol. 2, p. 112.
26. Rolando, Pombo, Braulio, *Diarios de Bolivia* (Argentina: Fuerte, n.d.).
27. Soria Galvarro, p. 112.
28. Cormier, p. 414.
29. Gadea, pp. 173–75.
30. Bonachea and Valdes, p. 426.
31. "Wanted" (above), "Good men" (below); "Read the Black Dwarf," "This Poster is for Eldridge Cleaver," publ. by Stones Posters (UK), c. 1971.
32. Cormier, p. 107.
33. See *Los Angeles Times* column on religion, 2 December 1972, where he is featured as one of a trio of religious leaders with Gandhi and Martin Luther King.
34. Kunzle, *Murals*, p. 108, no. 37.
35. Oriana Baddeley, ed., *New Art from Latin America* (London: Art and Design, 1994), repr. p. 88.
36. Martha Zamora, *Tomás Sánchez* (Mexico City: Petróleo Mexicano, 1994), pp. 87, 128.
37. Kunzle, *Murals*, p. 68 and color plates 18a and 18b.
38. Alexandre, p. 113.
39. Anderson, p. 504.
40. Betto, p. 229. For Betto's interpretation of the miracle, see p. 55.
41. Cormier, p. 437.
42. From "Son Cubano para Ernesto Guevara," poem by Victoriano Cremer, in *Poemas al Che* (Barcelona edition), p. 12.

Chapter 9. Che Dead, Che Vive

1. So designated and dated 1972–1975 with the three other titles used here, in Arnold Belkin, *Muertes Históricas* exhibition catalog (Mexico DF: Museo de Arte Moderno, 1975), no. 15. The set (nos. 15–18) has never otherwise been exhibited as such, and is now split up in four different places (Managua, Mexico City, New York, Puerto Rico). There is a short non-analytical discussion of the paintings which do not otherwise figure in the Belkin bibliography in Belkin's *33 Años de Producción Artística* (Mexico: Instituto Nacional de Bellas Artes, 1989), pp. 20–21, with our Figures 9.3 and 9.5 as catalog numbers 83 and 84, both dated 1974. In the version or state of the fourth painting reproduced here, the bodies of the guerrilleros are left blank (as it were unfinished, like the surgeons in the first painting), whereas in the version or state reproduced in the *Muertes Históricas* catalog they are painted as fully clothed. My thanks to Patricia Belkin for providing transparencies, and Shifra Goldman and Lisa Nuñez-Hancock for negotiating them.
2. This truncated corpse is almost identical, save for the Che head, to the victim in *Attica* (1973), where the executioners are architectonic robots (Belkin, *Contra la Amnesia, Textos 1960–1985*, Mexico City: Domes, UAM, 1975, pl. 18; and Belkin, *33 Años*, no. 75.)
3. The "surgeons" here resemble the explosively rhetorical "Gran Dictador," paraphrase of Ingres's Napoleon, 1977 (*33 Años*, p. 67, no. 94).
4. Curiously, the Dutch word *ontleding* means both analysis and anatomical dissection.
5. Repr. in *33 Años*.
6. Shifra Goldman in *33 Años*; and Kunzle, *Murals*, no. 1.
7. *Muertes Históricas*, cover.
8. John Berger's article first appeared as "The Legendary Che Guevara is Dead." *New Society 10*, 26 Oct. 1967, and has been much reprinted: in Berger's *The Moment of Cubism* (1969), and his *The Look of Things* (New York, 1972, pp. 42–53), with substantial additions dated December 1967, "prompted by another recent newspaper photograph," of a US atrocity in Viet Nam.
9. I owe this reference to Jacquelline Adams and thank the artist for providing photographs.
10. See Adrian Arguedas Ruano, exhibition catalog, Museo de Arte Costarricense, 1993, introduction by Eugenia Zavaleta, with three reproductions of series.
11. Repr. in Riva Castelman, *Printed Art: A View of Two Decades* (New York: Museum of Modern Art, 1980), p. 64. Thanks to Shifra Goldman for these two references.
12. This image, on a black ground, is paired with and placed over that of Che's feet. There are in the artist's archive photographs I believe unpublished, including one of fingers laid on Che's eyelids, preparatory to opening them, I assume. There are also paintings of the dead Che by Weisberg at the University of St. Thomas, Manila.
13. Translated by David Kunzle.
14. Andre Rouillé, "Paolo Gasparini," *La Recherche Photographique* 19, Autumn 1995, p. 50. Cf. Eliseo Sierra, "Los teatros de la muerte," in Paolo Gasparini, *La Pasión Sacrificada* (Caracas: Consejo Nacional de la Cultura, Museo Alejandro Otero, 1995).
15. Rouillé, op. cit.
16. *Le Monde*, 19–20 Feb. 1995, p. 27 (RTV).
17. *Le Monde*, 10–11 Nov. 1996, p. 37 (Télévision Radio Multimédia).
18. *Le Monde*, 1995, l.c.
19. *Le Monde*, 1996, l.c.

Alternative Views

1. Information and citation from the preface by Ernesto Santaloya to the Ikusager edition, and an interview with Breccia by Jan Baetens, held in 1992 just before the artist's death and printed in *Frigobox* 6 (February 1996), pp. 78–80. My thanks to Thierry Groensteen and Pascal Lefèbre for alerting me to this, and to Jan Baetens. For a "metarepresentative reading" of the comic book, see Baetens "Littérature et Engagement," *Cahiers Marxistes* 194 (1994), pp.162–77.
2. Vitoria-Gasteiz: Ikusager, 1987, with an introduction by Ernesto Sabato; the original edition included a text by Eliseo Verón.
3. Jan Baetens, *Cahiers Marxistes*, p. 168. Baetens also compares Breccia's Che brooding over the necessity of his sacrifice (Breccia, p. 69) with Jesus' Agony in the Garden.

Chapter 10. Demythification: The Twentieth Century Fox *Che!*

1. Twentieth Century Fox advertisement in *Los Angeles Times Calendar*, Sunday, 15 June 1969, p. 3.
2. H. Medved and R. Dreyfuss, *The Fifty Worst Films of All Time* (New York: Popular Library, 1978), p. 57–60.
3. Twentieth Century Fox press release, 9 Oct. 1968.
4. Twentieth Century Fox press release, 9 Oct. 1968.
5. Preliminary script (first draft) by Sy Bartlett and David Karp, 15 March 1967, Twentieth Century Fox archives, UCLA.
6. Tuckman, Mitch. "Michael Wilson," *Take One*, September 1978, p. 34.
7. Fleischer is quoted by the *New York Times Magazine*, 8 December 1968, p. 72, as describing Guevara as "a handsome, sexy guy. That's the secret of his appeal. He had animal magnetism...." Fleischer insists that he was severely misquoted in this article. *Newsweek*, 9 Dec. 1968, p. 110, quoted Fleischer, "As of this moment, he's a tremendous symbol for young people all over the world. But I'm not so sure that five years from now anyone will remember him, because there's no residue, no substance to the man. When you analyze it, Che's a big loser."
8. Michael Wilson archive, UCLA, 11 July and 24 July scripts (first draft and revised first draft).
9. Tuckman, op. cit.
10. Ibid.
11. *New York Times Magazine*, 8 Dec. 1968, p. 63.
12. *Hollywood Reporter*, 9 June 1969.
13. *Newsweek*, 9 Dec. 1968, p. 110.
14. *The Christian Century*, 6 Aug. 1969, v. 86, p. 1045.
15. *New York Times Magazine*, 8 Dec. 1968, p. 80.
16. *Politics and Film*, 1995, pp. 150–51.
17. See note 14.
18. Nene Montez, described as a "former captain in Fidel Castro's army" sued Twentieth Century Fox and producer Sy Bartlett for breach of an oral contract made in 1968 in the amount of $50,000 plus screen credit for his work on the film. The suit claimed that because of a secret agreement there was never a written contract (*The Hollywood Citizen News*, 27 May 1969). The suit was eventually dismissed because of lack of evidence (*Variety*, 30 Oct. 1972).
19. Wilson's letter dated 28 January 1969, from Wilson archive, UCLA.
20. Tuckman, op. cit.
21. Wilson's letter dated 1 March 1969, from Wilson archive, UCLA.
22. *Filmfacts*, 1969, v. 12, p. 308; *New York Times*, 29 May 1969, p. 47, col. 1; *Newsweek*, 16 June 1969, p. 102; *The New Yorker*, 14 June 1969, vol. 45, p. 83; *San Francisco Chronicle*, 26 June 1969, p. 47, col. 6.
23. *New York Times*, 30 May 1969, p. 17, col. 1.
24. *Daily Bruin* (UCLA) 26 June 1969, p. 5, col. 1.
25. *New York Times*, 9 June 1969, p. 49, col. 1.
26. Los Angeles *Herald Examiner*, 27 June 1969.
27. *Hollywood Reporter*, 24 June 1969.
28. *Hollywood Reporter*, 5 Sept. 1969.

Chapter 11. The Passion of Che: Capture, Death, and Disappearance

1. Volker Braun, *Guevara oder der Sonnenstaat* (Leipzig: Reclam, 1983), p. 18. The play was written in 1975 and first performed in 1977.
2. Taibo, p. 724.
3. Cormier, p. 415.
4. *Der Spiegel* 38, 16 Sept. 1996, p. 133.
5. Taibo, p. 736.
6. Soria Galvarro, vol. 2, p. 291; Cormier, p. 418; and Luis González and Gustavo Sánchez-Salazar, *The Great Rebel*, Helen Lane, trans. (New York: Grove Press, 1969), pp.192–94.
7. Taibo, p. 733.
8. Cormier, p. 420.
9. Soria Galvarro, vol. 2, p. 291.
10. Cormier, p. 421. An ophthalmologist tells me this can happen at death when loss of oxygen drains color from the eyes. Cf. Taibo, p. 738, who implies that Schaller never saw the corpse.
11. Taibo, p. 741.
12. Ted Cordova-Claure in Soria Galvarro, vol. 2, p. 314.
13. Che Guevara, *Poesía Trunca*, Mario Benedetti, ed. (Havana: Casa de las Américas, 1968), p.10.

References

Alexandre, Marianne
1968 *Viva Che*. London: Lorrimer.

Anderson, Jon Lee
1997 *Che Guevara, A Revolutionary Life*. New York: Grove.

Barrenechea Zambrana, Ramiro (ed.)
1995 *El Che en la Poesía Boliviana*. La Paz, Bolivia: Caminamos.

Berger, John
1967 "The legendary Che Guevara is dead." *New Society* 10 (26 October).

Betto, Frei
1990 *Fidel and Religion*. Melbourne: Ocean.

Bianqui, Matilde
1967 *Cantar del Che*. Montevideo, Uruguay: Comunidad del Sur.

Bonachea, Rolando E., and Nelson P. Valdes
1969 *Selected Writings of Che Guevara*. Cambridge, MA: Massachusetts Institute of Technology.

Breccia, A., E. Breccia, and H. Oesterheld
1987 *Che*. Vitoria-Gasteiz: Ikusager.

Camnitzer, Luis
1994 *New Art of Cuba*. Austin: University of Texas.

Chanan, Michael
1985 *The Cuban Image*. London: British Film Institute.

Cormier, Jean
1995 *Che Guevara*. Paris: Rocher.

Felipe, León (ed.)
1976 *Poemas al Che*. (Barcelona edition, facsimile of Casa de las Americas 1969 edition).

Fornet, Ambrosio (ed.)
1969 *Poemas al Che*. Havana: Instituto del Libro.

Fornet, Ambrosio and Winston Orrillo (eds.)
1972 *Poemas al Che*. Lima, Peru: Causachun.

Gadea, Hilda
1972 *Ernesto, A Memoir of Che Guevara*. New York: Doubleday.

Goldberg, Vicki
1991 *The Power of Photography*. New York: Abbeville.

Goldman, Shifra
1994 *Dimensions of the Americas*. Chicago, IL: University of Chicago.

González López, Waldo (ed.)
1989 *Como Jamás Tan Vivo* (Havana: Abril).

Guevara, Che
1960 *La Guerra de Guerrillas*. Havana: Minfar.

Guevara Lynch, Ernesto
1984 *Ernesto, Mi Hijo el Che*. Argentina: Sudamericana Planeta.

Kunzle, David
1995 *Murals of Revolutionary Nicaragua, 1979–1992*. Berkeley: University of California.
1975 "Uses of the Portrait: The Che Poster." *Art in America* 63:66-73.

Ladrón de Guevara, José G.
1976 *Romancero de la Muerte de Che Guevara*. Málaga, Spain: Arte y Cultura.

Lao, Meri
1995 *Al Che. Poesie e Canzoni dal Mondo*. Rome: Erre Emme.

Liberman, Arnoldo
1968 *Pero Che*. Buenos Aires: n.p.

Massari, Roberto
1994 *Ernesto Che Guevara, Uomo, Compagno, Amico*. Pomezia (Rome): Erre Emme.

Rodríguez, Félix
1989 *Shadow Warrior*. New York: Simon & Schuster.

Rothschuh Villanueva, Guillermo
1989 *Che Poeta Guerrillero*. Mexico: Ediciones Armella.

Sontag, Susan, and Dugald Stermer
1970 *Art of Revolution*. New York: McGraw Hill.

Soria Galvarro, Carlos (ed.)
1992–1996 *El Che en Bolivia*, 5 vols. La Paz: CEDOIN.

Szulc, Tad
1986 *Fidel: A Critical Portrait*. New York: Morrow.

Taibo II, Paco Ignacio
1996 *Ernesto Guevara: También Conocido Como el Che*. Mexico City DF: Planeta, Joaquín Mortiz.

Zeitlin, Maurice
1967 *Revolutionary Politics and the Cuban Working Class*. Princeton, NJ: Princeton University Press.

Zeitlin, Maurice, and Robert Scheer
1964 *Cuba: An American Tragedy*. Harmondsworth, UK: Penguin.

Further reading

The very recent book by Jon Lee Anderson, a not uncritical monument of original scholarship using untapped sources, now clearly supersedes previous biographical studies, notably the major one hitherto available in English, David James's *Che Guevara, A Biography* (London: Allen, 1970), which mixes much admiration with some outright hostility. Andrew Sinclair's *Che Guevara* (New York: Viking, 1970) is still an excellent short introduction, as is Richard Harris's summary of the life and more detailed account of the death in *Death of a Revolutionary* (New York: Norton, 1970). Also recommended are Donald Hodges's *The Legacy of Che Guevara* (London: Thames and Hudson, 1977) and David Deutschmann's *Che Guevara and the Cuban Revolution, Writings and Speeches of ECG* (Sydney: Pathfinder, 1987). *The Bibliografía Cubana del Comandante Ernesto Che Guevara* (Havana: Ministerio de Cultura, 1987) contains sections on Che in art, music, literature, sports, and a filmography. A supplement is planned.

Emily Hatchwell and Simon Calder's *Cuba, Guide to the People, Politics, and Culture* (London: Latin American Bureau, 1995) is a good, short, critical introduction to revolutionary Cuba.

UCLA Fowler Museum of Cultural History

Doran H. Ross *Director*
Clarissa M. Coyoca
Assistant Director for Administration and Finance

Accounting
Dina M. Ogle *Accountant*
Michael Bermudez *Accounting Assistant*

Administration
Betsy R. Escandor *Administrative Specialist*
Lori A. LaVelle *Administrative Assistant*

Center for the Study of Regional Dress
Patricia Anawalt *Director*
Barbara Sloan *Assistant Director*

Collections
Fran Krystock *Collections Manager*
Dwight Gorden *Assistant Collections Manager*
Aileen Dugan *Collections Assistant*

Conservation
Jo A. Hill *Conservator*

Curatorial
Patricia B. Altman *Curator Emeritus*
Roy W. Hamilton *Curator of Southeast Asian and Oceanic Collections*
Doran H. Ross *Curator of African Collections*
Glenn S. Russell *Curator of Archaeology*
Anne Summerfield *Visiting Curator*
John Summerfield *Visiting Curator*
Elisabeth L. Cameron *Visiting Curator*

Development
Kyrin Ealy Hobson *Director of Development*
Lynne K. Brodhead *Assistant Director of Development*

Education
Betsy D. Quick *Director of Education*
Stacey J. Hong *Assistant Director of Education*
Sheila Egan *Education Assistant*
Kristen Quine *Education Assistant*

Exhibitions
David A. Mayo *Exhibition Designer*
Victor Lozano, Jr. *Exhibition Production*
Ann McNamara *Graphic Technician*
Don Simmons *Exhibition Production*
Karyn Zarubica *Traveling Exhibitions Coordinator*

Information Systems
Donald H. McClelland *Director of Information Systems*
Eric Anderson *Imaging Technician*
Ledda J. Macera *Imaging Technician*
Branislav Unkovic *Imaging Technician*

Membership
Kathlene Kolian *Director of Membership*
Vickie Reese *Database Manager*

Museum Store
Polly Svenson *Museum Store Manager*
Sue Kallick *Assistant Store Manager*
Marilyn Liebman *Special Events Coordinator*

Photography
Donald Cole *Senior Photographer*
Jonathan Molvik *Photography Assistant*

Public Relations
Christine Sellin *Director of Public Relations*
Kara Lee *Public Relations Assistant*

Publications
Daniel R. Brauer *Director of Publication*
Anthony A.G. Kluck *Assistant Director of Publication*
David Svenson *Publications Processor*

Registration
Sarah Jane Kennington *Registrar*
Farida Sunada *Assistant Registrar*

Security
Francisco J. Muñoz *Director of Security*
Jose A. Garcia *Assistant Director of Security*
Emry Thomas *Facilities Supervisor*

Security Guards
Rene Padilla *Security Supervisor*
Fisher Thompson *Security Supervisor*
Roger Palmer *Console Supervisor*
Fernando Martin *Console Relief*
Michelle Oskoui *Cashier*
Pejman Akhlaghi
German Bracamonte
Domingo Caldona
Bob Cheng
Joseph Eubank
Steven Faison
Dylan Godmintz
Pablo Orduño
Francheska Peters
Gina Denora Ruiz
Fabian Torres

Interns
Karen Abend
James J. Clark
Aphrodite Dielubanza
Priscilla Herbilla
Alicia Katano
Taaji Rauf-Madyun
Luciana Scrutchen
Danielle Smith

Support Staff
Cathy Barrow
Angel Haro
Kathy Marquez
Paula Padilla

Volunteers
Ruth Parsell *Volunteer Coordinator*
Margaret Abraham
Lyn Avins
Jane Bardwell
Virginia Beckwith
Simone Civet
Linda Clougherty
Josey Dodd
Monica Eiserling
Doris Finck
Elaine Fleischman
Helen Goebel
Moonlight Gurfield
Kimberly Herzog
Marillyn H. Holmes
Betsy Keliher
Rose Korsak
Deborah R. Last
Mary Jane Leland
Roz Lipkis
Mickey Loy
Jovita Luglug
Frances Martin
Robert McClelland
Nancy McCreery
Rosemary Murray
Nancy Porter
Caroline Sakaguchi
Batyah Schtrum
Stuart Shaffer
Jill Stein
Ellen Vener
Andrea Williams